D1001154

EX LIBRIS
TSM

REDWOOD

LIBRARY

WITHDRAWN

Randolph Churchill

Randolph Churchill

The Young Unpretender

Essays by his friends
collected and introduced by

Kay Halle

HEINEMANN : LONDON

William Heinemann Ltd
15 Queen Street, London, W1X 8BE

LONDON MELBOURNE TORONTO
JOHANNESBURG AUCKLAND

First published 1971
Selection and introduction © Kay Halle 1971

Material by the late Sir Winston Churchill © 1969, 1971 C. & T. Publications Limited. Previously unpublished material included in this volume: 'Randolph in Oxford', © Roy F. Harrod 1971; 'Randolph', © John Betjeman 1971; 'Randolph Churchill', © Christopher Sykes 1971; 'My Friend Randolph', © John Sutro 1971; 'Randolph', © Stuart Scheftel 1971; 'Randolph with the Yugoslav Partisans', © Vladimir Dedijer 1971; 'Randolph as a Commando', © Fitzroy Maclean 1971; 'With Randolph in Yugoslavia', © John Blatnik 1971; 'Framed in the Prodigality of Nature', © Kenneth T. Downs 1971; 'With Randolph in Darkest Africa and Elsewhere', © Stephen Barber 1971; 'Randolph in Korea', © Ansel E. Talbert 1971; 'The Meeting of Prime Minister Churchill and his Son Randolph Churchill in Italy in August 1944', © Lyman L. Lemnitzer 1971; 'Randolph and the Law', © John G. Foster 1971; 'Ho! Ho! Ho! and a Bottle of Printer's Ink', © Henry Fairlie 1971; 'Randolph — Without the Boast of Heraldry, the Pomp of Pow'r', © Arthur Krock 1971; 'Electioneering with Randolph', © Julian Amery 1971; 'The Riddle of Randolph', © the Estate of the late Iain Macleod, 1971; 'Randolph', © Eliahu Elath 1971; 'Randolph as a Neighbour' © Viscount Blakenham 1971; 'Randolph and the Great Work', © Martin Gilbert 1971; 'The Lion in Autumn', © Franklin R. Gannon 1971; 'Could You Come Please . . .', © Barbara Twigg 1971; ' "Box On" ', © Michael Wolff 1971; 'Randolph Churchill', © Hugh Trevor-Roper 1971; 'Gardening with Randolph', © Xenia Field 1971; 'Randolph', © Isaiah Berlin 1971; 'Randolph Churchill', © Arthur Schlesinger Jr 1971; 'Randolph', © Jacqueline Onassis 1971; 'Randolph my Friend', © Aristotle Onassis 1971; 'Randolph: A Tribute', © Harold Macmillan 1971.

434 31260 6

Printed in Great Britain by
WESTERN PRINTING SERVICES LTD, BRISTOL

For
Randolph S. Churchill
my dear and lifelong friend

Contents

Contents

Illustrations

Acknowledgments

I wish to thank the family of Randolph Churchill, and his friends and colleagues who have recorded their cherished recollections of him expressly for this volume.

I am also grateful to those who have granted me permission to include their perceptive impressions of his unforgettable character which have appeared before in other publications.

My profound thanks to Elizabeth Beverly for her devoted and tireless labours in assisting with the arrangement and typing of this collection.

A diligent effort has been made to obtain permission to reprint copyright material and to make full acknowledgment for its use. Any errors or omissions in the list which follows are purely inadvertent and will be corrected in subsequent editions. I am grateful to the publishers and others listed below for having graciously given me their permission to use copyright material in this book: Philippe Barrès for permission to use the English version of his article in *Le Figaro* of 14 June 1968; Mrs Constance M. Broun and Heywood Hale Broun for permission to reprint 'Young Randolph Churchill' by Heywood Hale Broun from *The Collected Edition of Heywood Broun*, published by Harcourt Brace and Company; copyright 1936, 1963 Heywood Hale Broun; Curtis Brown Ltd for permission to quote extracts from *The Great Sahara Mouse Hunt* by Miggs Pomeroy and Catherine Collins, published by Hutchinson & Co. and Houghton Mifflin Co.; James Brown Associates Inc. and the Author's Estate for permission to reprint an excerpt from A. J. Liebling's article 'Monsieur Flandin's Domaine', first published in the *New Yorker* of 13 September 1958: © 1958 The *New Yorker* Magazine Inc.; Lady Jean Campbell for permission to reprint her article 'A Visit to Randolph', first published in the New York *World Journal Tribune* of 25 December 1966; Cresset Press for permission to quote four lines from Frances Cornford's *Collected Poems*; Doubleday & Company Inc. for permission to reprint an excerpt from *A Smattering of Ignorance* by Oscar Levant: copyright 1939,

1940, by Oscar Levant; Elek Books Ltd for permission to quote four lines from 'The Vatican Rag' from *Tom Lehrer's Song Book*; the *Evening Standard* for permission to reprint 'Randolph Churchill: Untamable, Outrageous, Unforgettable' by Michael Foot, first published in the *Evening Standard* of 7 June 1968; Granada Television Ltd for permission to use a few lines from the interview 'Profile of Randolph Churchill', broadcast on 24 April 1961; David Higham Associates and the *New Statesman* for permission to reprint 'In Defence of Randolph Churchill' by Malcolm Muggeridge, first published in the *New Statesman* of 28 April 1956; Clive Irving for permission to reprint his article 'The Shade of Churchill: Randolph in Retrospect', first published in *20th Century Magazine*, Vol. 177, September 1968: © Clive Irving 1968; Leonard Lyons for permission to reprint excerpts from 'Morsels From the Lyons' Den', first published in the *New York Post* at various dates; the *New Statesman* for permission to reprint 'Great Contemporary' by Alan Brien, first published in the *New Statesman* of 14 June 1968; the *New York Times* for permission to reprint the United Press despatch 'Report from Cairo' quoted by Kenneth Downs in his essay 'Framed in the Prodigality of Nature': the despatch appeared in the *New York Times* on 30 November 1941; The *New Yorker* Magazine Inc. and Harcourt Brace Jovanovitch, Inc. for permission to reprint 'The Sock Hunt' from *My Sister Eileen*, first published in the *New Yorker* of 16 January 1937: copyright 1937, 1965 by Ruth McKenney; *The Observer* for permission to reprint the *Observer* Profile of Randolph Churchill published 30 October 1960: the article also appeared in *Atlantic Monthly* on 19 June 1961; the *Sunday Times* for permission to reprint a short extract from Clive Irving's interview of Randolph Churchill of April 1964: © Times Newspapers Ltd, London E.C.4, 1964, and for permission to reprint 'Randolph—the Man who was Fun to have Around' by Harold Macmillan, first published in the *Sunday Times* of 9 June 1968: © The *Sunday Times*, London, 1968; A. P. Watt & Son for permission to reproduce the essay on Randolph Churchill by Xenia Field; Sir George Weidenfeld for permission to reprint an excerpt from *Twenty-One Years* by Randolph Churchill, published by Weidenfeld and Nicolson.

KAY HALLE, 1971

Introduction

When Winston Churchill was thirty-one, Lady Lytton cautioned his new Private Secretary, Edward Marsh: 'The first time you meet Winston you see all his faults, and the rest of your life you spend discovering his virtues.'

I could appreciate the truth of this beautiful tribute when tremors from the 'quake of first meeting his son Randolph had subsided into a close and lasting friendship.

I met Randolph at a wedding reception in Cleveland, Ohio. It would perhaps be more accurate to say I was commandeered into Randolph's presence by his bewildered host, who had been firmly directed to bring me, without my escort, to their table.

After the introductions, Randolph's opening gambit was to inform me that I would shortly accompany him and his host to Little Mountain, in the country, for a raccoon hunt that had been arranged for him later that evening. If I refused, he too would decline to go. As I was dining that evening in honour of Charles F. Kettering, the inventor, Randolph's campaign plans seemed about to topple. His host, a soldier, sportsman and businessman of fortitude, was rendered utterly helpless. There was nothing for it but that he and I should take our battle orders from Randolph, which meant striking a compromise. It was agreed that all three of us would dine first in town in honour of Mr Kettering and proceed later to the raccoon hunt in the country.

By good fortune our dinner host was an Englishman who had served in the First World War on the fore-turret of the dreadnought *St Vincent*, in the Battle of Jutland. So Randolph was delighted and delightful. That is—until after dinner as we were waiting for Mr Kettering's films on the Galapagos Islands to start. Randolph, who was seated behind me, apparently wishing to see my hair, which I had hurriedly pushed up into a Persian lamb turban, lifted my hat from my head. To my distress and embarrassment long lengths of it fell to the floor. Weeks later when he was a guest at my parents' house he cut my hair off to my shoulders as I lay asleep on the drawing-room sofa. As he attempted to stop the flow of my tears, his touching excuse was, 'Your long hair made you seem older than me!'

On our arrival at Little Mountain we were greeted by a group of sportsmen eager to show Randolph the wooded delights of the mountain trails where the raccoon is stalked. But, after one quick glance at the inviting lodge with its roaring fire, he decided against 'hunting those poor defenceless beasts'. So—waving off the crestfallen hunters—he stood before the fireplace and began rehearsing what he would say the next day to an audience of the English-Speaking Union.

He was then nineteen and of striking, classic Greek beauty. His virtuosity as a debater in the Oxford Union had attracted the notice of an American lecture bureau, who had signed him up for this, his first lecture tour in the United States. Among the high points of that dry run for his speech, I remember best his shock at what he termed, 'the barbaric, unlawful Negro lynchings in your South', and 'the outrageous treatment of your Red Indians whom you almost decimated while our Indians multiplied under benevolent British rule'. And he scorned our concept of ourselves as 'The land of the free and the home of the brave'. As for our youth—he found them untrained in logic and therefore unable to present or debate ideas as well as their English counterparts. I thought I could foresee storm signals ahead. But the following day his presentation of his views was such a *tour de force* that his audience, which included a son of President James Garfield, found it hard to refute him.

Some months later he debated with Will Durant, the author, in another Cleveland appearance on 'Should India have Dominion Status?' Starting with an array of statistics Mr Durant proceeded to decry Randolph's boldness in discussing India without ever having been there. Whereas Randolph opened his rebuttal by imploring, 'I beseech you, Mr Durant, in the famous words of Oliver Cromwell, "I beseech you, in the bowels of Christ, think it possible you may be mistaken".' He then suggested that many scientists had made computations about the moon who hadn't been there. College debating teams filling the galleries roared their approval.

I, too, was dazzled by Randolph's skill with words, his logic and ability to speak on the unpinioned wing. And so, it seems, was his father, who later at Chartwell spoke to me with pride tinged with envy of Randolph's gift of spontaneous rhetoric.

But it was up at Little Mountain while we waited for the hunters to return that I glimpsed in Randolph a promise of those virtues Lady Lytton enjoyed in his father: a keenly searching and brilliant intellect; utter honesty and a breathtaking directness; a passion for truth, and an almost blind courage. And above all a deeply concerned heart. But what I treasure most from that evening of provocative monologue was the vivid way Randolph inspired me to look above the hedgerows of my young life and explore the world beyond.

The dominant chord throughout his talk was always his father, who at that time was out of office, a prophetic voice crying in the wilderness about the horrors implicit in the Nazi threat. But there was even then an independence of thought and an originality of spirit in Randolph which, years later, was perfectly expressed by Alice Roosevelt Longworth, the brilliant and spirited daughter of another towering figure, President Theodore Roosevelt. 'Randolph,' she said, 'is not the Young Pretender*, he is the Young Unpretender.'

Later, in an interview with Clive Irving, Randolph was to sum up his relationship with his father:

> Much as I revered and reverenced him, I wasn't prepared just to be an A.D.C. and go along. I wanted to have a show of my own. So, struggling to establish my own individuality and personality, I often said and wrote rather reckless things, which I suppose if I hadn't felt this frustration I would have tempered down. I suppose I am a markedly extrovert person and I like to cultivate and display my own personality. I try and think things out for myself. Substantially I went along with my father all the way, but I was always looking for opportunities to establish an individual position, and it's very hard to do so, obviously, when you're living under the shadow of the great oak—the small sapling, so close to the parent tree, doesn't perhaps receive enough sunshine. Of course, I had wonderful opportunities and to begin with everyone was very kind and helpful to me. But I became sort of bloody-minded, I suppose, and wanted to strike out on

* Bonnie Prince Charlie.

my own and adopted possibly rather an arrogant attitude towards people and institutions at a time when I didn't really have the ammunition or the skill to hit the target. But I hold neither guilt feelings nor reproaches about that. I think anyone can see that there were difficulties naturally inherent in the situation.*

With this frank self-analysis Randolph took the couch right out from under any amateur psychoanalysts.

But that evening on the mountain top, as he charted his dreams of a career in Parliament, he looked so young and hopeful he made me think of Frances Cornford's lines† on Rupert Brooke:

> A young Apollo, golden haired
> Stands dreaming on the verge of strife
> Magnificently unprepared
> For the long littleness of life.

Highlights from his childhood laced Randolph's talk, beginning with his birth on 28 May 1911, when he was christened Randolph Frederick Edward Spencer Churchill. The weight of these names did not daunt Randolph. Unlike many English children, he was not sent off to the nursery but enjoyed instead a close relationship with his father and his father's gifted friends.

I could sense that, as a child, Randolph 'could not understand how it was possible to reconcile the omnipotence of the Deity with the doctrine of free will', as he once put it to me. As I grew to know him it was inevitable which would triumph. His father when he was once asked if he was a pillar of the Church defined his position as 'a flying buttress, I support it from the outside'. During the Second World War Randolph was attached to Marshal Tito's Partisan forces and shared a small farmhouse deep in the woods of Croatia with two wartime companions and boyhood friends, Freddie Birkenhead‡ and Evelyn Waugh. In an attempt to stem Randolph's non-stop conversation his two comrades bet him £50 each that he could not read the Bible through in a week and prove it by submitting to a quiz. Though he completed the assignment 'like a devouring flame', in less than the time allotted him, the torrent of words continued. His first reaction to the Holy Book was one of

* *The Sunday Times*, April 1964.
† Frances Cornford, *Collected Poems*, London: Cresset Press, 1960.
‡ The 2nd Earl of Birkenhead.

such overwhelming horror at the many instances of God's thunderous wrath and punishments that he exploded, 'God, wasn't God God-awful!' But he was also impressed with how well the Bible was written and wished that it had been brought to his attention before! In his more reflective moods he would quote Disraeli's view that 'Sensible men are of the same religion—Sensible men never tell.'

Randolph admitted he was a naughty, unmanageable child, 'unable to brook authority or discipline'. William Cowper's lines:

> Born a disputant, a sophist bred,
> His nurse he silenced and his tutor led

were as true of Randolph as of Charles James Fox, about whom they were written. So, at the age of nine, he was packed off to Sandroyd, a preparatory school. At fourteen he went to Eton and was appointed a fag for Freddie Birkenhead, who described one occasion when Randolph became so bellicose he was tossed from a first-floor window into the street, which apparently left him unharmed, for on landing he went right on talking as if he had not been interrupted.

Like his father, Randolph was not a brilliant scholar. He was eighteen when he went to Oxford, where he spent four terms and later admitted he had been lax in both sports and studies. Aware of the coincidence that Randolph shared the same birthday as the Younger Pitt, who had been Chancellor of the Exchequer, First Lord of the Treasury and Prime Minister of England at twenty-four, Winston Churchill once reminded one of Randolph's tutors that though there might have been two Pitts there would be three Churchills.

Randolph liked to point out that he had been born at 33 Eccleston Square, within the sound of Bow Bells, which made him a Cockney, and that at the time of his birth he 'came from poor but honest parents'. This was indeed true, as his father's salary as Home Secretary in Asquith's Liberal Government was about all Winston Churchill could then draw upon to support his family apart from what he earned by speaking and writing. 'I live from mouth to hand!' he would say.

Though Randolph strove seven times to win a seat in Parliament he succeeded only once, on his third attempt, in 1940 after the death of Adrian Moering, when he sat for the Lancashire cotton weaving town of Preston. On that occasion he was unopposed because of the political armistice between the Conservative and Labour Parties during the Second World War when seats were uncontested. In spite of the frustration of his appetite for a career in government, his interest in politics remained undiminished to the end of his life. The late Commander Anthony Kimmins used to recount an instance of Randolph's absorption with politics when they were together on a warship in the Mediterranean during the Second World War. With shells exploding and falling all around them Randolph was in the middle of a dramatic account of a particular political campaign and seemed unaware of the shellfire. He talked on, almost convincing the Commander that nothing could compare in excitement with an election. Not even the battle raging around them!

On his return to his constituents in Preston after the war, he spoke to them of his aims that 'all thinking people of all classes wanted the abolition of unemployment, equality of education and opportunity and the removal of class distinction'. It was then that he toyed with the thought of forming a centre party in the spirit of his grandfather Lord Randolph Churchill's Tory Democrats, which might replace the Labour or Tory Party. When Labour chieftains responded that a centre party had no place in the British political system as it would weaken democracy and fertilize dictatorships, Randolph retorted that Labour's Trade Unions 'were more anxious to have political power than to achieve desirable public ends'.

When he failed as a candidate for Bournemouth in another election he rationalized his defeat, saying, 'I do not wish to represent a lot of stuffy old ladies from Bournemouth. I want to fight for really hard-pressed people.' One of Randolph's Labour opponents, Michael Foot, once described him as 'an eighteenth-century Whig' and 'a political buccaneer; with in one part of his outlook a deep hatred for Conservatism'. Throughout his life, Randolph, like his father, always fought on the right side of the moral issues of the day, whether the subject under discussion was Hitler, unfair exploitation or a concern for privacy.

He came to realize, however, that he lacked the discipline and continuity of performance necessary for a life in politics. On his failure to achieve it, his friend Malcolm Muggeridge was later to write of him that 'worldly success has no surprises, and supreme success is always supremely commonplace. Failure on the other hand is incalculable and therefore entertaining'.

Randolph was always a realist so he decided on journalism as a career, where, as he put it, 'few credentials or examinations are required'. The variety of British and American newspapers and magazines that carried his by-line ranged from *The Times* to the publications of the Hearst Press and the *New Statesman*. As a polemical journalist his attitude of fearless independence of his editors and newspaper owners often caused him to be dismissed but as often rehired. It left him unmoved to be accused of biting the hand that fed him. When the 15 May 1955 issue of the *People* called him 'a paid hack' no one was surprised when he sued for libel and was awarded £5,000. His brilliant performance under cross-examination in court came to be known as 'Randolph's Finest Hour'.

For nearly a quarter of a century he waged his own colourful brand of crusade to improve the ethics of journalism. In his passionate condemnation of the invasion of privacy it was his view that:

> . . . every human being in this country of ours whether he be a politician, a journalist, a plumber, a carpenter, a bricklayer, or even a member of the Royal Family, is entitled to some genuine privacy in his private life and that it is complete abuse in the name of the so-called Freedom of the Press for rich men to try to get richer by allowing their editors to send underpaid reporters into people's homes in order to ask impertinent questions.

Just a few weeks before he died, Randolph had the great satisfaction of knowing that the Press Council had upheld his complaint against the *Daily Sketch* and one of its reporters for what he called 'two of the vilest and most intrusive stories . . . in almost every detail fabricated', concerning the break-up of the marriage of Mrs Jeremy Fry. Though Randolph had never met Mrs Fry he came up to London to hear her own version of the 'story', 'sentence by sentence', and became so convinced of its truth that he championed her against what he charged was a trumped-up interview and a misleading photograph, representing 'a gross intrusion into people's private lives and a flagrant breach of journalistic ethics'.

The writer of the *Daily Sketch* article issued a writ of libel against Randolph and the *Spectator* magazine in which he expressed these views in June 1964. Mrs Fry in turn issued a writ of libel against the *Daily Sketch*. Two years later the newspaper paid Mrs Fry £5,000 damages and offered sincere apologies. Almost another year passed before the reporter's action against Randolph was dismissed and the reporter was ordered to pay the court costs. Once the law courts had finished with these cases, Randolph asked the Press Council to adjudicate. Its Report, published on 9 April 1968, strongly condemned the *Daily Sketch* 'both for the manner of the interview and the publication of resultant articles'.

Two years after his death, it was surely Randolph's crusade in the cause of privacy that helped generate two proposals that were introduced into the House of Commons in 1970 to create by Act of Parliament a general right to privacy. It was Randolph's view that, 'It is a curious thing that while the wealthy men who own papers set themselves up to criticize every kind of institution, they themselves are the one institution which is totally immune from criticism. They have the power not only of the Press but of the *Sup*-press.' And, he used to repeat over and over again, 'I am one of those who believe there is a fifth freedom—freedom from the Press.' When an American reporter in London asked him why he was suing the provocative British weekly *Private Eye* for libel, he told him, 'We don't have trial by Press as you do in your country. In this country we have trial by jury and the case is *sub judice*.' To the purveyors of pornography he would quote a withering phrase which Stanley Baldwin had levelled at Lord Rothermere and Lord Beaverbrook: 'Power without responsibility—the prerogative of the harlot through the ages.'

As a roving reporter Randolph covered the Spanish Civil War and assignments in Germany where, six months before Hitler came to power, with Churchillian foresight, he wrote in the *Sunday Graphic*, 'They are determined once more to have an army. I am sure that, once they have achieved it, they will not hesitate to use it.' In 1938 he left journalism to be commissioned in his father's old regiment, the Fourth Queen's Own Hussars, and in 1939 he was transferred to one of the early Commando units. In 1941, with the rank of major, he was placed for a few months in charge of Army Press Relations at Middle East Headquarters, Cairo, where he managed to abolish certain fatuous rules of British and Egyptian censorship, which won him the respect of his journalistic colleagues and the enmity of the military authorities.

Britain's fortunes were then at their lowest ebb. One disaster after another was occurring in Libya as Rommel advanced through the desert. It so happened that a staff officer at Cairo Headquarters made a series of foolishly misleading and over-optimistic statements to correspondents and they quoted him as the Cairo military spokesman in subsequent dispatches. This caused the Prime Minister, Winston Churchill, to come under heavy attack in Parliament from Opposition members who believed his son Randolph had been guilty of misleading the Press and the British public. Randolph was utterly blameless, for at the time in question he had been taking a group of important American journalists to the front, which was part of his job, as the U.S. had not yet entered the war. He could have denied the implied charge of lying to the Press. Instead he said nothing, believing more was at stake than his personal reputation.

In 1942, as a member of the First Special Air Service Regiment, he was the first M.P. to join the parachute troops, and took part in the raid on Benghazi deep behind enemy lines. On this, his favourite mission, he and six others were assigned to blow up ships anchored in Benghazi harbour in Libya.

Randolph also took part in the North African and Sicilian invasions, and landed at Salerno with the Commandos. Following these actions he was attached to a tank regiment, the North Irish Horse, and remained with it until the capture of Tunis in 1943. In 1944 he parachuted into Bosnia in Yugoslavia where, under Brigadier Fitzroy Maclean, he served as British Liaison Officer to Marshal Tito's Partisans.

A few months after his arrival, in company with other Allied officers, Randolph escaped with Tito to the mountains, where their headquarters were raided by German parachutists and airborne troops.

On a flight with a group of comrades he crashed in a plane on a bleak mountain top in the interior of Yugoslavia, an accident in which ten were killed and nine were saved. Though some were rescued from the burning plane through the bravery of a Yugoslav, Sergeant Pavelic, Philip Jordan attributed his and Evelyn Waugh's escape to Randolph's mad heroism when, with his bare hands, he forced open parts of the burning fuselage, causing a gap through which his friends dropped to safety. Two Partisans and Randolph, who was in shock with an injured spine and water on the knees, were evacuated by plane to a British hospital in Italy. Later Randolph was awarded the M.B.E. for his daring and courage. In 1951 he completed his last military assignment as a war correspondent for the *Daily Telegraph*, in the Korean War, in which he was wounded.

Randolph's first wife, Pamela Digby (now Mrs Leland Hayward), bore him a son, Winston, with whom he collaborated in one of his last literary ventures, *The Six Day War*, a vivid account of the Israeli–Arab conflict. Pride in his young son—a flyer, adventurer, author, journalist and now a Member of Parliament—moved Randolph to express the hope that it was his son who would become that 'third Churchill' that Sir Winston had warned was on his way. June Osborne, Randolph's second wife, is the mother of his daughter Arabella.

Believing with his father that 'there was small hope for the world unless the United States and the British Commonwealth worked together in fraternal association' Randolph made many visits to his grandmother's native land, lecturing over most of the United States, and becoming an expert on the variety of its regions. After covering Presidential conventions and campaigns and versing himself in the nuances of American politics, he was unable to resist 'intervening in our affairs', offering one Presidential candidate, Alfred Landon, advice on how to win. He expressed his admiration for President Truman by likening him to 'a vulcanized Indiarubber ball'. After the Suez crisis, Randolph was the first British correspondent to say a word in praise of John Foster Dulles; an act which took a certain courage at a time when international tempers were still inflamed.

At the unveiling ceremony for the bronze statue of Sir Winston Churchill that stands before the British Embassy in Washington, D.C., Randolph remarked to the sculptor, William McVey: 'I see you are putting up statues to British statesmen. How nice! Of course, we have statues in England to George Washington, Benjamin Franklin, Franklin Roosevelt and others. I've looked everywhere in Washington for a statue of Lord North or George the

Third, but I can't find them anywhere. No! Those, of course, are the men to whom you should be erecting statues. It was on account of their stupidity that you won your independence!'

During interviews at the White House with each successive President, Randolph developed a reputation for putting blunt and unadorned questions to them all. With none was he closer or more direct than with President Kennedy, of whom he wrote after his death, 'I loved him as a brother'. Their last meeting at the White House, forty-five days before the President was assassinated, fell on 9 October 1963, the day after Randolph, with weird prescience, expressed his premonition that something was wrong with Britain's Prime Minister, Harold Macmillan. Randolph's anxiety over his forebodings made him decide to put in a transatlantic call to the Prime Minister's son-in-law, Julian Amery, a Member of Parliament, who was in Blackpool attending a Conservative Party conference. The call revealed that Mr Macmillan had that very day, after a two-hour Cabinet meeting, decided to resign his premiership because of a sudden illness. Randolph, then, was the first to bear 'the unbearable news' to President Kennedy at the White House. After exchanging mutual expressions of affection and admiration for Harold Macmillan and deep concern for his health, I was startled to hear Randolph ask President Kennedy how he could face the thought of having to deal with Harold Wilson were he to become Prime Minister. Obviously amused by Randolph's unabashed directness the President assured him that he could, of course, work with anyone who represented Great Britain as Prime Minister.

Like his father, Randolph dismissed his mounting physical ills with complete disdain. When Sir Winston, at eighty, became Prime Minister for the second time in 1951 Harold Nicolson found him 'looking white and fatty, . . . most unhealthy . . . but somehow out of this sickly mountain comes a volcanic flash'. I saw that same phenomenon repeated many times in Randolph in his later years. Especially in 1964 in New York City when he accepted, in his father's stead, the Theodore Herzl gold medal award from the Zionist organization in America for Sir Winston's long record in supporting the Jewish homeland. Exhausted from illness, his skin of fish-belly pallor and his chin almost resting on the long table before him, Randolph endured endless speeches before his turn came. Then, after being introduced by Lord Caradon, the U.K. Representative at the United Nations, he rose miraculously and gave one of the most splendid acceptance speeches his audience of over a thousand people could remember hearing. Though he dropped the gold medal on receiving it, he picked it up, put it between his teeth, bit it and assured his audience that it was real, which brought him a second uproarious ovation.

Sometime after his return to England, Randolph went to hospital for the removal of what proved to be a non-cancerous part of a lung. On hearing the Press release from the Brompton Chest Hospital that 'Mr Randolph Churchill today underwent an operation for a non-malignant condition of the lung', Evelyn Waugh was heard to exclaim at the bar of White's Club, 'Trust those bloody fool doctors to cut out of Randolph the only part of him that wasn't malignant.' When this was reported back to the Brompton Hospital, Randolph wired Evelyn on 28 March 1964: *Enchanted by your benignant thoughts about me in Holy Week. Happy feast of Resurrection.* This brought about an immediate reconciliation between Randolph and Evelyn, who had been separated over a minor quarrel and were to die within so short a time of each other.

The day following his lung operation Randolph was drinking champagne and smoking cigarettes to the disbelief of the nurses and his stream of guests. On the following evening he was informed that blood had appeared on his pillow and he would have to return to surgery. He refused to do so. Recounting it all to me later, he explained that the 'blood' was dried drops from the chocolate-covered mints he was in the habit of eating before going to sleep. 'As they did not examine the "blood" I had no intention of enlightening them with the truth,' he told me. Randolph was not a particularly enthusiastic admirer of the medical profession, though he did respect and enjoy discussions with certain members of it—especially with Dr George Crile, Chief of Surgery at the Cleveland Clinic. Both were ever hot for arguments in which they would carve up opponents they considered ill-equipped for a rational discussion leading to the truth. Both delighted in throwing out what they deemed to be the false facts and specious arguments of their adversaries as if they were dealing with bad tissue. Sometimes they would turn their tactics on each other.

Throughout the years of our enduring friendship I was able to look forward with joy, though not without some trepidation, to Randolph's yearly visits to Washington, when he would turn my house into uproar with tumultuous round-table debates and fact-finding discussions with his most old and admired friends. Scotty Reston and Arthur Krock of the *New York Times*, Robert McNamara, Joseph and Stewart Alsop, and Eric Sevareid, 'the Montaigne of T.V.', were among the regulars, with many odd and interesting irregulars thrown in. Randolph had a way of crashing into the heart of the matter, no matter what was under discussion, infusing the talk with such an electric quality, dropping so many depth charges and challenges, that after he departed Susan Ford, my housekeeper, would say, 'When he leaves the oxygen seems to go out of the house. Everything seems so dull.' And so it did! Susan loved her early-morning dialogues with Randolph when, seated on my drawing-room sofa, shaving with his cordless electric razor, he would discuss the menus for the day with her. He loved cherrystone clams, unknown in England, and ate his first ear of sweet corn at our table in Cleveland with the comment, 'We feed it to the hogs.' Thereafter, he became a willing hog and would often serve corn at his own table in London.

After he had departed I would find myself taking the measure of our friends and visitors by the manner in which they either met, stood up to or tolerated Randolph's over-heated lapses of good manners in arguments. If his adversaries, critics or mere bystanders took his slings and shots personally, I knew they were missing his true intentions as he never meant to be personal in his drawing-room jousts however targeted his thrusts may have sounded and seemed. He preferred ideas to people, and in arguments considered his opponents as envelopes for their ideas—worthwhile or worthless. He went into a battle of words with his sword unsheathed and expected the same from his friends as well as his adversaries. If he learned later that he had been wounding or outrageous he was disturbed, and hastened to make amends. I know, as I've paved the way for some of his heartfelt apologies. 'I must never be allowed out in private,' he would sometimes say—in mock despair.

In sharp contrast were the hours I spent with a mellower Randolph during the last years of his life, at his beloved Stour, in East Bergholt, on the Suffolk–Essex border, overlooking the beautiful valley where John Constable lived and painted. In the late afternoons we would sit under the deliciously scented tangle of climbing roses, wistaria, honeysuckle and clematis that crowned the columned arbour above us—all of his own design—and I could sense his joy as we listened to little Arabella reciting in her clear child's voice the same familiar poems so beloved by her father and grandfather.

Randolph was at his most endearing with his adored pug dogs, always at his feet or on his lap, especially Captain Boycott, whom he named after the question that blacked him out when he appeared on the $64,000 television quiz programme on a visit to the United States in 1956. My sister Jane Crile and I must surely be held accountable for Randolph's freeze-up on that programme as we persuaded him to deny himself alcohol on that day. Alas, our over-solicitous concern resulted in throwing him off his equilibrium.

Always a delightful part of Randolph's household was his research team of 'Young Gentlemen', as he lovingly called those journalists, history and English scholars who laboured with him on his massive biography of his father. His deep concern for their lives and careers was touching. When the time came for one to leave, Randolph would help him towards some new and rewarding job. All of his 'Young Gentlemen' remained his close friends, which is true of most young people who really knew him.

Tending his beautiful gardens and publishing provocative pamphlets under the imprimatur Country Bumpkins Ltd took up the little time that was left after his labours on the major work of his life—his father's biography. Everything that came before seemed a prelude for that great adventure for which his father had designated him. His volumes *The Fight for the Tory Leadership* and *Lord Derby: 'King of Lancashire'*, helped to prepare him for his *magnum opus*. Over the years he wrote books with such disparate titles as *They Serve the Queen*, *The Story of the Coronation*, *Fifteen Famous English Homes*, *The Rise and Fall of Sir Anthony Eden*, *What I Said About the Press* and *Twenty-One Years*. He also edited three volumes of his father's speeches.

Away from London and the tumult of politics, journalism, idle hours at White's Club and the waste of misplaced energies, Randolph created a new and rewarding life for himself at Stour. At the entrance of his house he placed a plaque which expressed his own new style of life:

I am come to a determination
to make no idle visits this summer
nor to give up any time to commonplace people
I shall return to Bergholt
—John Constable

Randolph's long search for a true career became his style of life, which became in itself a career. In an age when the dizzying advance of the sciences has created a widespread and deadening conformity, Randolph, always a life enhancer, remained unswervingly individual, one of the few Grand Originals.

He died in his sleep on the night of 6 June 1968. His ashes rest near his family's ancestral Blenheim in the lovely little churchyard of St Martin's at Bladen, at the side of his father and of his grandfather, Lord Randolph Churchill.

In 1924 Lord Birkenhead put down some of his thoughts about his close friend Winston Churchill:

Only his friends understand him well. And they know that there is no man in public life in England with a heart so warm, with a simplicity so complete, with a loyalty so unswerving and so dependable. He has indeed, in the intimacy of personal friendship, a quality that is almost feminine in its caressing charm. And he has never in all his life failed a friend, however embarrassing the obligations, which he felt it necessary to honour, proved at the moment when he honoured them.

And Winston Churchill, after the death of his great friend Lord Birkenhead in 1930, wrote:

Some men when they die after busy, toilsome, successful lives leave a great stock of scrip and securities, of acres of factories or the good will of large undertakings. F.E. banked his treasure in the hearts of his friends and they will cherish his memory 'til their time is come.

These sentiments by Randolph's father and godfather about each other serve, decades later, as the truest epitaphs for their son and godchild, who also 'banked his treasure in the hearts of his friends', and they 'will cherish his memory 'til their time is come'.

KAY HALLE

Washington, D.C.

Childhood

Excerpts from the Letters of Sir Winston Churchill to Lady Churchill

W.S.C. to his wife

23 July 1913   H.M.S. *Enchantress*

. . . Tender love to you my sweet one and to both those little kittens and especially that radical Randolph [aged two]. Diana is a darling too: and I repent to have expressed a preference. But somehow he seems of a more genial generous nature while she is mysterious and self-conscious. They are vy beautiful and will win us honour some day when everyone is admiring her and grumbling about him.

15 December 1915

I see photos of Diana & Randolph [aged four] in all the papers. They will be getting quite vain.

27 February 1921

I gave the children the choice of Randolph [aged ten] or the Zoo. They screamed for Randolph in most loyal & gallant fashion.

Schoolboy

W. M. Hornby
A. G. Huson
H. G. Babington Smith
J. D. Harford
A. H. G. Kerry
C. R. N. Routh
Sir Robert Birley

Reports on Randolph by his Headmasters and Tutors at Sandroyd Preparatory School and Eton

1922—W. M. Hornby, Headmaster of Sandroyd, on eleven-year-old Randolph:

> A quick boy, at times too quick as he is apt to answer before he thinks. . . . He likes to dash ahead too fast. He must learn to digest things more slowly and to be tidier. . . . His clumsy pen does not keep up with his quick brain and makes for slipshod work. . . . His thoughts appear to fly from one thing to another with an uncontrolled rapidity that spoils his chances of achieving his best.

1924—A. G. Huson, mathematics tutor at Eton, on thirteen-year-old Randolph:

> He is hideously ingenious for a boy of his years. I hope this bodes well for the Country. I must say he is extremely good fun; one does not talk much when he wants to.

H. G. Babington Smith, mathematics master at Eton:

> Obstinacy appears to be one of his more prominent characteristics. He has shown himself to be possessed of a natural capacity in many directions but he does not take kindly to being taught.

J. D. Harford, Classics master at Eton:

> His chief fault at present is to strain to breaking point a natural adroitness of mind, by indulging in constant interruptions in the form of queries and quibbles. He shews at present no sign of realising that one of the best forms of discrimination and to develop criticism is self-criticism, a faculty which would

enable him to see that his remarks, wasteful of time and fraying to everyone's patience, are very largely cheap, pointless and irrelevant.

1928—C. R. N. Routh on Randolph Churchill, who was not yet fourteenth out of the fourteen of his division in mathematics:

> The reason for this humble result is not entirely that he is the worst mathematician in the Division—though I think it probable that he is. But he is further handicapped by his obsession for the sound of his own voice. At first I dared to answer him back (in fear and trembling) but, finding I was not completely withered, I persevered and have managed to keep his effusiveness slightly in check. It has been good fun (but poor Maths).

1928—C. R. N. Routh on Randolph Churchill, who was not yet seventeen:

> He seems to me to be a boy whose ideas and ambitions have outrun his years and capacities. . . .
>
> My chief criticism is that at present Churchill has very little use for mere facts. He is obsessed with the beauty of theories, but he forgets that historical theories without facts to prove his theories are mere vapourings. And it is this almost scorn for facts which leads people to think that he does less work than he really puts in. He has only had one failure this Half with me, but with most other boys three or four of his essays must have meant a 'tear-over'. I am a little frightened that Churchill may not turn his gifts to advantage unless he can bring himself to do some drudgery.
>
> And that he has some gifts even his poorest work proves. He brings to his history what very few other boys bring—ardent enthusiasm. He is overflowing with ideas, he has passionate likes and hates, he is as courageous as they make them in defending his theories, and he has a dialectical skill which is often needed if he is going to get out of some of the holes into which he gets himself. But he does get out of them!
>
> His literary style is lively and bold. It often degenerates into melodrama, but it is always interesting and always fresh. He has more sense of balance and rhythm in prose than anyone else in

the division, so that I have always turned to his work with relief. But some of the views that he expresses are too reactionary even for me!

Altogether I have enjoyed making his acquaintance, and I hope to meet him again. Is it unkind—it is not meant to be—to suggest that he is too quarrelsome, that he likes being in a minority, and enjoys, not rubbing people up the wrong way, but the result of having rubbed them the wrong way?

Robert Birley, who was later to become Headmaster of Charterhouse and of Eton, wrote the following report in July 1928, just before Randolph left Eton:

Let it be said at once that his work was not always satisfactory. There was a period when he seemed to be reading the books extremely sketchily, though he certainly improved in this, and he is very careless about showing up his work in time. But he answers fairly well to expostulation. He is not by any means a bad worker, and there is all the difference between a boy who takes a holiday and then does nothing, and one who reads widely and does not waste his time. But he needs discipline and he must not get into the habit of working only when he wants to.

His real trouble is his facility. He finds it a great deal too easy to do moderately well, and he is developing too early the journalist's ability to 'work up' a little information or a solitary idea. I can give a good, though rather an unfair example. The other day, when he was with me we talked for five or ten minutes about Shaftesbury, and I told him one or two points. The next morning one of the questions in the trial paper was on Shaftesbury's career. As he is up to me in trials [examinations] I happened to look at his paper and saw that he had done the question. He had served up just the few things I had said, turned into a longish answer. It was extremely well done. There were some excellent allusions and the whole thing was thrown into the form of a good summary of his character.

The trouble is it was far too well done. There is nothing wrong in his putting down the ideas given him or in his expanding them. But for all the allusions and the good writing there really was hardly any original thought or real thought at all in the whole answer. It was, in fact, a piece of very good journalism.

There is no need for him merely to do this. He has a first-rate brain. But he must be prepared to do some hard thinking for himself and not to take an easy course. His easy course will not be a dull one, in fact it will be an amusing and interesting one. But it will be second-rate for all that.

There is one other matter which is a little disquieting. He seems to find his friends entirely among people who are either more stupid or much younger than himself. I am really more worried about the former. He really must not search out foils. It is far too easy a way to be clever. This fact is due, of course, to the difficulty he finds in getting on with his contemporaries. Here I think he has shown great improvement. Knowing that he was likely to become unpopular in any division he was in, I was rather uneasy about mine this half [term]. But he behaved really well, without aggressiveness and conceit. This is a very good sign. I am asking him to join the Essay Society, which should I think be useful to him.

I have attacked him pretty often about his style, though I am not really very alarmed about it. It is at the moment abominable, extremely rhetorical, windy and involved, full of clichés and pomposity. All these, however, are faults on the right side. They are due partly to his reading a good deal of Macaulay, mostly to an attempt on his side to form a style (which is to be commended). I think that he should try to get out of it and write more simply. It makes his answers now very heavy and rather jaded.

He is trying I think to improve his handwriting, but not very steadily. He must persevere in this. He is quite one of the most interesting pupils I have had, and he is a very pleasant one. His mind is very vigorous and his interests are wide. At the moment he is going through a mental crisis. I consider it almost inevitable that a boy with a mind as logical as his should experience very real religious difficulties. It is almost a sign of mental honesty. But while it is good that he should be honest in this, and that he should be ambitious, I hope he will not become too self-centred. There *is* a danger of this.

University

Sir Roy F. Harrod
Sir John Betjeman
Christopher Sykes
John Sutro
Stuart Scheftel

Randolph in Oxford

by

Roy F. Harrod

(*Eminent British economist: former President of the Royal Economic Society; author of* The Life of John Maynard Keynes, 'The Prof' (*A Personal Memorial of Lord Cherwell*), Money, *and other works*)

'The Prof' (Lord Cherwell)* sometimes brought Randolph, when he was a schoolboy at Eton, to dine at Christ Church High Table and subsequently to drink port in the Senior Common Room with the dons of Christ Church. Randolph was quite exceptionally good-looking as a schoolboy, and, it need hardly be said, he was quite at ease in talking with the learned professors. On these occasions 'the Prof' always sent him back to school with a large box of chocolates.

One evening the conversation seemed to be lagging—after all there was not all that much in common between the schoolboy and the learned men—and I suggested to the Prof that he and Randolph should come round to my rooms. I thought to myself—what shall we talk about? In my enthusiasm, I extracted from a file some charts that I had recently made, depicting the state of the British economy, and explained to Randolph how to read them. To my surprise, he immediately controverted me—in a flash—and affirmed that my charts did not mean what I said they did, but something different. I was quite taken aback. Reflecting upon that episode, it occurs to me that my charts purported to present rather a gloomy view of the British economy, as they have so often done since, and that he, being the son of the then Chancellor of the Exchequer, felt it his filial duty to demonstrate that, rightly interpreted, they

* A very great friend of Winston Churchill and his most important adviser during the Second World War. See my book *The Prof*, London: Macmillan & Co., 1959.

showed that the economy was in good shape. He was quite polite, but stuck firmly to his point that his interpretation of the charts was correct and mine wrong.

Some two or three years after that he became my official pupil at Christ Church. When first there, he passed his preliminary examination in history for which I was not responsible—he had a blinding row with one of our history tutors, a very distinguished scholar—and then came on to me to be generally supervised and, in particular, to be taught economics, for the Final Honours School of Philosophy, Politics and Economics. He was a delightful pupil and I was very happy with him. There was no more criticism of my charts. He did not do much work, but I felt that it was within my powers of persuasion to correct that in due course.

Randolph came up to Christ Church in the wrong term. Looking back, I think that this was the biggest factor—paradoxical though it may be to attribute so much importance to a seemingly trivial event—that accounted for his failure to achieve all that he might have achieved in his subsequent life. Almost all undergraduates arrive in Michaelmas Term (October). He came in Hilary Term (January). Why could he not have come at the proper time? Whose fault was it? Winston's? Clementine's? His own? It is possible that Winston, lacking knowledge of university routines, would have supposed that his son might be allowed to come up to Christ Church at whatever time in the year best suited family plans.

But it was not so. The point is that almost all the 'freshmen' arrive on the same day. Together they all have to do a lot of things for the first time. They inquire of one another and get to know one another while going through identical experiences. You make quick friendships with those on your own stair or on neighbouring stairs. But if you come up in an odd term, the others have all settled down into their own friendships and do not pay much attention to a newcomer, except to advise him in a superficial sort of way, like the policeman at the corner of the street.

Of course Randolph was not lacking in friends or good fellowship at Oxford. He had his friends from Eton. There was Basil Ava,* who, although he was at Balliol College, happened for a time to be my pupil, and was, in some respects, the most brilliant one I

* Later the 4th Marquess of Dufferin and Ava. He was killed in Burma in the Second World War.

ever had. There was Freddy Furneaux,* a fascinating figure. And there were others. But they did not suffice. One cannot get the benefit of Oxford without making deep and intimate friendships with many coming from different schools and different strata of society. I do not believe that Randolph did this—and that just because he came up in the wrong term.

I kept a watchful eye on him. I was Senior Censor (chief administrative officer) of Christ Church at that time, and got a good view of the life of the college as a whole. So far as I could see, Randolph was not mingling enough in it, and this distressed me.

About half-way through his prescribed time at Oxford, he came to me and said that he wanted leave of absence (for two terms or a year?) to give lectures in America. He had gone around with his father on a lecture tour during the vacation and, on the side, made contracts amounting to more than £2,000. This would represent, perhaps, more than £6,000 today. Rather good for a young man aged about nineteen or twenty! It is to be remembered that the Churchills were by no means rich. I remember Winston once saying to me, 'I believe that, if I did not have to spend so much time earning money by writing, I could one day become Prime Minister.' Doubtless Randolph was helped in securing his contracts by his father's name, but this did not boom as loud in the U.S.A. in 1930 as it did in 1945. Anyhow, he must have shown some enterprise. So I congratulated him, but urged him not to go. I said, 'Randolph, you will not come back to us.' He assured me that he would. I had my own conviction that he had not struck deep roots in Christ Church, or in Oxford, such as would pull him back. He did not have to come back to Oxford to maintain contact with his old friends, like Basil and Freddy. And in fact he did not come back.

I very much wanted Randolph to complete his degree. I felt that he had a certain pride that would make him *wish* to get a good class. A great many undergraduates at Oxford do no more work than Randolph did in the first year or two. Then the more determined among them get down to business. I believe that Randolph would have done so, and that he would have understood the requirements —precision of language, accuracy of thought, citation of references for factual statements, due humility in the face of unresolved

* Later the 2nd Lord Birkenhead and author of a number of distinguished books.

problems. These were the qualities that during his life he most lacked, but he could have acquired them by the traditional disciplines of Oxford—he had the brain to do so. On some occasions in later life, for example in legal suits, he did show himself capable of very accurate thinking. But not so in his more general writings on contemporary affairs. I believe that, if he had subjected himself to the disciplines necessary to obtain a good class in his Honours degree, he would have achieved an understanding of the prerequisites for effective intervention in wider matters. Thus I was very keen that he should submit himself to the fierce discipline of an Honours examination at Oxford. And I think that the world lost something through his not having done so.

Winston was against his going on the lecture tour. Randolph has stated the opposite, but his memory must have been at fault. (Of course he may have over-persuaded Winston at a later date; or Winston may have acquiesced with a good grace, so as not to quarrel with his son.) I already had, independently of Randolph, friendly contacts with the Churchill family. Winston rang me up and suggested that I should go and stay with him for a weekend at Chartwell, so that we might combine our forces in dissuading Randolph from accepting the proposal for a lecture tour in the U.S.A.

Naturally in that weekend it was Winston who did most of the talking. After dinner on the Saturday, or it may have been the Sunday, he stood up with his back to the chimneypiece and delivered a great oration. He discoursed on the nature of a university and on the merits of a university education. He spoke of the ripe judgement and mellow wisdom of the university teachers. They had devoted their lives to reading, study and reflection. They were unique in this respect. Through their teaching one could learn to be a wiser man. Then he talked about his own experience, in a modest and charming way, about how his lack of a university education had handicapped him in his political career, about how, in the cut and thrust of debate with someone like Arthur Balfour, he had felt himself at a disadvantage for lack of the weapons, and the tools of thinking, that a university education could have given him. It was the most splendid eulogy of the university function that I have ever heard. How I wished that I was a Boswell who could go back to my room and write it all down! I will only say in self-defence that Boswell's subject was more terse in his epigrammatic comments than Winston. But Winston's quality of judgement was no less good.

I was watching Randolph during Winston's discourse. It was all flowing over him, so it seemed to me, like water off a duck's back. Perhaps he had heard it all before. He sat on the sofa alongside one wall of the room, looking rather bored. I envisaged his thought— 'mellow wisdom, ripe judgement, my foot!' For him the 'mellow wisdom' had so far meant mainly me, a youthful personage. He was obviously unshaken in his resolve to go out to the U.S.A. and earn that £2,000 plus.

Finally, when he went out of the room, Winston turned to me and said, 'Well, we have got down to brass tacks.'

Thinking back on that great evening, I have sometimes wondered whether Winston, on occasions of high affairs of State, in the British Cabinet or at international conferences, overestimated the receptiveness of his audience as regards his own 'mellow wisdom', and wrongly supposed that they would translate his superbly poised judgements into 'brass tacks'.

Randolph did not come back to Oxford. But we remained friends, and I saw him occasionally. My wife and I once spent a weekend with him in his country house. I believe that, whenever he came to Oxford, he usually called in to see if I was at home. I always enjoyed seeing him. He somehow braced one up and gave one a sense of the worthwhileness and meaningfulness of life. It was worth making a real effort in a good cause. Although I did not see him all that often, I regarded him as a friend in the true sense. Had I been in some difficulty in which he could have helped me by doing a kindness— though the occasion did not arise, because our paths of life did not often cross—I should have gone to him without hesitation and in complete confidence that he would comply, if humanly possible, with what I asked of him.

There was an amusing coincidence that may be worth recording. Shortly after he returned from the U.S.A. there was a telephone call from Randolph. On the previous day Basil Murray had rung me up with a request—granted—that he might use my rooms in Christ Church for the day, for the purpose of doing some telephoning and writing an article for the Beaverbrook Press on the topic of who should be the Chancellor of Oxford University. No definite resolution as regards this had yet been made; but the people under consideration for the position were Lord Halifax and the Prince of Wales (subsequently King Edward VIII and later still the Duke of Windsor). Basil seemed to be rather considerably in favour of the Prince of Wales and slanted his article accordingly.

It occurs to me that there was a certain resemblance between Basil Murray and Randolph. Both were the sons of great fathers,* both had the greatest personal charm when in good form, both could be difficult and even 'impossible' on other occasions, both had considerable literary gifts, both were very intelligent; neither knew how to orient his life and neither achieved what his talents should have rendered him capable of achieving. Basil Murray died, at a younger age than Randolph, of a sickness contracted when he was reporting on the 'government' (liberal) side in the Spanish Civil War. It must be said, in fairness to Randolph, that he achieved rather more than Basil Murray.

The next day Randolph rang me up with a request—granted— that he might use my rooms in Christ Church for the day, for the purpose of doing some telephoning and writing an article for the Rothermere Press on the topic of who should be Chancellor of Oxford University. Thus for two whole days I could not use my rooms either for teaching or for studying. It turned out that Randolph was much more violently in favour of the Prince of Wales and more violently against Lord Halifax than Basil Murray had been. He used my telephone for much propaganda.

And then he made a fatal mistake, against which I warned him. He rang the residence of the Prince of Wales to ascertain if the Prince would be willing to serve as Chancellor. Of course, if the Prince of Wales had expressed willingness, this would almost have settled the issue. Or, anyhow, it would have caused dreadful embarrassment to those who wanted Lord Halifax.

Randolph was told that he must on no account refer to the Prince of Wales's willingness or unwillingness to accept this

* Basil Murray's father was Gilbert Murray, an eminent classical scholar, a distinguished poet—as exemplified in his verse translations of Euripedes—and a passionate liberal and sponsor of the League of Nations. He had what may be a unique distinction in having had two *Festschrifts* written in his honour, one by classical scholars and the other by liberal and internationalist political associates. Basil's mother was also a great personage, Lady Mary Murray, on whom the title role in Bernard Shaw's *Major Barbara*, was based.

appointment. It is my understanding that the Palace immediately rang up the newspaper in question and warned it against publishing any reference to the Prince of Wales.

Basil Murray's article recommending the Prince of Wales was duly published. Randolph's was not. Of course Basil was Randolph's senior by some eight or ten years. Randolph was just at the beginning of his journalistic career. All the same, even at the beginning, Randolph ought to have had more sense. It illustrates how his excess of pushfulness, his tendency to 'go too far', could frustrate what he wanted to achieve.

In the event, only Lord Halifax was nominated and he was elected without contest.

In reference to Lord Rothermere, I recall that shortly afterwards there was a late-evening gathering of some eight or ten people in the rooms of 'the Prof', Winston amongst them, when Randolph referred to Lord Rothermere with some unprintable words of abuse. Winston piped up: 'Randolph, you can't talk about your employer like that. Unless you withdraw the words and apologize, I shall leave the room and go to bed.' We were all against this, as we wanted Winston to go on talking. At first Randolph held out, with the plea that his scabrous epithets were factually correct. But Winston would have none of it. Randolph in due course apologized.

Nearly thirty years had passed, since this double use of my rooms, when Lord Halifax died, and there came up the question of a new Chancellor of Oxford University. My telephone bell rang, and Randolph asked whether he might spend a day doing some telephoning and writing in my room regarding the election of a new Chancellor. Granted.

The circumstances were not quite the same. On the previous occasion no one had as yet been nominated; Basil and Randolph had arrived while discussions were going on in university circles as to who should be nominated. On the second occasion two people, Harold Macmillan and Oliver Franks, had already been nominated and it was polling day. Randolph wanted to write an article for the *News of the World* on the events of polling day.

When he arrived in my rooms I said, 'Well, Randolph, this is like old times. History repeats itself.' Oddly enough, he had *entirely forgotten* that he had used my rooms for the Prince of Wales versus Lord Halifax issue nearly thirty years before. Perhaps his failure to get his article published had led to a Freudian repression of the incident.

During the day his son Winston came in to help him with his writing and telephoning. I thought that that was rather nice.

After Randolph had been in my room for an hour or two another old pupil arrived. He had been responsible in London, whether duly authorized or not I do not know, for the issuing of a sticker which read

M ac's your an

This might have been suitable for a general election, but was not so for persuading the former undergraduates of Oxford, all of whom had votes, many of whom were V.I.P.s, almost all of whom were a sort of élite, to vote for Macmillan. When Randolph heard the name of my old pupil he rose into an instant rage. 'Damn you, are you the person who issued that sticker? What the —— right had you to do so? Who the —— are you? Do you realize that, if Macmillan doesn't get in, it will be entirely due to you?' His fury seemed to mount. He got very pink in the face. Having had reports of Randolph's behaviour on occasion, I feared that he was going to strike the man. He approached him in a menacing way. I took Randolph rather firmly by the arm and said, 'Randolph, this is the study of a quiet scholar; it must not be turned into a rough house.' He desisted *immediately*, and my other former pupil tactfully slipped out of the room. I think that Randolph had some right on his side; middle-of-the-way folk who had not quite made up their minds how to vote might have been disgusted by the thought that Macmillan supporters were campaigning in such a manner and have voted against him.

Some time later in the day, A. P. Herbert, who had journeyed to Oxford to vote for Macmillan, came into my rooms. He had soon to catch a train. I told him that he *must* come and look at the splendid redecoration in the hall of our library. I took my key to show him. It was a Saturday afternoon and the library would presumably be locked up. When we came out of the library we ran into a colleague with two friends who had travelled a long distance to vote for Oliver Franks. My colleague had no key, but wanted to give his friends a glimpse of the library. I said that I just had to put A. P. Herbert into a taxi, would return with my key in ten minutes or so, and locked them in. It was a beautiful afternoon and I said to A. P. Herbert, 'I must show you our college garden.' It was at its loveliest. A.P. had an urge to walk to the station. I said that I thought that he could get there in time for the train if he went through the back streets. 'But I may lose my way.' I had to admit that this was so. 'I will take you.' And, having got him to the station, I saw him off on the train. It was a glorious day. There was no particular point in getting back to my rooms quickly, as Randolph was in occupation and rendering serious work there impossible. So I decided to saunter back slowly, enjoying the sunshine. I should think that my expedition took about three-quarters of an hour. Then, suddenly, as I approached Christ Church, I remembered the men locked up in the library!

They had eventually got on to Randolph by telephone. He had replied, 'I am not Roy Harrod's keeper; he left these rooms half an hour ago in the company of A. P. Herbert; that is all I can tell you.' There was some breakdown in college communications. Perhaps the porters on duty had not got the key of the library. The visitors had managed to extricate themselves only two or three minutes before I returned.

Randolph seized on this story, and, giving it a twist, reported in his article that Roy Harrod had incarcerated some Franks supporters in the library at Christ Church, to prevent them from voting for him. Well, what did it matter? It was a good story. I do not recall if it was ever published.

But when, in the heat of controversy, I referred to Franks by a pejorative expression which was very good journalese, Randolph at once took up his pen. I said: 'Randolph, you are not to publish that; Oliver Franks is an old friend of mind.' He immediately complied. One could *trust* Randolph not to do an unfriendly thing.

When the long day's work was done, I accompanied Randolph up St Aldates. In the course of the walk I was greeted by the then Chancellor of the Exchequer, Derick Heathcoat Amory. He was walking along in a rather forlorn sort of way. He sought my advice as to how he could register his vote for Harold Macmillan. I said, 'Well, you will need a gown; I will take you to the Christ Church lodge, where the porters will provide you with one and give you the necessary information about time and place.' I thought it was typically British that the Chancellor of the Exchequer, V.I.P. No 2 in the political arena, should have just taken the ordinary train to Oxford—no official car—and walked up from the station—no use of his status to get a taxi—and was meandering along down St Aldates without having required prior briefing about where to go or what to do. He was just a plain citizen.

Meanwhile Randolph had shaken him warmly by the hand, congratulating him on having taken the trouble to come to Oxford to vote for Macmillan, and making some rhetorical comments, which seemed to me to be unnecessary, on the importance of Macmillan becoming Chancellor of Oxford University. I told Randolph to wait for a few minutes on the pavement, while I did my stuff for Heathcoat Amory by securing him a gown, etc. When I rejoined Randolph, he said, 'Who was that man? I seemed to know his face.'

It was rather endearing to me that Randolph, who had the flimsiest of connexions with Oxford, and whose father had none, apart from having been made an Honorary Doctor of the University, should care so deeply about Oxford getting the right Chancellor.

Perhaps I may be permitted to refer to something that he said to me, which should probably be discounted as typical Randolph overstatement. None the less it naturally moved me very much. Winston and Randolph both came to the funeral service for Lord Cherwell in Christ Church Cathedral. I have referred to Winston's behaviour there in my book *The Prof*. But I did not refer to Randolph's. Christ Church thought that I was the appropriate person to read the lesson on that occasion. I chose the long passage in the Corinthians, '. . . O death, where is thy sting? . . .'. Although 'the Prof' had no religious belief, he was deeply traditional, and I felt sure that he would like to have the most traditional lesson read. I have read lessons many times in Christ Church; and I have always tried to comply with my uncle's* dictum that the great thing is to try to understand what the words mean and, by that understanding, to convey their sense to the listeners. After we came out of church, Randolph said, 'Roy, hearing you read that lesson gave me my first inkling of what the Christian religion is all about.'

More years passed, and it was in deep sorrow that I went to

* Johnston Forbes-Robertson.

Randolph's memorial service in St Margaret's, Westminster. That evening I was due to receive a gift from Christ Church and, having already made numerous retirement speeches on this and that, I resolved to concentrate on this occasion on my old pupils. When it came to the point that day, my mind reverted to the service in the morning and I devoted some three-quarters of my speech to Randolph. I know that some friends occasionally experienced rough treatment at his hands. I never did. It may be that I stood in his mind as an especially privileged person owing to having been his tutor. If so, that was a good mark for him. At the end of my Christ Church speech I said of Randolph that, in so far as I was concerned, 'a very parfait gentleman was he'.

Randolph

by

John Betjeman

(*English poet; author of* Mount Sion, Ghastly Good Taste, A Few
Late Chrysanthemums, Summoned by Bells, *and other works*)

When I think of Randolph, I see him in terms of noise, light and
laughter. I can't remember when we first met. It was probably in
the room of Edward James in Canterbury Quad, Christ Church,
Oxford, in about 1927, when we were undergraduates. There was
a set of people in that Quad who were neither aesthetes nor hearties
but above both. Randolph was one of them. They included peers,
commoners and rich Americans, and were a continuation of the
world described by Evelyn Waugh in *Decline and Fall* and *Brides-
head Revisited*, and by Cyril Connolly in his famous parody, *Where
Engels Fears to Tread*. I do not associate Randolph with a college,
though he must have been at one. I associate him with people who
just as they transcended the division of aesthetes and hearties, also
transcended the divisions of colleges. Most of them seemed to
have known one another since nursery days. I would even go so
far as to say that these people were above University. Some of them
may have come over from Cambridge. Certainly two of them
edited a short-lived periodical, the *Oxford and Cambridge Review*.

The tutelary God in Oxford of these men was Professor Lindemann, later Lord Cherwell. In his bowler hat above his inscrutable
yellow face he was to be seen driving to the best country houses.
His deputy was Roy Harrod, nearer the age of us all, and, to me
at any rate, more approachable and patient. I can see now, though
I did not see it at the time, that what bound Randolph and this set
of people together was politics. They were Ministers of State in
embryo. The furious discussions Randolph used to have when
voices grew louder and louder and tables were banged were about
political personalities of the twenties. I did not know who they

were then and I am no surer now. I do recall that if ever his father was attacked in these discussions, Randolph spoke in his defence.

This was all the noisy Randolph of the lunch and dinner tables. There was the other side of him which came out in his love of poetry and his eye for landscape. When I say his love of poetry, I must mention that it was mine which he liked, which some people would not call poetry at all. He liked rhyme and rhythm and a bit of satire. How he first came to know my poetry, I cannot recall. What I am quite certain of is that it was through his early encouragement that it came to be published. He used to make me recite the stuff at lunch parties, and at dinners he used to ask for special favourites and then listen with his eyes wide open, and laughter in his face, and lead applause at the end. It was through him that I gained self-confidence, and I think he had much to do with persuading Edward James, who used to write poems himself and publish them privately, to put mine into print, under the imprint of the James Press.

The time for sitting for a degree came round and I could not sit for mine because I had failed to pass the examination for Holy Scriptures, which was then a necessary preliminary. Randolph advised reconciliation with my mortified father, which was something he certainly would have sought with his own father. So I became a prep-school master and Randolph kept in touch, and when terms were over for both of us, Edward James arranged that we should share a house of his in Culross Street, London. This was small, luxurious, with limewood walls and pale carpets. I think it was then that Randolph must have started his life on the telephone. Ever since then, when I have seen him he has either been on the telephone or about to telephone. There were dinner parties given in Culross Street, and I remember Lord Castlerosse as a frequent guest. We then had the galley proofs sent in of my first book of poems, *Mount Sion*, and Randolph corrected them. One of the poems, called 'The Wykehamist', I dedicated to him. Randolph was never a carping critic, he liked everything I wrote in verse, and he never ceased to read it out to his friends. Then one day the bound editions of my first book were delivered to Culross Street and filled up the little hall. We did not know what to do with them. I hardly liked to sell them and take money for them, it didn't seem gentlemanly; so we used to give them away to people who came to the house. Then somehow they got into the hands of a book distributor, but I am quite sure that if it had not been for Randolph the edition would not have sold out as it did. He was a tireless and wholehearted advocate of my wares.

Life with Randolph was not of course always peaceful. I remember being woken up one night by terrific thunderings on my door, and an American saying, 'It's Mr Vanderbilt, it's Mr Vanderbilt, Randolph has cut himself.' I went up to Randolph's bedroom and there was a doctor putting stitches into a cut on his head, and Randolph murmuring to the doctor, 'Don't puncture me.' I don't know how he cut himself or which Mr Vanderbilt it was who was there. In fact the reason why I find it so hard to remember anecdotes about Randolph is that I took him for granted, and expected him always to be the same, which he was. He had no self-pity and great energy and unbounded loyalty. He used to shout at his secretaries because he was a nervous and excitable person, but there was nothing mean or vengeful about him. If you had a row he bore no grudge.

His eye for landscape was an unexpected thing in him, of which he was hardly conscious. When he lived at Oving, near Aylesbury, in Buckinghamshire, he rented the house because of the view from the windows. This was of lawns and trees, a very eighteenth-century sort of view. When he moved into Suffolk he chose a house with a similar view and took great pride in the planting of trees there, so as to give romantic vistas. It may be that the park at Blenheim was always in his mind's eye as inspiration.

I look through these words and realize that I have not conveyed the glorious buoyant company he was. I saw him before he grew really ill and still saw in him the exuberant undergraduate. His outrageous remarks to people to their face, which I so much enjoyed, would lose their pithiness in print, and might well bring in libel actions from those still living to whom they were addressed. I always sensed a certain loneliness in him, and I remember how badly he needed company. A great friend to him in the Culross Street days was his aunt, Mrs Romilly, whom he used to like to go round and see, bringing me with him. When I saw him in that large house in Suffolk, he still seemed a lonely figure.

Randolph Churchill

by
Christopher Sykes

(*Scriptwriter and producer for the B.B.C. 1950–68; author of* Four Studies in Loyalty, Two Studies in Virtue, Orde Wingate, Cross Roads to Israel, Troubled Loyalty, A Biography of Adam von Trott, *and other works*)

I knew Randolph so long, so well, and so variously that he was part of my life for nearly forty years. I first met him when he was an undergraduate at Oxford, after my own Oxford days, in 1929 or thereabouts. He was remarkably handsome, reflecting in a youthful, mannish way the beauty of his mother. He was polite, gay, and gentle. My first impression, a most misleading one as I later found out, was of a modest, charming young man.

We were related in an indirect way as I am a descendant of the Leslie family and Winston Churchill was connected to them by marriage. Churchills have a weakness for genealogy, and I dare say that our distant relationship was in part responsible for Randolph's mild manners at our first meeting.

During the thirties we often met in the company of two friends of his and mine, Tom Mitford, who was killed in Burma in 1944, and John Sutro, one of the great humorists of my generation. It was not long before I came to know a more real Randolph than the deferential young undergraduate I remembered at Oxford. He was argumentative, shouting-down and arrogant in his opinions. He seemed a caricature of his father at his worst. Faced with this vociferous young politician, I was tempted to join the common opinion that Randolph was 'intolerable'. But I had the advantage of seeing him most often with our two friends, who stood no nonsense from him at all. I think that was why the affection I first felt was never very seriously endangered.

Tom Mitford was adept in firm, severe, comic and decisive con-tradiction. 'My *dear* Randolph!' he would cry in his loud tenor voice, very Oxfordish in intonation, 'I have heard a great *many* stupid remarks, but this is a *masterpiece* of its kind.' Then Tom would overwhelm Randolph with swift, clever and merciless counter-argument, broken with shouts of laughter. John Sutro would use an entirely opposite technique. He usually affected agree-ment with Randolph. 'You make an interesting point, Mr Churchill,' he would say in the drawl of an elder statesman, 'and what you have to tell us leads us to an important speculation.' And then, often adjusting an imaginary pair of pince-nez spectacles, he would pur-sue Randolph's latest enormity to some inconceivably preposterous conclusion, of which he would express his complete approval. Such out-manœuvring scenes left no room for rancour.

What was hardest to forgive in Randolph was his passion for intrigue and mischief-making. This was extremely prominent, and it puzzled me because his essential nature contained so much of kindliness and good nature. Perhaps this weakness was fed by frustration. In Randolph's childhood his father was a great national figure, but during Randolph's receptive years of early manhood, his father was not only in the political wilderness but looked upon by the party in power, and by its Opposition, as a disastrous relic of the past, a dangerous has-been.

Intensely ambitious, Randolph's formative years were spent in a household of frustrated ambition. More than that, his ambitions were stifled by the versatile gifts of his frustrated father. Randolph wanted to be a politician. His father had excelled as a politician in spite of criticisms. Randolph wanted to be a first-class journalist. His father was one of the ablest journalists in the English-speaking world. Randolph wanted to be a fine public speaker. His father was an orator to be compared only with Chatham or Gladstone. Failure never made Winston obscure, famous as he was from youth to death. Randolph suffered frustration from this too, though in an inverted form. Long before he had the experience needed for good journalism, Randolph was offered, thanks to his father's fame, tempting contracts to write, both in Europe and America, and he accepted. He was the heir to an enormous and excessively awkward inheritance. Small wonder that some of the results were destructive to himself. But in this connexion one thing must always be remembered to his immense credit. Most men who are over-shadowed by greatness in a father tend to denigrate the father. If it is a mean reaction, it is a most natural one. Nothing of this was ever found in Randolph. Throughout life he gave his father respect, honour, loyalty and love in abundance.

When the war broke out Randolph's regiment, stationed in Beverley, was close to mine, stationed in Bridlington. He had recently married. We saw a lot of him and his wife. Indeed my wife stayed with the Randolphs in Beverley for a while when, after I had been detached for special duty, we were temporarily homeless. I have two opposite memories of him at that time. He was thrust as an officer into a new milieu and he was determined to learn the ropes. Again, I saw the modest, interesting, delightful young Oxonian of ten years before. But that was not the whole story of Randolph in that time of quiet. Not by a long way. I also remember a lunch party in a country house near by when Randolph did every-thing he knew, and he knew a lot, to distress, anger, exasperate, and make miserable his host and every one of his fellow-guests! Randolph was a man of many moods.

I next remember him in General Headquarters Middle East, where I saw him from the summer of 1941 to the spring of 1943. When he arrived I was one of relatively few staff officers there whom he knew. Soon after taking up his duties in Cairo he paid me a call, and I introduced him to my departmental chief and others of my colleagues. Again he made a delightful impression. But it was not long before my peppery chief, a former officer of the Army of India, was bursting into my room with cries of 'This damned fellow Randolph Churchill! *Your* friend! What the devil does he think he's doing?'

As far as I knew, Randolph's terms of reference at that time were somewhat vague, and with characteristic vigour, and characteristic love of intrigue, he was establishing his own department in various political fields, and showing, as was his way, complete disregard of other claims. I don't think he did harm in Cairo, as was often alleged at the time. Whether or not he took unfair political advan-tage of his right to communicate direct with his father, the Prime Minister, I do not know, but what I do know is that many political departments of G.H.Q., mine included, were riddled with chican-ery, and I dare say that Randolph's unorthodox irruptions let in needed fresh air, and were thus an influence towards healthy and long-overdue reorganization.

I saw a great deal of Randolph in those Egyptian days, and he was a joy. He made mistakes in plenty, issuing an anti-Communist Press hand-out, for example, at a crucial point in the German campaign against the U.S.S.R., when something of the opposite seemed to be necessary, and really was at that time. When I remonstrated with him on this subject he defended himself with a bellowing display of logic which may have convinced him but had no such effect on me. Nevertheless, it must be remembered that he showed, on numerous occasions then, particularly in regard to the Gaullist French, a remarkable sense of political tact. He infuriated many and there were times when I wondered if he was mad. Just as I was deciding he was, I would suddenly be forced to reverse my opinion, on noting a flash of his father's brilliance. I found consolation in him. To meet him at dinner at the end of a wearying day was entertainment and refreshment. He stood up to generals, much as his father is reported to have done in the India of long ago, and in political argument, in the French-speaking society of Cairo, he would, with no conscious imitation, reproduce his father's unusual performances as a linguist. I remember hearing him say to a lady at dinner one evening: '*La difficulté avec lui, madame, comme avec si beaucoup des générales americains, c'est qu'il est terrifié du State Department.*'

Our ways parted early in 1943, but in the spring of 1944 I was in White's Club in London one morning when Randolph burst in roaring: 'Where's Evelyn Waugh? I've got to get hold of him! Where the devil is he?'

I knew the answer, as Evelyn was then training in Scotland, with my regiment. I knew that my Colonel was in some perplexity as to how to place Evelyn, never the easiest of men for whom to find advantageous military employment. I said to Randolph: 'I know where he is, and he can be with you here tomorrow morning.'

'You mean it?' cried Randolph.

'I think I do,' I said, 'if you let me get to the telephone. Why do you need him?'

'Because,' said Randolph, standing by the bar and in a very loud voice, 'my father has agreed to me taking charge of a mission to Croatia under Fitzroy Maclean, and Fitzroy and I have been hunting for Evelyn everywhere, because I need him. I can't go to Croatia', he added, 'unless I have someone to talk to.' Discretion was never one of Randolph's virtues. I found it a reason for liking him.

I telephoned to my colonel and the deal was settled there and then. I was thus instrumental in organizing the raw material of Evelyn Waugh's best and last work, the three novels of his war trilogy.

After the war I saw rather less of Randolph than I had done before and during it. I used to meet him at clubs I belonged to in London, usually with Evelyn Waugh. Then, sometime in the early fifties, I had a meeting with him which was painful.

I had arranged to dine with John Sutro. On arriving at his flat he told me he had arranged for us to join Randolph and his wife at a restaurant near Sloane Square. There we found Randolph's wife and another person, but no Randolph. We waited for five minutes and then sat at our table. Soon after we were settled, Randolph turned up, far from sober and in a furious rage.

It was a very rainy night and Randolph was dripping. After curt greetings he turned to his wife and in a voice like a trumpet asked why he had been kept waiting in the rain on his own doorstep for so long a time before anyone could be found to open the door to him. To her quiet reply that since he came back so late she had assumed he would come straight to the restaurant, he responded in yet louder tones. The trombones took over. Randolph fairly yelled that this was not the reason at all, and went on in language which was anything but restrained.

At this time Winston Churchill was Prime Minister and Randolph a well-recognized personality in England. The diners in the restaurant could hardly not be interested in this deafening and extraordinary scene. A hush descended on the room, and all eyes were on our table. But unhappily for us, no hush descended on Randolph. Ever louder and more recklessly Randolph roared.

One is always told not to interfere between husband and wife, but this unspeakable scene, louder at every moment, before a large, shocked, and appreciative audience, seemed to provide an exception to the rule. I should have felt a worm for ever had I not done something to stop it. In vain the others had tried to divert Randolph's attention. It was my turn. 'Randolph,' I said, 'you should not talk to your wife like that in a restaurant.' Randolph turned to me with an enormous renewal of wrath, and, as though an orchestral conductor had summoned up the whole of the brass, *fortissimo*, he let fly. 'What the hell!' he bellowed, 'what the HELL do you mean by butting in on this *purely private conversation*?' 'I am sorry to have made a mistake,' I said, 'but I had the impression that it was a public one.' Mercifully this reply took Randolph aback. John Sutro laughed loud and long. Quite suddenly the storm was over, as though a switch had been turned off. The dinner was not the most convivial that I remember.

Many people only know Randolph through the recounting of such scenes, and therein lay the basis of his unfortunate reputation. The fault was his entirely. But if only his angered critics could have seen the other side of Randolph which, though this violent side was real enough, gave the truer indication of what sort of man he was! Randolph's early death was one of the most tragic. He longed to be as great a writer as his father. Given more years he might have proved a greater. His life of Sir Winston Churchill, so far as Randolph is the author, can only remain a fragment, but it is a fragment of a great book. In this biography he had clearly found himself. He showed himself to be uninhibited but without any trace of vulgar exhibitionism, and he was armed with the merit without which no biographer should undertake his task, an unswerving determination to tell the truth. He faced the facts with all his natural courage and never feared to set them down. The distressing as boldly as the creditable, the embarrassing as plainly as the splendid. He showed the self-assurance of a writer who has such faith in his subject that he rightly believes that only truth can serve.

Everyone who knew Randolph heard him take up arms in defence of his father, but usually in a fierce, even frenzied partisan spirit. He could wreck his cause by overstatement—Heaven knows! It was a wonderful revelation of the depth of his love for that great man, when he brought so fine a spirit to the record of his life.

I remember the last time I saw my old friend. It was in his country house at Stour, where he spent his last years. I came down with a B.B.C. colleague to take a recording of him for a radio programme I was organizing on the subject of Evelyn Waugh, a subject which he and I both had very much at heart. Randolph was at his best, gentle, amusing and charming, reminding me again of the delightful young man at Oxford. Even so, at lunch he gave us a fierce touch of the familiar, combative Randolph when he learned that I was working on the biography of Adam von Trott, an anti-Nazi German. Why hadn't the anti-Nazis eliminated Hitler long before the war? Why all this procrastination? What was the difference between an anti-Nazi and a 'henchman of Hitler'? All in vigorous staccato. And then, in the accustomed style, be began so to overstate his case as to demolish it. Anti-Nazis were worse than Nazis, he said, and of the latter he began a perverse defence.

'Well,' I said, when I could get a word in, 'I never thought to have heard a Churchill defending the "final solution".'

He was at a disadvantage and he knew it. 'No, no, my dear Christopher,' he said, 'I didn't mean that, of course.'

'I don't know if you meant it,' I said, pursuing my advantage, 'but it's what you said.'

'Did I say that?' he turned to his friends.

'I'm afraid you did,' said one of them.

And then there came the infectious giggle. 'Well, I'll give you the hell of a good recording,' he said, and thus inconsequently brought the argument to a close.

He did give me a very good recording, but I noticed a weakening in his broadcasting technique. Once or twice a phrase was nearly inaudible, or slurred over. I asked him to repeat these, but each repetition was weaker than the preceding one, and more slurred. I was sure of what I had suspected from the beginning, that he was a very ill man.

He showed a signal courtesy on this occasion, having been to the trouble to search out all the correspondence between Winston Churchill and my father, in the years of the First World War, and this he showed me. Not long after this visit I wrote to him to ask for guidance concerning a problem involving his father and relative to the subject of my biography which he had so crazily denigrated. I had no answer. Then I got news of his death. Not long after that I heard from his researchers that he had given instructions for me to be given access to the information I needed. He had been beyond writing.

I shall always miss Randolph. He was like no one else. It may be that in his uniqueness one may solve a riddle of his character, for, though he was no Hamlet, he had a riddle, as do most men of high quality. He was determined to be something more than the worthy son of a mighty father. He tore asunder the bonds which held him from freedom, but, with true Churchillian excess, he tore them with needless violence. He thus became not so much a man on his own but a separate species. He might have become a monster under the stress of his predicament, but he saved his name, his reputation, and confirmed the trust of his friends, by the excellence of his last work.

My Friend Randolph

by

John Sutro

(British film producer: associated with Alexander Korda in London Film Productions (later Two Cities Films) and now Director of Constellation Investments)

How vividly I recall Randolph—it seems impossible that he is gone. I met him for the first time at Oxford, some time after I had gone down, and we went river bathing at Godstow together with his cousin Johnnie—Randolph was wonderfully handsome and bubbling with ideas. Then I was to meet him frequently between the wars, especially with the Mitford sisters, Nancy and Diana, to whom he was related. He invited me to a dance at the Ritz, given by the Winston Churchills, at which I knew scarcely a soul, but Randolph and Sarah looked after me and introduced me so I had an agreeable evening, memorable to me as the first and last occasion when I had a few words with Lord Beaverbrook. However, later on, Randolph's imitations of the voice and manner of 'Max' brought to such vivid life this extraordinary man of genius that I began to feel that I had known him well.

My principal memories of Randolph belong to after 1945 when he returned to England after a vivid and picturesque war. His absolute personal courage both in peace and war has always been admitted even by those whom his caustic tongue or pen offended. I must however first mention a period around 1933, when for some reason, perhaps because Alexander Korda wished Winston Churchill to make a series of short films, Randolph had joined the staff of London Films at our office in Grosvenor Street. There was little for him to do, but one day he said to me, 'John, I want my salary raised.' 'But Randolph, why?' said I; 'you seem to be reasonably remunerated for not working very hard.' 'For working in the same building as X,' he replied, naming a mutual acquaintance also employed in Grosvenor Street with less justification than Randolph.

At Oving, the house near Aylesbury which Randolph took after the war, I spent many happy weekends and got to know him well. On one occasion we stayed talking until four o'clock in the morning and he told me from the heart many intimate thoughts and recollections which are engraved in my memory and must still remain sealed. But I can say that he suffered deeply from the inevitable change in his relations with his father after the outbreak of the war. Before 1940, and during the period when Winston Churchill's views were sometimes opposed by the Conservatives, and when indeed after the Abdication he was treated with contumely, Randolph was so close to his father that he was his confidant and adviser. Inevitably, after Churchill became Prime Minister this relationship abruptly ceased and Randolph, though understanding the reasons, could not help being hurt. Indeed one can add that had Randolph's advice been taken in the 1945 election campaign, such blunders as the 'Gestapo' broadcast would have been prevented.

In the later years Randolph spent more and more time in the country, which he came to prefer to London, though once he had been a great frequenter of White's Club. He bought Stour, a lovely house in Suffolk, and became an enthusiastic gardener as well as working on *The Life of Lord Derby* and, later, on his Life of Winston Churchill and writing articles for the *Evening Standard*. I remember staying there on the night of the General Election in 1959, after Suez, when Harold Macmillan became Prime Minister for the first time—we were to spend the evening listening to the results on the wireless. That evening he arrived home in the car accompanied by a young Swiss and his girl friend. The two had been walking in the lanes, hoping for a lift; Randolph picked them up and brought them back to Stour. They had dinner with us and he invited them to listen to the results and spend the night. The next day he sped the delighted couple on their way, having behaved with the greatest courtesy and informality—so much for the rumour that he was distant and impolite to strangers! Incidentally it turned out that Randolph had made an astonishingly accurate prophecy of the final voting—for he was a real expert in politics.

I remember a comical and bizarre happening at an evening meeting of the short-lived John Gordon Society which Graham Greene and I formed as a tease on John Gordon, Editor-in-Chief of the *Sunday Express* and author of its influential Sunday column 'Current Events'. Graham had chosen Vladimir Nabokov's *Lolita*, which had been published by Olympic Press in Paris, as one of his three favourite books of the year, though the book was then virtually unknown in London and New York. John Gordon read and denounced it in his column as prurient and criticized Graham Greene's praise of it. As many of our friends had joined the Society we decided to hold a public meeting to put forward the differing views. The source of our difference with John Gordon was over the morality or immorality of *Lolita*. He agreed to be present and speak when we met that evening in a private room in the Horseshoes Hotel, Tottenham Court Road, on what proved to be the hottest night of the year.

Graham Greene, A. T. Frere of Heinemann and I presided on the platform. Randolph, streaming with perspiration, was in his shirtsleeves—the most prominent of all the audience. Though he was there to review the meeting for the *Evening Standard* he could not resist haranguing all the participants in the debate with vehement irrelevance. When John Gordon read out a passage someone interjected, 'Read it at dictation speed!' When a lady began to protest, Randolph observed, 'Madame, if you continue in this way, I shall have you removed.' Anita Loos and Lillian Gish, who were present at the meeting, declared it to be the most diverting and uproarious evening they had ever spent in London. *The Spectator* recorded one side of the debate, while John Gordon gave the other in his column in the *Sunday Express*. The evening's events caught the attention of Putnam's, the New York publisher, thus bringing about *Lolita*'s global fame.

Then there was Randolph's libel action against the *People*, which in some acrid exchange of views called him 'a paid hack', which he certainly was not. Randolph brought an action saying the words were defamatory and he invited me down to Stour the weekend before the hearing in the Law Courts, to discuss details and give him advice. I should add that I was called to the Bar and became a member of the Inner Temple in about 1929 but had hardly started to practise as a barrister when I was somehow, for better or worse, sucked into the maelstrom of film production through representing my father Leopold Sutro on the board of Korda's London

Films, which my father financed. Anyway, I had spent much time in the courts, and read my *Gatley on Libel and Slander*, and was amazed in the course of our discussion by Randolph's absolute knowledge of and mastery of his own case, so rare for a litigant. Each day I would cross-examine Randolph in detail; I could not, try as I might, shake his conviction and veracity, but often had to tell him to stay calm and not lose his temper. For instance, he would turn to an imaginary judge and say, 'My Lord, must I go on listening to this insufferable nonsense?' 'No, Randolph,' I said, 'you must say, "My Lord, may I have guidance?"' and so on. The following week I saw my pupil so much impress the jury and judge that he was awarded £5,000 damages.

Finally, let me mention an instance of Randolph's magnanimity. There was a plan to start a magazine on the lines of *Time* magazine, and the suggestion was made that Randolph should become its editor—an admirable idea, for he was a first-rate journalist and had the gift of inspiring others. I was to join the editorial board, and out of the blue on the telephone Mr Onassis offered to put up a substantial sum of money to join the other sponsors in launching the magazine. We spent the weekend planning and had many good ideas—the position would have been the salvation of Randolph and occupied his eager and creative mind. Then, at the last moment, when all seemed settled, some enemy of Randolph, or someone whom he had offended—we never knew who—torpedoed the whole plan and he was excluded. Instead of being angry and vindictive Randolph behaved with dignity in spite of the crushing disappointment, 'I wish them the best of luck,' he said. It only remains to say that after a few months the magazine failed completely and a very large sum of money was lost. Randolph would have made the magazine a success—it was a shame.

In Randolph courage, loyalty, wit and gaiety were mingled with a certain intransigence, sometimes too fiercely expressed. He was, none the less, always honest and sincere, and I am proud to have been his friend.

Randolph

by
Stuart Scheftel

(*American journalist and businessman: formerly a reporter for the* New York Times; *co-Founder of the Pan Am Building in New York; now Chairman of the New York City Youth Board under Mayor John Lindsay*)

Someone once said you don't meet Randolph, he just happens to you. This was certainly true in my case and therefore I am unable to describe the exact occasion of my first encounter with him beyond saying that my 'happening' took place at Christ Church College, Oxford, in the early thirties, when we were both freshmen. Randolph, even then, took no exercise, and spent the better part of his time eating, drinking and talking politics. And while I was more athletically inclined, I shared with him a total disinterest in the academic life of the university and this made a bond between us, besides giving us plenty of leisure in which to get to know each other and become close friends.

It was an agreeable time for both of us, and if I sometimes wondered about the outcome of a way of life in which two young men disported themselves in an ancient seat of learning as though it were a sort of restaurant cum political club cum golf hotel, Randolph seemed to have no such qualms. He appeared to be completely insulated from even the possibility that his behaviour might arouse any adverse criticism. I was therefore surprised, when, one evening, in his rooms (which was where we usually met owing to his habit of seldom completing his toilette before nightfall) he indicated that he did not feel 'completely' accepted by the professors . . . or even by the other first-year men. I pointed out that walking across the quadrangle wearing a bathrobe and smoking a cigar at three o'clock in the afternoon, might not be the best way of gaining the respect of others more seriously inclined who had been about their academic or other worthwhile pursuits since early morning. Randolph wondered how, without having to go to some such extreme as attending a lecture, or opening a textbook, this unfavourable impression might be changed. I then asked if he had any athletic attainments of any sort, and after listing the obvious ones and getting a negative response I was about to search down other avenues when suddenly he said, 'Of course you know I ride very well?' I didn't know, but I agreed that that should do the trick, and as I happened to know that Oxford was having a point-to-point race the following Saturday, I suggested that Randolph take part. Randolph now said that he had no horse and no money to rent one, but as I had had a success on the turf on that day (as a result of what Randolph had referred to as a 'judicious wager') I offered to provide the funds and the matter was arranged.

Unfortunately I could not be present on that historic occasion (I was playing an 'away' match for the university golf team), but on my return I sought out Randolph in his rooms, where, had it not been that I knew the rooms we were in to be his, I might not have recognized him, so heavily were his head and face bandaged. Naturally I was eager to learn how my friend had been transformed from an English undergraduate into an Egyptian mummy, but beyond growling that he was 'bloody but unbowed', Randolph seemed far more interested in finding an aperture in his bandages into which he might introduce his cigar than in describing what clearly had been a narrow escape from death. So I had to wait until later to hear what had happened; when I also found out that not only was Randolph's experience with horses extremely limited, but he had never before ridden in a race of any kind, much less a steeplechase. Despite this handicap he had made such an excellent showing for himself that he had held the lead all the way to the stands. He had come a cropper at the water jump, receiving a bad roughing-up from those following behind.

This for me was the first demonstration of the absolute fearlessness and courage for which Randolph was later so justly admired by those who were with him during the war. As for the hoped-for result of this early feat of derring-do it seemed to have little effect on his colleagues, and so Randolph returned to his unpopular habits, but without any further evidence of a troubled conscience. He felt, I suppose, that he had made sufficient contribution to the *esprit de corps* of his college. Nor, after that, did I ever see him show the slightest interest in the opinion that others might have of him. This attitude was in evidence on the occasion of that year's rugby match between Oxford and Cambridge. The Prince of Wales (later Duke of Windsor) asked me and my brother and any friends to come to St James's Palace for a snack and then go to the game in our own car but behind his police escort. I warned Randolph not to be difficult but, to my horror, heard him say to the Prince on being introduced, 'It's a bit disappointing to meet my future King by courtesy of an American.'

Despite the devotion with which he applied himself to making his life at Oxford one of pleasure, it became plain to me by the end of the spring term of that first year that Randolph was bored; and thus I shared in his satisfaction when one day a cable arrived from a Mr William B. Feakins inviting him to make a lecture tour of the United States.

This was pretty heady wine for a nineteen-year-old, particularly in view of the handsome financial reward which accompanied the offer, and it would have been quite understandable had Randolph, while looking forward to the prospect of his first American appearances on a platform, felt some little uncertainty. However, far from showing any such misgivings, Randolph approached his forthcoming departure with that sublime self-confidence that I was coming to recognize as his major characteristic. Indeed he adopted an attitude so casual that his father, although he raised no objection to the tour, felt obliged to warn him that it would be no more than prudent for Randolph to prepare in England the basic speech that he intended to deliver in America.

Randolph's response to this suggestion was to inform his father that, since his first engagement was not to take place until a week after his arrival in the States, there would be more than enough time for him to compose a brilliant address *after* he arrived in America. Not necessarily so, countered Winston, who knew from his own considerable experience of the lecture platform in America that the speaking schedules were frequently expanded, and Randolph might expect to find himself appearing well in advance of the first date on his itinerary. In that case, said Randolph, although he thought such concern quite unfounded, he would indulge his father's whim by devoting the sea voyage (which he reminded Winston took several days) to the organization of the many splendid ideas he had for the tour. Hearing this did nothing to reassure Winston, for, as he said, he was sufficiently aware of his son's propensities to know that Randolph would spend the first day on the boat on the prowl for girls; the second day seeking an introduction to one of his choice; the third day in making himself agreeable to the young lady; the fourth in making a pass at her, while the fifth and sixth days would be used for consolidation of any previous gains, finally arriving in New York with nothing (nothing, that is, in relation to the proposed work) accomplished!

The first time I saw Randolph after his return from the States I asked him if his father's projections had been accurate. Uncannily so, Randolph replied, for not only had the activities on the boat been exactly as his father had outlined, but no sooner had he disembarked at the port of New York than he was informed that he was expected to go immediately to Princeton, where, it had been announced, he was to be one of two speakers, the other being André Maurois, then at the height of his fame. And now, for the first time, Randolph told me, he began to wonder if he hadn't made a mistake in having nothing prepared. However, when he arrived at the lecture hall at Princeton and was informed that he was to speak first and for a maximum of half an hour (to enable André Maurois to deliver one of his celebrated lectures and still make a train connexion) he cheered up considerably, for he had decided to tell 'all he knew' in lieu of a prepared speech, and he felt sure that he 'knew' enough to fill half an hour in an interesting fashion.

And so it was with confidence restored that he arose and launched into what he believed was an instructive and amusing address; and then having done what he believed to be justice to his subject (i.e. himself) he prepared to sit down, first glancing at his watch, where, to his astonishment, he noted that the passage of time since he commenced speaking had been something less than five minutes! More than ever now, he wished that he had taken his father's counsel, but realizing that vain regrets would not help, he decided that the only recourse open to him would be to tell 'all he knew' again from a different angle, and with certain embellishments; and so, while he began to search rapidly through his memory, he delivered the results of his rummage with unnatural slowness, punctuated by frequent protracted pauses, and many sips of water from the carafe on the podium; and having so grossly misjudged himself earlier, he did not even look at his watch when he came to the end of this second sorting through of his store of knowledge, but even though he had the impression that he had been speaking for a very lengthy period, he forced himself to give one last pressing to the grapes in his cerebral vineyard. After that, he told me, the water carafe and his mind both being completely empty, he *had* to sit down, only then permitting himself another look at his watch, where, to his horror, he saw the hands on the face to be in the identical position in which they had been when he had made the earlier check! Too late he realized that his watch had stopped when he first got up to speak, and that there was nothing to do now but to learn the worst; and so, under cover of what might generously be described as very 'light' applause, he received, in answer to his whispered query, the information from the noticeably tight lips of the moderator, the information that he had been speaking for a time in excess of one hour and forty-five minutes, and that as a result the great M. Maurois would be obliged to cut his much-anticipated lecture to its opening and closing remarks.

It was, I suppose, an unavoidable corollary to Randolph's lack of concern for what people thought of him that he nursed a lifelong belief that others were equally indifferent to his opinions; seeming to think that if he didn't give a hoot what was said to him, others possessed an equal detachment; and even though this was an assumption which was baseless, he continued to react with seemingly genuine astonishment when the reactions to what he pleased to call his 'teases' would run the whole gamut from a stony stare of outraged dignity to a maddened roar portending mayhem. At that point, since Randolph was not a cruel man, but rather a carelessly playful one, he would be quite ready to offer to make amends. Offers, which I may say, were invariably turned down by anyone who had had any previous experience of his attempts at atonement; for Randolph's apologies had the curious property of being, usually, even more offensive than his original provocation. One such was the one he proffered a pretty young movie star, when by way of placating her rage, aroused by his asking her if she really was 'interested in acting', he told her he did not like her to frown at him 'because it makes you look *so* ugly!' Or when he tried to calm an almost hysterical dowager by assuring her that when he had said that he was sure that *her* daughters would commit 'adultery with the utmost discretion' he had been merely trying to compliment her on the excellence of the early precepts with which she had so clearly inculcated her offspring! Or the time when, having told me that Evelyn Waugh (who, at one time, had an almost phobic dislike for the U.S. and with whom I had had a serious disagreement during the war) had said that he based his 'whole dislike of Americans' on me. Noting from my expression, I suppose, that the pleasure this confidence gave me was less than total, Randolph hastened to mollify me with the assurance that he'd done his 'loyal' best to convince Waugh that Scheftel was 'not *that* bad'.

Perhaps the topper in the tease and amends department occurred during the war when Randolph, who spent most of the time out of England, came home unexpectedly on leave. On arrival he found that his father was going to be busy that night presiding at a dinner for the Joint Chiefs of Staff. No one under the rank of lieutenant-general was to be present. However, it was wartime and, after all, the presiding officer was the Prime Minister, and if Randolph, who was a major, promised to say not a word he could come along. The dinner was hardly under way when Winston had reason to regret his misplaced hope in Randolph's ability to remain silent for even a short period, for the meal had proceeded no further than the soup course when during a lull in the conversation the following was heard as Randolph leaned across the table to Field-Marshal Montgomery: 'It's not as if I'm accusing you, Field-Marshal, of *personal* cowardice.' I never did discover Randolph's original remark that brought forth this stunning 'apology'.

Returning to Evelyn Waugh, it may be noted that he was so well aware of Randolph's propensity for disruptiveness that when Father D'Arcy—the well-known Jesuit who had been responsible for the conversion of many distinguished non-Catholics (including Evelyn Waugh himself)—had suggested that Randolph, as the son of one of England's most distinguished Protestants, might be a good 'target' for conversion, Evelyn disagreed vehemently, telling Father D'Arcy that, in his opinion, Randolph would be less an ornament to Mother Church than a 'rogue elephant trumpeting in the Sanctuary'!

While my wife and I were on our honeymoon I introduced her to Randolph, who, the first moment he found himself alone with her, suggested an assignation. When she refused with indignation, adding that she was going to tell her husband, Randolph told her that he agreed that Scheftel ought to know that he was married to a woman whose moral standards were so 'boringly middle-class'! Despite this and his habit of telling her not to 'interrupt' if she so much as opened her mouth, she had a genuine fondness for him, though she admitted that in her case it was something in the order of having a taste for Bombay Duck or Bird's Nest Soup.

As someone once remarked, the lights went up a little higher when Randolph came into a room but soon thereafter, figuratively speaking, he almost always put them out altogether.

If this sounds as if Randolph's attributes were visible mainly on the level of outrage, I must point out several that I found disarming and even loving. One that combines his always-present courage was when I was recuperating from an illness at Chatham on Cape Cod and he telephoned to say he would charter a plane from Newport, where he was staying, and come and see me. I really was not expecting him, as one of those late August Cape Cod fogs had settled in and nothing was flying, but at just about his predicted arrival time I heard the motor of a single-engine plane going back and forth obviously trying to find the airport, and pretty soon there was Randolph as large as life. I understand the pilot, who had not wanted to make the trip in the first place, was not in nearly such good shape. I must add further that Randolph did have an appointment after our lunch with President Kennedy in near-by Hyannisport.

And there is also the occasion when my stepson was sent down from Christ Church for failing an examination. Randolph asked him to stay and, what is more, volunteered to tutor him for the exam that would get him back to Oxford if he passed.

He was unique, often maddening, sometimes disarming. He was a special taste. If things had turned out differently, if it all hadn't been so easy, he might have been anything, perhaps even another Winston Churchill.

A Lecture Tour
in the United States

Ruth McKenney
Heywood Broun
Oscar Levant

The Sock Hunt*

by
Ruth McKenney

(American journalist and playwright: author of the highly successful play
My Sister Eileen)

I suppose, what with the passing years and the girls he's met
since, that young Mr. Randolph Churchill, the scion of the London
Churchills, does not remember me. Still, looking back on it all, I
should think he would. I certainly do. Precisely as I can never, for
so long as I walk this earth, forget the time I fell down at my high-
school senior prom, right smack in front of the orchestra, with my
best beau sprawled beside me, so can I never put aside the memory
of young Mr. Churchill. My flesh still crawls. Not that Mr. Churchill
is anything to make a girl's flesh crawl. Not at all. In a certain way,
like the men in the breakfast-food ads, he is quite handsome.

Mr. Churchill and I met in a purely professional capacity. It was
the late fall of 1930. He was touring America, speaking before
literary clubs, Rotary Clubs, university clubs, and the like on a
variety of light topics, including 'Fate of an Empire' and 'Why I
Am a Conservative'. He was then nineteen, and I was the daisy-
eyed star reporter on the *Ohio State Lantern*, a newspaper published
daily, except Saturday and Sunday, by the students of journalism at
Ohio State University.

Young Mr. Churchill arrived in Columbus, Ohio, on the flood
tide of a lot of awe-struck advance notices. He was to address a local
men's dinner club which for pure hauteur would make the Union
Club look sick any day. All the speeches before this tony outfit
were dead secret; no reporters allowed. Furthermore, celebrities
who appeared before these hallowed few were never interviewed

* Reprinted from *The New Yorker* of 16 January 1937.

by the Columbus press. The editors of the papers were all members of the club, and that was that.

Well, my mouth watered to interview Mr. Churchill. I had never seen a real Englishman in the flesh, for one thing. For another thing, my deadly rival on the *Lantern* staff, a chap of considerable energy and no ethics, had publicly stated that he considered the feat of obtaining an interview with Mr. Churchill too great even for his remarkable talents. After this, nothing could hold me. I marched forward with determination to my doom.

I arrived at the hotel lobby at 4.35 p.m. and briskly set about finding out Mr. Churchill's room number. Then, with success almost in the hollow of my hand, I collapsed on a lobby lounge with an attack of acute panic. This lasted until 5.22 p.m., when a man insulted me. At least he came directly over to my lounge and said, in a chummy tone, 'Waiting for somebody?'

This drove me to Mr. Churchill. I fled from my insulter and arrived at the forbidding door of Mr. Churchill's hotel room, still unnerved. I knocked valiantly. I had mapped out my strategy well in advance. When Mr. Churchill asked, 'Who's there?' I intended to reply, 'Maid, with towels.' Then, when he opened the door, I planned to stick my foot in the crack and ask him a lot of questions very fast. I think a scene such as this had been in a newspaper film about that time.

Anyway, Mr. Churchill ruined my pretty plans by replying, to the knock, 'Come in.' I hesitated, getting a burning sensation in my throat. I was nineteen and lived with my grandmother, who would have been absolutely horrified at the thought of any young woman traipsing into a man's hotel room alone.

'Come IN!' roared Mr. Churchill from behind the door. He sounded rather angry. I kept telling myself that after I got out of school and got a real job on a newspaper, I would look back on this moment and laugh. As it turned out, however, in spite of a lot of jobs on newspapers, genuine daily ones, the mere thought of that frightful moment, with Mr. Churchill bellowing 'Come IN' on one side of the door and me trembling on the other, has never brought even the sickliest of smiles to my face. It still makes my hair prickle.

Finally I opened the door very timidly indeed, and beheld Mr. Churchill, surely the blondest young man in the world, seated at a desk writing. He wore a smoking jacket over his dinner trousers, black vest, and starched shirt front. His bare feet were stuck in floppy leather slippers. Mr. Churchill looked so very public-school English he was faintly incredible. Maybe he's grown out of that now, but in 1930 he was certainly breath of Empire. You could—or at least I could—just see him wolfing down supper off in the tropics, dressed to the teeth in tails and white tie. Mr. Churchill's eyes were a china blue and his smoking jacket was the same, over-laid, however, with old rose and gold.

I stood by the door for several seconds while Mr. Churchill continued to scratch away at his desk. Now, a cynical old interviewer of ripened years, I fear that Mr. Churchill was attempting to impress me. But on that trying evening I felt that I had intruded on the literary labors of a young genius. Finally Mr. Churchill lifted his blue eyes to mine.

'Ah,' he said, leaping gallantly to his feet, 'a lady! I beg your pardon. Pray do forgive me.'

My mouth sagged. Mr. Churchill drew up a chair beside his desk and, with a cozy gesture, beckoned me over. I went.

'Pray excuse me,' said Mr. Churchill. 'I must finish this wireless message.' On his desk lay eleven or twelve Western Union blanks covered with writing.

'What?' I said. The reason I said this was that I could not understand very much of what he said. His accent, which I had so longed to hear, a real, bona-fide Oxford accent, was so broad that unfortunately he might as well have spoken French. I can get every other word a Frenchman says, too, which is fairly good, considering I studied French in the Ohio public schools for only eight years.

Young Mr. Churchill now turned to me and said in a fierce tone, 'What would you say if you wanted to tell your manager you did not want ladies to give you flowers at lectures?' At least that is what I thought he said. It was so difficult for me to decipher Mr. Churchill's accent, and the question seemed so entirely improbable that, after agonized reflection, I simply shook my head.

Mr. Churchill didn't note my silence. He apparently hit on just the right words, for he signed his name with a flourish I am sure no American operator ever spelled out, and turned briskly to me, saying, 'Now what may I do for you?'

I explained haltingly that I was a newspaper reporter. Mr. Churchill didn't ask, so I didn't find it necessary to tell him that the paper I was interviewing him for was only, alas, the university daily. I simply trotted out all my carefully prepared questions. I asked him about Ramsay MacDonald and Hoover and Briand and a few other such people. Mr. Churchill roundly denounced them all, for different reasons. MacDonald was too far left, and even Mr. Hoover was pretty much of a Socialist. I asked him about the future of English youth, and Mr. Churchill said that if only a few more young people of his class would awaken to their responsibility, the future of England was safe. I was slightly shaken at Mr. Churchill's firm Tory opinions. He seemed quite young to be so fierce.

However, I drew a breath and started off on the English public-school system. Just at this point Mr. Churchill created a diversion.

In an ordinary speaking voice, as distinguished from the voice in which he denounced Mr. Hoover or Mr. MacDonald, he said, 'Would you care for a drink?'

This unnerved me again. I could explain the interview to Grandma and my conscience, but drinking with a total stranger in his hotel room certainly seemed excessive. In those days, most college students—at least at my school—still thought drinking, no matter where, was pretty darned daring. Mr. Churchill, however, had already unearthed from his suitcase a bottle of what he assured me was fine Scotch, straight from England.

I was no judge. Up to that very moment I had never tasted anything in alcoholic beverages except a variety of bootleg liquor called 'New Straitsville corn', because it was distilled in some abandoned mines near New Straitsville, Ohio. New Straitsville corn burned your throat and made you sick. Also, it hurt so to choke down New Straitsville corn that you were acutely conscious of every drink. It was the suave, sneaking quality of Mr. Churchill's fine liquor which undid me. You hardly knew you were drinking it, until afterward.

Mr. Churchill and I soon forgot serious topics. I asked him whether he really enjoyed lecturing about 'Fate of an Empire'. He said he did not, and also that he hated America and couldn't wait to get home. After a while Mr. Churchill thought we ought to eat something.

'I say,' he said, 'how about a spot of food, what?' He really talked just like that.

'O.K.,' I said. 'Let me order, though. They can't understand you over the phone. You talk so funny.'

Mr. Churchill glowered. He said I was the one who had a peculiar accent.

'You talk through your nose,' he said, with truth, 'and you pronounce all your "r"'s. They aren't supposed to be pronounced.'

'That's what you think,' I said, feeling hilarious, 'Old Mushmouth.'

For some reason, Mr. Churchill thought that was very funny. ' "Mushmouth!" ' he shouted joyously, amid peals of real upperclass English laughter, very high-pitched, like a whinny. ' "Mushmouth"! Deah me, I must remembaw that.'

We ate lamb chops, a lot of them. 'Tell them to send up a bally lot of them!' Mr. Churchill roared while I telephoned. 'I want six lamb chops all for myself. After all, I must lecture on the "Fate of an Empire".'

While we were gnawing on lamb-chop bones we traded opinions on moving pictures. Mr. Churchill was a fan, and so was I. It turned out we both adored Vilma Banky. Suddenly Mr. Churchill said, 'What about my lecture?'

'Well,' I said, 'what about it?'

'I won't do it,' Mr. Churchill said. 'Let the Empire go rot for tonight. Let's go to the cinema. You and I.'

For a moment I was sorely tempted. Then I pictured the fearful scandal. The lecturer disappears. The town's leading citizens are left waiting. Among the leading citizens was the publisher of the Columbus *Dispatch*. I was the campus correspondent for the Columbus *Dispatch*, and I lived—in a very meagre way, to be sure, but still I lived—on the weekly wages the *Dispatch* paid me. In my fancy I saw the publisher of the *Dispatch* discovering that his most minor employee had practically kidnapped young Mr. Churchill.

'No,' I said firmly. 'You have to make that speech.'

Mr. Churchill sighed. 'Well, then,' he said, 'I have to put on my dinner jacket.' He found that all right; also his white scarf and his black overcoat and his two patent-leather pumps. But alas, as the hour approached nine, he could find only one black sock. The club was to send a committee at nine, to escort Mr. Churchill to the lecture hall.

'What shall I do?' Mr. Churchill inquired frantically. 'I can't lecture with only one sock.' I rose from the dinner table, still gnawing a bone, and cast a quick look over the room.

'Be calm,' I said. 'They'll never notice.'

'Oh, yes they will,' Mr. Churchill said. 'Besides, I won't go unless we find that sock. And I only have one black pair with me. The rest of them are in Pittsburgh.'

'Wear another color,' I said lightly. 'What's happened to the socks you had on this afternoon?'

'Tan socks,' Mr. Churchill shouted, 'with a dinner coat?'

I observed Mr. Churchill's frenzy with a motherly eye. 'There, there,' I said. 'Relax. I'll find it.'

Mr. Churchill sat down, putting a childish faith in me. I failed. I trotted around in circles, afraid to look in his luggage—for after all, that would hardly be proper—and unable to spot a stray black sock in the immediate surroundings.

Suddenly Mr. Churchill shouted, 'I bet it's under the bed. I unpacked my things on the bed, and maybe it fell off on the floor.' He threw himself down beside his bed and stuck his head under the springs.

'I can't see it,' he said dismally, sounding muffled. 'You have a look from the other side.'

I obligingly sprawled out under the wall side of the bed, and peered around, coughing in the dust. At this moment precisely, there was a knock on the door.

'Come in!' bellowed Mr. Churchill, before he thought. I gave a faint scream, and too late Mr. Churchill considered the informality of his position. He tried to get up, too suddenly, and bumped his head severely on the bed slats. He relapsed, groaning, just as the committee of super-leading citizens walked in.

Fortunately, I do not now remember the names of those three well-starched, beautifully tailored citizens who marched in on that sock-hunting expedition. It would be frightful to be haunted all my life by their names as well as their faces.

'Mr. Churchill?' said the first leading citizen, in a tone of pained surprise.

Young Mr. Churchill showed the heritage of generations of gentlemen. Still reclining on the floor, he turned his head, nodded an acknowledgement, and said in a loud, belligerent voice, 'I'm looking for my lost black sock.' The second leading citizen went directly to the bureau and picked up the lost black sock.

'Your sock, sir,' he said. Mr. Churchill rose, bowed slightly, and said, 'I thank you very much.' Then he shouted to me, 'Get up! We've found it.'

I hesitated. I wanted to stay under that bed and just die there peacefully, without ever having to rise and face those three leading citizens. I did get up, though, feeling the way you do in dreams when you have no clothes on at a gala performance of *Aïda* in the Metropolitan. I suppose, from the expression on the faces of the three leading citizens, that they had not realized until the moment my face slowly emerged from behind the bed that there was a young lady in the room. Each leading citizen did a combination gasp and snort.

'She's coming to hear my lecture,' Mr. Churchill announced as he put on his sock. The purple staining my cheeks now rose to my hairline.

'I couldn't,' I said weakly. 'I couldn't, indeed. It's private. They don't allow women in.'

'Nevertheless,' said Mr. Churchill briskly, 'I don't speak unless you come.'

The three leading citizens looked so grim I thought I should really faint, although I never had in my whole life. Mr. Churchill and I and the committee now left the room and boarded the elevator. All the way down, Mr. Churchill maintained his position. I was to come or he wouldn't speak. The three leading citizens took turns saying, 'But that is impossible, Mr. Churchill. The rules of the club do not permit ladies.'

As we got off the elevator, one of the leading citizens, a tall, white-haired man with a large stomach, managed to fall in step with me while the two other leading citizens took Mr. Churchill by the arms.

'Now,' said my sudden escort, 'you go away fast, and stop bothering Mr. Churchill.'

'Me?' I said in honest astonishment. 'I never bothered him.'

The leading citizen did not stop to argue. 'Go away,' he hissed, giving me a slight push into the lobby. I went. I was never so glad to leave any place in my life. I wrote my interview that night, and it was a big success. My rival, Ernest, was a picture of jealous confusion when he read it next day. But even the sweet rewards of college fame and my colleagues' envy did not erase the memory of that hideous moment when I was caught, red-handed, looking for Mr. Churchill's sock. It is comparatively easy to recover from honest sorrows, but I wake up in the dead of night at least twice a year and my heart fills with agony, remembering that unspeakable moment when, like a rising moon, my face slowly appeared from behind Mr. Churchill's bed, to confound the three leading citizens of Columbus, Ohio.

Life can hold no further terrors for me.

Young Randolph Churchill *

by
Heywood Broun

(American journalist and columnist: formerly a reporter for the New York
Morning Telegraph, *the* Tribune *and* World. *Died in 1939)*

Randolph Churchill, England's ambassador of ill will, has gone
home breathing maledictions upon our native press. . . . It is an
art with him, and since I recognize it as such, he cannot get my
goat any more.

When first we met, young Churchill was about sixteen.† He was
engaged on a lecture tour and went about the country telling
women's clubs what was wrong with American politics, customs
and cookery. He was even then a journalistic delight, because if any
ship news reporter asked him what he thought of our skyline or
the American woman Randy would tell him in no uncertain terms.
I rather gather that young Churchill thought the American woman
looked best in a heavy fog. But, of course, it was seldom if ever
necessary to ask Randy. He was the first to volunteer.

At the age of sixteen† I observed him in drawing-rooms inter-
rupting his elders and telling them where they got off. But it came
to be so magnificent that you could hardly call it bad manners.
It was Promethean, and one could almost hear the flapping of the
vultures on their way home to peck at little Mr Churchill's liver.

Distinctly I remember a historic occasion in the home of Herbert
Bayard Swope.‡ At that time I was in the employ of Mr Swope and
regarded him with great awe. In fact, I still regard Mr Swope with
great awe. Only for a space of some five minutes did he seem to

* Reprinted from the *New York World Telegram* of 15 December 1936.
† *Editor's note:* Randolph was in fact nineteen.
‡ *Editor's note:* American journalist. The executive editor of the New York
World, he died in 1939.

me neither a god nor a devil, but a man. This brief deliverance from the thraldom of hero worship I owed to Randolph Churchill. He sawed through one bar in the window of my cell, and I tried to slip out but got stuck in the middle.

At the time Mr Churchill had just turned seventeen.* Mr Swope and I were somewhat older. I forgot what the argument was about, but as a trusted employee I took no part in it. Suddenly the chill English voice of the young visitor smote upon my ear saying, 'Herbie, you talk like an utter idiot.' I could hardly believe my ears, and I turned my eyes. Mr Swope was slowly and gracefully growing a little purple.

The room was bathed in that silence which comes before the crack of doom. Only on one other occasion have I experienced such a stifling stillness. It was during a hurricane in Florida, and it is called a lull. For the space of fully a minute Mr Churchill and Mr Swope sat without saying a word. This in itself constituted a new world's record, and has since been accepted by the A.A.U. [Amateur Athletics Union.]

Naturally I held my peace and gripped the arms of my chair. I averted my face. At any second the lightning would come through the roof and strike Randy dead or Mr Swope would rise quietly and strangle him. I did not want to be struck or held as a material witness.

Instead I gazed out the window, and to my great surprise pedestrians were going about their business as usual and trying to get into a speak-easy just across the street.

A well-remembered voice shouted, 'Heywood!' Indeed, the voice said 'Heywood!' a second time before I jumped and replied, 'Yes, Mr Swope.' And that was another's world's record.

'Heywood,' said Mr Swope. 'I've been wanting to talk to you about your review of *Processional* for some time. The trouble with you as a dramatic critic, Heywood, is that you are always reviewing the play the dramatist intended to write but didn't get around to doing. I might add while we're on the subject that your column isn't holding up very well, and I didn't like your last couple of baseball stories. Besides, your book reviews are getting a little dull. I wonder if maybe you are doing too much work. I think perhaps you're staying up too late. Come down to my office around midday

* *Editor's note:* Randolph was nineteen.

tomorrow and we'll go out to lunch and have a nice friendly chat about what's wrong with your work.'

'Yes, Mr Swope,' I answered, but for a fraction of a second I was almost inclined to give him a slightly more contentious reply, because Randolph Churchill had made him change the subject.

A good many years elapsed before I saw Randy again. This time we were on a train following Franklin Delano Roosevelt through New England. We were sitting in the dining car, and several other newspapermen joined the party. I introduced Randy as a visiting British journalist to the group of White House correspondents, all of whom were pretty much fans for the President. Randolph Churchill acknowledged the introduction and started to lay down the law. Perhaps somebody had dropped a hat, although Randy never needed any such encouragement.

'I think,' he said, 'your American press is most peculiar. Your greatest journalist, of course, is William Randolph Hearst, and yet his conduct in this campaign amazes me.'

Several of us nodded in agreement.

'Yes,' said Randy, 'it amazes me to observe the way in which Mr Hearst leans over backwards in order to be fair to Mr Roosevelt.'

That broke up the debate. We had to shout for the porter to bring spirits of ammonia. Three Hearst men had fainted.

Randolph in Hollywood*

by
Oscar Levant

(American pianist, composer and writer: author of A Smattering of
Ignorance, The Unimportance of Being Oscar, *and* Memoirs of an
Amnesiac)

Regardless of whether a visitor to the coast was a Cabinet
member, a banker or the dean of a university, he rarely appeared in
Hollywood without a letter of introduction to Harpo. In due course
he would make his way to the Marx dinner table where Harpo
presided over his cluster of disciples like a mute Socrates.

Only on one occasion did we encounter someone who could
euphemistically be described as our match. This was the youthful
Randolph Churchill, son of England's First Lord of the Admiralty,
Winston Churchill. He came with the reputation of being even
more than a London equivalent of me—the most bumptious, loud-
mouthed, impertinent person that English society has produced in
our generation. At dinner he succeeded in insulting everybody at
the table before the main course had arrived. It was at the time
when Landon was contesting Roosevelt's right to a second term
in the White House, and Churchill argued vehemently for the
merits of the Republican, as if the election had not already been
decided two days before. Since one of Harpo's most treasured
possessions is an inscribed photograph of the President, it may be
understood how popular this made Churchill with his host.

After dinner we attempted to exact retribution by taking
Churchill to a ping-pong parlour and imposing on him the labor
of retrieving the balls, which, mysteriously, were being batted
consistently to the most inaccessible corners of the room. This did

* Reprinted from *A Smattering of Ignorance*, New York: Doubleday & Co.
Inc., 1939.

not faze him, however, nor did it diminish his capacity for the querulous.

News of his behaviour at Harpo's filtered back to New York, and especially to Swope, whose letter of introduction had effected his invitation to Harpo's. In the morning Churchill received a wire:

'Don't forget you're not only representing the Empire. You're also representing Swope.'

Despite this admonition Churchill was hardly chastened when we invited him on the following evening to one of my favourite Hollywood houses—Salka Viertel's. Salka, I should point out, is Garbo's personal representative and wife of Berthold Viertel, the celebrated poet and director. As an old Berliner, she automatically had become the social arbiter in California for the many refugees, both German and Austrian, in Hollywood—such as Korngold, Schoenberg, Tock, Klemperer and Reinhardt. Her house was the gathering place for all of these, comprising what I called the 'fast-drinking Schwartzwald set.'

With scarcely any important exception the wives of all of these, and most of the other guests that one was likely to encounter there, were ex-Reinhardt actresses, in consequence of which all valuations were couched in terms of Greek drama.

'What was she like as a young girl?' I once heard Salka ask, in discussing the youth of a mutual female friend.

'A rather poor Klytemnestra,' replied her informant.

Mrs. Klemperer, too, was hardly more proud of her husband than she was of the fact that in her youth she had been 'a fine Medea.' Salka herself once reported that she had won the 'most-beautiful-legs contest in Vienna' before embarking on her studies with Professor Reinhardt. She had her first quarrel with him shortly after that when she insisted on playing Lady Macbeth.

It was into this atmosphere, redolent of the theatre, that Churchill was projected on the occasion of his visit with us. Actually, the torch of the drama was burning with particular brightness that night, heightened by the reflected glow from Ernst Lubitsch, the evening's particular lion. The air was thick with talk of parts, roles, great performances, the mystery of the footlights and so on, when Salka turned to our companion and said,

'And you, Mr. Churchill, do you like the theater?'

Economically, almost aggressively, he answered:
'No!'
In the audible silence that descended on the room Salka found
voice to inquire,
'Why?'
'Because,' said Churchill, 'you can't smoke in the theater.'
Despite the egregious impudence of this young man, whom
Heywood Broun immortalized as 'England's ambassador of ill-will',
I confess that I had a fondness for his breezy impertinence, his
indifference to anything describable as public opinion—and also
for his really sharp intelligence.
On the day following his triumph at the Viertels' he was
scheduled to receive the press at the Brown Derby during lunch,
and I accompanied him. It was November, but an exceedingly
warm day which made me uncomfortable in my vestless suit.
Churchill, however, turned up in an imposing fur-lined greatcoat,
giving him all the aura of statesmanship.
He handled himself well with the newspapermen, even if he did
seem a little insensitive to the satire of one young reporter who
kept referring to him constantly as the 'future Prime Minister'.
Churchill accepted the nomination placidly, even appearing indifferent to the fact that his one sortie into politics as a candidate
for Parliament resulted in his defeat, as he himself phrased it, by
'the largest majority in English governmental history.'
I was abundantly impressed, too, by the lunch he had on this
day. Despite the hour and the heat of the day he began with mush-
rooms under glass, followed by shrimp, as preliminaries to a double
order of pork chops with extra potatoes, leading to salad, an impressive dessert and, of course, the usual cheese and coffee. Virtually a whole meal served Under Bell.*
When I expressed my wonder at this and asked him how he did
it Churchill responded airily,
'Americans just pick at food. I like to eat heartily.'
As a final touch in his campaign of ingratiating himself with the
film colony came Churchill's encounter with Jack Warner of
Warner Brothers. It was then that he established his true claim to
be described as the 'irrepressible Churchill.' Warner was holding
forth on some subtle point incident to the intricate art of produ-

* Under a heat-retaining cover.

cing, not without difficulty, owing to the incessant interruptions of Churchill, who was full of suggestions for improving Warner Brothers' output.

Finally, in exasperation with Churchill's eighth interruption, Warner turned to him and said heatedly,

'Young man, when you're my age——'

'You'll be eighty,' interjected Churchill blithely.

TELLING THE WORLD

(*From a* Daily Express *cartoon by Strube. Reproduced by courtesy of London Express News and Feature Services.*)

TELLING THE WORLD

At the Front Lines

Vladimir Dedijer
Sir Fitzroy Maclean
Congressman John Blatnik
A. J. Liebling
Kenneth T. Downs
Stephen Barber
Ansel E. Talbert
General Lyman L. Lemnitzer

Randolph with the Yugoslav Partisans

by
Vladimir Dedijer

(*Yugoslav author: fought with the Partisans under Marshal Tito; Yugoslav delegate to the United Nations 1945–52; Visiting Professor to Cornell, Harvard, Manchester and Oxford Universities; author of* With Tito through the War, Tito Speaks, Stalin's Lost Battles, *and other works*)

The first time the Yugoslav Partisans heard about Randolph Churchill was at the beginning of January 1944, when Brigadier Fitzroy Maclean brought a letter to Marshal Tito from the British Prime Minister, Winston Churchill.

At that time a turning-point had come in the relations between Great Britain and the Yugoslav Partisans. For almost three years London had backed the Royal Yugoslav Government and General Draza Mihailović, its War Minister, in occupied Yugoslavia. But after the unsuccessful German offensive against the main Partisan forces at the Neretva and Sutjeska rivers in the spring and summer of 1943, it became obvious to the outside world that the Yugoslav Partisans were the main military and political forces in Yugoslavia. This fact was recognized at the Teheran meeting of Roosevelt, Stalin and Churchill at the end of 1943.

The Headquarters of the Yugoslav Partisans at the beginning of 1944 were in the mountains of Western Bosnia. Marshal Tito was naturally very pleased to receive that hand-delivered letter from the British Prime Minister in which Mr Churchill expressed great admiration for the contribution of the Yugoslav Partisans to the common struggle against the Nazis. He was doubly pleased with the news that Churchill had decided to send his only son to join us on the battlefields of Yugoslavia. He wrote to Marshal Tito:

Sir,
 I thank you very much for the kind message about my health

from yourself and the heroic patriot and Partisan Army of Yugoslavia. From Major Deakin, who is a friend of mine, I learnt all about your valiant efforts. It is my most earnest desire to give you all aid in human power by sea supplies, by air support, and by Commandos helping you in the island fighting. Brigadier Maclean is also a friend of mine, and a colleague in the House of Commons. With him at your Headquarters will soon be serving my son, Major Randolph Churchill, who is also a Member of Parliament.

One supreme object stands before us, namely, to cleanse the soil of Europe from the filthy Nazi-Fascist taint. You may be sure that we British have no desire to dictate the future government of Yugoslavia. At the same time we hope that all will pull together as much as possible for the defeat of the common foe, and afterwards settle the form of government in accordance with the will of the people. . . .

The snow in the Bosnian mountains was too deep for the landing of the Allied D.C.3 which usually brought the medical supplies to the Partisans, so Randolph had to parachute in. His arrival made a deep impression on the Partisans for two reasons. While he was being escorted by a group of Partisans to Marshal Tito's Headquarters a German plane flew overhead. The Partisans—wondering whether he would duck or not—looked at him, a British officer, with suspicion. Randolph remained standing, as still as the Rock of Gibraltar, and that was that! The Partisans realized that he was brave, which was always the first quality they looked for in a man. Also the fact that the Prime Minister of Britain had sent his only son to fight with our Partisans created a great impression not only among the fighters, but even more upon the people of Yugoslavia. Randolph's arrival was, for the Yugoslav highlanders, the best proof that Britain had decided to change its policies and back the Partisans.

In his talks with Tito, Randolph was very outspoken. He mentioned that he was authorized to say that the British Government would no longer help General Mihailović, and that there existed great possibilities that the Royal Yugoslav Government would openly denounce Mihailović. Randolph also hinted that there was a chance that even King Peter might do the same thing. It is clear from the Memoirs of Sir Winston that Randolph's task was to explore what advantages could be obtained for King Peter and the Karadjordjević dynasty after the dismissal of Mihailović.

As soon as the harsh winter was over, Randolph roamed around the liberated territory of Yugoslavia. He was full of dynamism and always ready for a good argument and a joke. He often went on those rovings all alone, on foot. Once when he was tired he went into one of the offices of a People's Liberation Committee that was billeted in a half-ruined house near the River Una, where Arthur Evans, during the uprising of 1875, had helped the insurgents and gathered material for his articles in the *Manchester Guardian*.

The peasants could not speak any English, and Randolph's Serbo-Croat was rather poor, but he rescued himself by means of paper and a pencil which he had in his pocket.

He drew a sketch of a horse. Half an hour later he was riding back to Tito's Headquarters at Drvar on a Bosnian pony. I still possess Randolph's famous sketch in my war diary* as a happy souvenir. The impressionist tendencies of Randolph's sketch would have shocked his father's insistence on realism in painting.

At the beginning of May 1944, Randolph represented the young generation of Great Britain at the Second Youth Congress of Yugoslavia. It was held in a wood-processing factory at Drvar and attended by more than 850 young men and girls from all parts of Yugoslavia. The best young sharpshooters of the Partisan brigades were there, as well as couriers and illegal workers in the German-occupied cities. Some of them had walked for months through the German lines and over many ranges of mountains, in order to attend the Congress.

In my war diary I have recorded that Randolph greeted the Congress and expressed his sadness that the British delegates could not come from Britain. During the recesses between sessions of the meetings, which were held during the night in order to evade the attacks of German bombers, Randolph spent his time talking to the Partisans about their way of life and their ideas of complete austerity during the war so far as both drinking and sex were concerned.

On 25 May 1944, by order of Hitler, the German parachute units

* *With Tito through the War* (Partisan Diary 41–44), condensed by Alec Brown, London: Hamish Hamilton, 1951.

specially trained for the occasion tried to capture the Partisans' Headquarters at Drvar, together with Tito and the Russian and Anglo-American missions. This daring plan did not materialize, despite the combined air and land attacks. Randolph, who was in a near-by village, succeeded in withdrawing with a Bosnian Partisan Unit.

When the Partisans' General Headquarters were established on the Adriatic Island of Vis, Randolph, fearful of enduring a boring life in a secure spot, asked to be transferred back to Yugoslavia where he would have more action and excitement. He chose the Headquarters of the Croat Partisans and had a high time with them from the very first day. During the landing on an improvised air-strip, not far from the small Croat town of Topusko, his D.C.3 overshot the runway and a fire broke out. The Partisans saved Randolph in the nick of time, as a few seconds later the plane exploded.

Randolph used to spend a good deal of time with Dr Vladimir Bakarić, the leading Croat Partisan. Although Topusko was only some ten miles south of the main Belgrade-Zagreb railway and not far from Zagreb, the capital of Croatia, the Germans and their satellites did not dare to move against the Partisan-liberated territory around Topusko. Life in the small town was very quiet. Randolph once told Dr Bakarić, 'I have just written a letter to my father, telling him if he wishes a peaceful place he should come here to our Headquarters.' Dr Bakarić remembers Randolph as a brave man. 'He was indifferent to discussions of bravery or cowardice,' he would say.

Randolph did not concern himself with Yugoslavia's internal affairs and warned Partisan leaders several times about possible provocation from the Royalist sides. One must remember that he was a Whig gentleman after all.

The leisurely days at Topusko were disturbed one day by noisy demonstrations and Randolph hastened to ask Dr Bakarić what it was all about. 'People are demonstrating against King Peter and for the Republic,' answered Dr Bakarić. Randolph saw a good deal of action on Partisan fronts that year. He was always gay and ready for argument. Several of the Partisan officers knew some English and he liked their company, teasing them because of their atheism and egalitarianism.

'You look like a bunch of Levellers. If they had been any good, Cromwell would never have banished them!' Randolph once told a group of Partisans.

Thanks to Randolph we heard for the first time about the secret agreement between his father and Stalin on the division of Yugoslavia into 50–50 spheres of influence. At the beginning, as sincere Marxists, we could not believe this. We regarded Stalin at that time as a pure revolutionary and the leader of the oppressed in the world, but the information we got from Randolph was soon confirmed by other sources.

Partisans cherish fond remembrances of Randolph. I once asked Tito what he thought of Randolph. He answered,

On 12 August 1944 I met Winston Churchill in Naples. He said that he was sorry he was so advanced in years that he could not land by parachute, otherwise he would have been fighting in Yugoslavia.

'But you have sent us your son,' I said.

At that moment tears glittered in Churchill's eyes.

Randolph as a Commando

by
Fitzroy Maclean

(British statesman, soldier, diplomat and author: Brigadier commanding the British Military Mission to Marshal Tito's Yugoslav Partisans, 1943–5; author of Eastern Approaches *and other works)*

My first memory of Randolph is of coming into a room at Eton and seeing an excited small boy with golden hair and shining eyes leaning over a bewildered master's desk and arguing with him, arguing, clearly for the sake of arguing and arguing with no holds barred.

In the years that followed there were fleeting encounters at parties in London and Paris, but my next substantial memory is again of an argument—this time in the summer before the war—at luncheon at Chartwell. I had just come back from two years in Moscow and had been summoned to tell my host and the assembled company (which included Randolph) what I thought the Russians were likely to do in the immediate future. My forecast (which was to be proved painfully correct a few weeks later) pleased no one, least of all the Churchills, father and son, and I was subjected to a shattering barrage of obloquy and, what is more, held personally responsible for every aspect of Mr Chamberlain's foreign policy, of which in fact I disapproved as strongly as they did. Outnumbered and outgunned, I argued back as best I could. It was a stimulating experience and one that, at any rate in retrospect, I thoroughly enjoyed.

Three years later, in the desert, in the spring of 1942, Randolph joined David Stirling's newly formed private army, the Special Air Service Regiment. When he arrived, six of us were on the point of leaving on a raid on the docks at Benghazi, at that time several hundred miles behind Field-Marshal Rommel's lines. On hearing of the impending raid, Randolph at once said he wanted to come. He had not done the necessary training and was told that he couldn't. He at once began to argue. He could, he said, get fit in three days and immediately started on a frantic series of setting-up exercises and early morning runs. For the next two or three days, wherever one went at our base camp, one met Randolph puffing strenuously but stertorously about. In the end David Stirling relented. He could, he said, come with us as far as our lying-up place in the hills above Benghazi, but not on the actual raid. This, clearly, was better than nothing, and when we set out he was one of the party.

On the long drive through the empty desert, far to the south of where the Eighth Army faced Rommel's Afrika Korps, I began to realize what a marvellous companion Randolph could be. Maddening, of course, in a dozen different ways, but endlessly stimulating and entertaining. Sitting round the fire under the stars where we stopped to brew up and open one of our precious bottles of whisky, the conversation ranged over a score of subjects on all of which Randolph held (and expressed) the strongest and the most controversial possible views. Meanwhile the day when we were to part company with him was approaching. Or so we thought.

On the evening before we were due to go into Benghazi, we were lying up in the Gebel Akdar, the scrub-covered hills outside Benghazi, checking our arms and explosives. Suddenly there was a sharp report and a cry of pain. A detonator had gone off by mistake and one of our party had lost a finger. Clearly he would have to stay behind with the rearguard. We were one man short.

The crack of the exploding detonator had hardly died away and the wounded man's hand had not been dressed and tied up, before Randolph emerged from behind the nearest sand dune, bristling with lethal weapons and ready to start. There could be no stopping him now.

The story of our adventures in Benghazi, of how we drove past the Italian Guard Post into the enemy-held town in an open staff car in British uniform and spent twenty-four hours in a derelict house opposite a German Headquarters before coming out again, has been told elsewhere. Randolph, needless to say, enjoyed every moment of it, never showing a moment's fear or hesitation in a whole sequence of hair-raising situations. The only trouble was that even at the most ticklish moments it was almost impossible to stop him talking and that, when he wasn't talking, he literally yelped with pleasure and excitement, like a dog following a hot scent.

On our return, unfortunately, the car in which we were travelling turned over and we all ended up in hospital in Alexandria. As a patient Randolph was not at his best and the nurses were on the whole glad when he was sent back to London for further treatment. I was not to see him again for about eighteen months.

In the meantime I had been entrusted by the Prime Minister with the command of the British Military Mission to the Yugoslav Partisans and towards the end of 1943 I came out of German-occupied Yugoslavia and flew to Cairo to report to Mr Churchill. With him was Randolph, by now completely recovered, but unhappy at not being nearer the fighting and, as usual, arguing indefatigably with everyone in sight from his father and Commander-in-Chief downwards.

Naturally, the first thing he wanted to know was what it was like in Yugoslavia, and the next, whether I would take him back with me when I went. I weighed up the pros and cons, and, despite massive opposition from all sorts of quarters, decided to take him. I knew that, with Randolph around, there wouldn't be a dull moment. Not that life with the Partisans was particularly dull anyway. I just thought the two would go well together.

They did. Randolph's year in Yugoslavia was an unqualified success. From the moment when his parachute deposited him in a sitting position in a puddle of melting snow in the highlands of Bosnia, until the day some twelve months later when he attended Tito's victory celebrations in liberated Belgrade, Randolph brought to his job as British Liaison Officer with the Partisans an infectious mixture of courage and enthusiasm. It was, I believe, one of the happiest periods of his life. He liked the excitement of the guerilla war. He was also fascinated by the political implications of everything that was happening around him. Altogether wartime Yugoslavia was full of the kind of problems on which he enjoyed sharpening his wits. He also got on well with the Yugoslavs. There was an explosive, Balkan, side to his nature which endeared him to them and them to him. They recognized in him, too, some of the qualities they had learned to admire in his father—pugnacity, generosity, curiosity, and a sense of style. And then the very fact that Winston Churchill should have let his own son join them was, they felt, a token of the importance that he attached to them and to their fight.

Finally to those of us who shared his life—sometimes at very close quarters—he was, as ever, a stimulating, if on occasion an exhausting, companion. The story is well known of how, when they could no longer stand the flow of conversation, anecdotes, political arguments, insults and 'jolly jokes', two of his brother officers, Freddy Birkenhead and Evelyn Waugh, bet him a hundred pounds he wouldn't read the Bible in a week. Needless to say, they lost their bet. Randolph not only read the Bible right through, but repeatedly woke them up in the middle of the night to tell them of the fascinating literary, theological and, for that matter, scatological discoveries he had made in the Good Book.

Randolph spent the early part of 1944 at Tito's Headquarters in Bosnia and was there at the time of the German airborne attack, which so nearly achieved its objectives. For his courageous and resourceful conduct in the ensuing fighting he was awarded the M.B.E. (The recommendation had been for a Military Cross.) He was later in charge of my Mission to the Partisans' Croatian Headquarters. While he was there an aeroplane in which he was flying crashed and caught fire and he had a narrow escape from being burnt alive. The other survivors of the crash told of his coolness and of the courage with which he helped them fight their way out of the blazing fuselage.

In the early summer of 1945 Randolph and I found ourselves back in the House of Commons and later that year fought the General Election in neighbouring constituencies. Unfortunately he was defeated and never got back to Parliament.

Randolph brought to politics the same dash, pugnacity and tactlessness that he brought to everything else. He also brought courage, an inborn political sense, a natural eloquence, an active and inquiring mind and a dogged determination to get to the bottom of things at all costs. Had he been re-elected then or later, these qualities would have been a most enlivening and valuable addition to peacetime political life and to a House of Commons which would have been none the worse for a few fireworks. And, for his part, he would have enjoyed, more than anyone, the thrust and parry of Question Time and the rough and tumble of debate. I shall always be sorry that this was not vouchsafed to him or to us.

With Randolph in Yugoslavia

by
John Blatnik

(American politician: Member of the U.S. House of Representatives; a member of the O.S.S. Mission to Yugoslav Partisans in Croatia in the Second World War)

In the spring of 1944 Yugoslavia had been at war, both internally and externally, for seven years. The country was divided by such factions as the Partisans, Chetniks and Ustashi. Their allegiances ranged from Communism in the Partisans, to royalism and later Nazism among the Chetniks, to frank collaboration among the Ustashi. Paradoxically, while part of the population fought to prevent a takeover by Hitler's armies, another strove equally hard to bring about that very thing. The country was surrounded by enemies. Italy to the west and Austria to the north were aligned with the Axis nations. The Russias to the north and east were an Ally. Each was determined to bring Yugoslavia to its own political ideology.

In the spring of 1943 the Allies, sensing that Yugoslavia was teetering on the brink of total collapse, undertook to support Tito and his Partisans, who were waging guerilla warfare against the Chetniks and the Ustashi, and ultimately against the Germans and the Italians.

This was no small undertaking, since the Partisans were almost completely lacking in even the most basic items of warfare: shoes, clothing, ammunition, weapons and medical supplies. Only their indomitable courage and will to survive kept them going. The project, then, undertaken by the United States, British and Russian forces, demanded concentrated co-operation between the three allies and the guerilla fighters hidden in caves and scattered over the country like gypsy bands. It was in the woods of Bosnia, in assorted caves and primitive camps, running from Germans, and living like gypsies, among people I have come to love for their spirit and respect for their incredible courage, that I met Randolph Churchill.

Randolph and I had been parachuted into Bosnia by our respective commands to help co-ordinate the Allied support of the Partisan movement. Before that, Randolph had been a major in a British Commando Unit, and the Officer in Charge of British Press Relations in Cairo. Anxious to see more action, and conscious of the heroic swath cut by his father in Cuba, India, North Africa, and in the Boer War, Randolph volunteered for paratroop duty. He had participated in the raid on Benghazi and the invasion of Sicily before parachuting into Bosnia to join the other Allied troops there with Marshal Tito.

All this formed the background for the sudden and lasting friendship that developed between the heir of the Prime Minister of Great Britain and the son of a Yugoslav miner from Chisholm, Minnesota, on the Mesabi Range.

I came to Bosnia with the American Special Forces Unit several months after Randolph's arrival. By that time his reputation had not only preceded him, it had galloped ahead at full pace. I was no sooner settled than I was given a colourful version of his eccentricities. Most of his acquaintances agreed that the son of the Prime Minister had inherited some of his father's ability, much of his ambition, and a good part of his arrogance. As a result, Randolph had made few friends, and lost some of them because of his irrepressible penchant for argument.

Randolph, when I met him, was a loner, and lonely. His fellow officers avoided him and he, by choice, avoided those on a different scale from his own. It was, then, something of a strange compliment that he and I came to be friends.

The start of our friendship was based on two of the most impermanent bonds men have devised to hold friendships together—politics and booze. As a Conservative he had stood and been defeated three times for a seat in Parliament. Finally he won an uncontested election in 1940, representing Preston, a Lancashire cotton-weaving town. But he was unable to take his seat, since the previous year he had been commissioned in the Queen's Own Hussars, his father's old unit, and had been in action since. Politics fascinated Randolph and he was impressed when he learned that I had recently been elected to the Minnesota State Legislature, and was at that time the youngest State Senator in America.

Our friendship began in peasants' huts, where Randolph and I sat for hours over cups of slivovic, the potent Yugoslav 'white lightning'—matching each other drink for drink. Relaxing during the tedious hours between military engagements, we traded stories, argued politics, and figured the odds, and the means, of making it our career after the war was over. I can honestly say that Randolph made the war, with its discomfort and ennui, almost enjoyable during those hours. He was a gifted monologuist and went on for hours, recounting wonderful and outrageous stories of people I had often heard of, but never dreamed of seeing. After listening to him, face-to-face meetings would have been an anti-climax.

Some of his stories might have been heightened by his imagination, but I knew that those he told of his adventures in battle were all true. In Benghazi, for example, he raided the port with the Long Range Desert Group, that heroic bunch of freelance Commandos, and performed feats of daring which made me wince then, and even more today. On one such raid—there were two, I believe—he spent the night in the town and, with other members of the party, passed himself off as an Italian member of the General Staff to the Italians stationed there—full beard, British desert uniform and all—thus bringing off a dangerous reconnaissance which laid the way for a later full-scale raid.

He had an inquisitive bent, as well as a taste for danger, an insatiable curiosity, and a remarkably retentive memory. He was fascinated by American politics, and embarrassed me, an American politician, by knowing more about the basics of American politics than I did. I had never been to a political convention. Neither had he. But his apparent familiarity with the protocol of American campaigning left me completely speechless. I could only listen and admire.

Though he did not adhere to any one strict party discipline, he was committed to democracy, and was philosophically sympathetic with the efforts towards self-determination of any people. In this we agreed, and the peculiar situation of the Yugoslavs furnished us many an hour of discussion. Randolph was a perceptive observer of human nature, and admired Tito and his Partisans for their courage, and for the real aim of their struggle, which he saw, correctly, as a struggle for independence, rather than an economic ideology. He thought, simplistically perhaps, that the Yugoslavs were caught between two alternatives: Nazism under Hitler, or Communism under Stalin, and although the latter was distasteful to many of them, the former was abhorrent to all. There wasn't much of a choice. Randolph distinguished between the man and his politics, and could genuinely respect Tito the man and simultaneously despise Communism, which he did loudly and often. He had a favourite description of the Communist line, reminiscent of his father's colourful use of metaphor: Communism is like a man talking on a cold day: it looks like he's breathing fire when he's really breathing ice.

This facility for the colourful word picture, the perfectly-aimed verbal dart, was one of Randolph's characteristics and still figures clearly in my memory of him after twenty-five years. When he arrived in Bosnia, he was accompanied by Evelyn Waugh, a quiet, slender young man, who even then had acquired a literary reputation. They were very close, almost inseparable, and the reasons were clear. Randolph enjoyed using the English language as an admirably refined mechanism for precise expression of thought. He had the perfect opponent in Evelyn Waugh, a man who could appreciate the cut and thrust of argument and the pointed witticism. All too often, however, Randolph's wit was directed more at provoking his audience than at entertaining it. As time wore on, the friends seemed to grow further and further apart until all that remained was silence. I learned later, though, that Evelyn and Randolph went through these periods often, and that their friendship, somehow, flourished under these conditions. But Randolph's fellow officers were not quite so understanding of their distinguished colleague, and the silences that grew between them were rarely broken again.

As I grew to know him, I saw that his arrogance was largely a mask. He wanted desperately to achieve something constructive even if not on the scale of his father's achievements. He was too much like his father to admit his own sense of frustration, even to himself. He distinguished himself at Benghazi and Drvar as a soldier of great bravery and endurance. During the German parachute and ground attack on Tito's headquarters at Drvar, Randolph fought with the Partisans in defending the Marshal, and narrowly escaped when Tito moved his headquarters. Stoyan Pribichevich later reported that the Yugoslavs called Churchill 'the incredible Englishman' and that despite his splenetic streak, 'he never fussed about the cold, hunger, thirst, sore feet, or German bullets, and only raised hell when the Partisan barber wanted to give him a shave without hot water'.

Another story will illustrate his style. During those autumn months in Bosnia, the days were pleasant enough, but the nights were very cold, and it was necessary to have a fire, when we could, for warmth as well as for cooking. On patrol, it was customary for one man to stay in camp tending the fire while the others scouted for Germans. When Randolph's turn came around he flatly refused—such work being clearly beneath him. He was a fighting machine, not a fire-tender. The rest of us were in no mood to argue, so we left him sitting stonily beside the dead fireplace and set off on our patrol. When we returned at dawn, we found a huge fire blazing merrily away, and enough firewood, neatly stacked by size, to burn for a month. He had grown cold, and decided that building a fire was a small price to pay for warmth. And, finding that the job was challenging and fun, he had thrown himself into the project. From then on, he would let no one else touch the fire, and we had a permanent fire-tender—an excellent one, too.

Both Sir Winston and Randolph were fascinated with words and appreciated a fine turn of phrase, their own or another's. Both earned their living as journalists and writers. Both enjoyed good food and plenty to drink. They loved argument, the art of politics, and the study of the human species. And each man admired the other.

Yet, for all his conscious or unconscious emulation, Randolph could not approach his father's success. It occurred to me later, after the war, that it was far easier for the son of a Yugoslav miner to make his personal mark on his times than it would be for the son of a man who had made his mark for all time.

Randolph was all that has been said and written about him— irrepressible, arrogant, rude, argumentative—and much more. He had a natural eloquence, a deeply inquisitive intelligence and a retentive memory; he was a marvellous story-teller, and—when he wished to be—one of the most charming men I have ever known. He had courage that went beyond bravery, because he had to force himself to the front, and he did so consistently. He needed, most of all, approval and love, but found it hard to win either. Perhaps this was one reason why he liked me. I had no reason to cultivate him. I liked him for himself alone, and I admired him for his achievements, apart from any reflected glory cast by the glow from his famous father. He was, above all, a good comrade, an entertaining friend, and a sensitive human being who was a slave to his strange pride. Perhaps he is best defined by his father's description of Russia as, 'a riddle, wrapped in a mystery, inside an enigma'. He was a mystery to himself, I think, an enigma to all who met him, and an object lesson, that human greatness and goodness may reside in deceptive forms not always recognized by those who are looking for them.

A Visit to M. Flandin— grâce à Randolph*

by

A. J. Liebling

(*American writer: correspondent for* The New Yorker *Magazine; author of* Between Meals, Jollity Building, Molly and other War Pieces *and* The Most of A. J. Liebling. *Died in 1963*)

The way I became acquainted with M. Flandin needs a bit of recounting. On a day early in February of 1943, I was sitting at a sheet-metal table in front of the Hôtel Aletti, in downtown Algiers, writing a letter.

. . . As I drank wine and wrote my letter, a British officer approached my table, verified my identity, of which he was certain, and announced his, with which I was familiar. It was Captain Randolph Churchill, dressed in a Commando cover-all that fitted like a greengrocer's bag around a single onion. We made a plump pair of rumpled amateur military figures; Algiers was full of such. Churchill, having accepted an invitation to have a glass of wine, began by saying that, for an American, I showed an astonishing understanding of the French, and that I wrote very good English for a fellow who wasn't English. I immediately began to like him. Churchill also said that he had heard I was a *bon-vivant*, citing as his authority an Englishman who wouldn't know a *grenouille au vin blanc* from a toad-in-the-hole.

'*Monsieur mon Père*,' he said, 'has a friend on the Riviera here who has a *cordon-bleu* cook. Pierre-Etienne Flandin. Charming fellow, charming wife.'

'Flandin?' I said. 'The fellow who was Premier? I didn't know he was in North Africa.'

* Reprinted from the *New Yorker* of 13 September 1958.

'He came here shortly before the Allied landings,' said *le fils de Monsieur son Père*. 'Bought a place on the coast near Philippeville to grow wine. Living the life of a squire. Elder statesman, you know. Pleasure to talk to him, full of wisdom. *Monsieur mon Père* would like you to meet him.'

This flattered me, because I had never met *Monsieur son Père*. I wondered if Flandin could be the candidate that *Monsieur son Père* was readying to pull out of the hat when the Allies, executing the Churchillian strategy of the long way around, finally arrived in France. The Allied heads of government did not like de Gaulle; Giraud wouldn't do; and Darlan had been shot—by a Gaulliste agent, according to the Americans, or by an American agent, according to de Gaulle. Of Flandin I remembered little from my newspaper reading between wars except that he was tall and had in his day been considered an Anglophile. But political speculation was not my specialty. I said I had a lot of writing to do and then wanted to return to the front, to the units I knew. (It was a small, intimate war, compared to what it afterward became, and personal loyalties were engaged.) Therefore I would have no time to visit M. Flandin.

Fils was prepared for that. He said that I could take my typewriter with me; the *domaine* of M. Flandin was an ideal scenic retreat for literary composition. Also, it was in the east, about three hundred miles away—and thus well on my way to the front. 'I have a new vehicle at my disposal,' he said. 'A lorry just out from England that I have to take to a Commando training site on M. Flandin's domain. We could be off tomorrow. If you get bored, I'll lend you the lorry and a driver any time, and you can pop off to the nearest airfield—it's at Constantine, I believe—and get a transport plane to where you're going.'

Recklessly I said that I would go. Churchill *fils*, I knew, had spent several months in a hospital the previous spring after overturning a car in Egypt, and it didn't occur to me that the British Army would let him drive. I expected him to have a driver, but when I brought my gear to the front of the Aletti at the appointed hour the next day, I found him alone and triumphantly smiling in the high cab of a khaki Bedford lorry; his driver, Corporal Williams, he said, was out at the camp catching up on his Commando training. I, a non-driver myself, found no reason to take exception to

Fils's performance at the wheel, though it did seem a bit odd to me once when he tried to go around a two-and-a-half-ton General General Motors truck on a *corniche* road and the driver, a Moslem soldier, crashed his truck into the cliffside in order to avoid putting us over the edge. The driver had been trying his best to stay ahead of us, apparently in the futile hope of getting to the next widening of the road, but his truck was heavy-laden with 105-howitzer shells, while our Bedford was racing-light. 'Get on with it, get on!' I could hear *Fils* saying impatiently when we were within a foot of the G.M.'s tailboard, and I thought at first that his plan was to hurdle the truck, but he decided to pass with our starboard wheels over the abyss. We made it, thanks to the truck driver's choice of two evils, but thereafter the Bedford limped slightly on the near forewheel.

In the evening, we reached a place called Azazga, in the coastal region of Kabylia, where there was a comfortable hotel (*des Touristes*, thirteen rooms), as un-African in aspect as possible, being built of wood in a mountain-summer-resort style. Azazga was in a forest a couple of thousand feet above sea level. Here it was winter again, and cold. The proprietress, a Frenchwoman, operated the hotel alone with her Kabyle servants; the only guests in residence when we arrived were another woman and her several small daughters—a family from Algiers who had retired into the country because of the superior nourishment available, the mother told me.

Azazga is only about a hundred miles from the Aletti, but Churchill and I agreed that we might not find as comfortable a place to stay if we pushed on. 'The feature of my military record of which I am proudest,' Churchill said, 'is that I have never, even in the most difficult circumstances, found myself compelled to sleep in a bed without two clean sheets.' It was hard for me to control my admiration. I had always cherished the same objective, but in the port of Tunisia where I had lately campaigned I had been unable to find a bed, or even a cot. I had graded billets by the hardness or softness of the floors, and outdoor sleeping surfaces by the geological quality of the terrain. As for sheets, when Lieutenant-General Anderson, the commander of the British First Army, visited Gafsa, the American battalion there had to borrow a pair from the local bordello to tuck the General in. When the Germans and Italians launched a brief delaying offensive and we abandoned

Gafsa temporarily, the madame and her *pensionnaires* departed in a
truck to escape the embraces of the invaders, for whose currency
they saw no future in Africa.

The hotel at Azazga was comfortable and *familial*, although we
didn't get a meal worth remembering. Philippeville was about two
hundred and twenty miles away by road, and we made it by twi-
light the next day. The *domaine* of M. Flandin, Churchill explained
en route, was on the other side of a rather large mountain just
beyond Philippeville, and was accessible only by a tricky unpaved
road that twisted all the way. If the lorry went into a ditch, we
would be benighted on the mountain. He suggested that we stay
over with some friends he had made in Philippeville—the family
of Senator Paul Cuttoli, a statesman who had once represented the
Department of Constantine in the Upper House of the French
legislature. In the Department of Constantine, as in Mississippi,
only a small percentage of the population voted. A few great
families of proprietors, with a firm grip on agricultural credit, could
bring the small European farmers to heel as they wished, and the
only political competition was among the big fellows, some of
whom even gave themselves the luxury of being left-of-center in
Paris—on all save Algerian issues. Cuttoli, a Corsican, had been one
of these pre-war liberals, I think, but he had voted at Vichy for the
abolition of the Republic, and had then retired to Algeria to cultivate his oranges and vines. The great man was not at home—he
had business interests all over Algeria—but his family made us
welcome to the palace. There were daughters, daughters-in-law,
and assorted children, besides the Moslem servants who, I did not
need to be told, were devoted-because-they-were-understood. I had
been over the same line of country in another hemisphere. 'A question of race', one of the ladies said. 'They are just like children.' (St
Augustine was a Berber from Bone, the next port east along the
coast.) Churchill and I dined with the family, and well. Later, in a
redundant wing of the enormous house, we briefly visited the
senior officers' mess of the Philippeville Base Section of the British
First Army.

. . . The next day, Churchill and I went around the mountain.
He put the lorry into the ditch only once, but we were fortunately
within hailing distance of a road gang—a score or so of barefoot
Kabyles. They got us onto the road again by taking hold of the

wheels and heaving. Happily, we encountered no vehicle coming in our direction, and after an hour or less we descended into a pirate's cove, about a mile across, where a stream ran down into the sea between two mountains. There was a crescent beach cupped in the amphitheatre of curving mountain flanks. The valley, wide at the beach, where it was nearly level, narrowed as it climbed into the interior. It was the broadest expanse of terrain I had seen since leaving Algiers and much of it, I noticed, was under neat vines. There was a low, wide-spreading white house on the west side of the cove, and out near the eastern headland there was a clump of tents—the Commando camp. 'Splendid place for landing exercises,' Churchill said. 'Hidden. Pity the chaps haven't a boat.' He had selected the site himself, he said, while visiting the Flandins, and then had had a bit of a time selling the idea to his superiors. I could see that the place offered advantages for small-scale amphibious maneuvers—not only concealment and a shelving beach but rocks to be scaled, which are a *sine qua non* of all Commando operations. ('If there are no cliffs to climb, move to another part of the coast and ruddy well find some' was, I believe, the first rule in the Commando tactical manual.)

We headed for the white house, and when we arrived, M. and Mme Flandin were waiting for us on a trellised terrace in front of the door. The former Président du Conseil was extraordinarily tall —six feet five, according to one obit I read the other day, or six feet six, according to another. That could have made him an inch or two taller than General de Gaulle, whom the newspapers have agreed to call six feet four. Flandin didn't look as tall as de Gaulle, though, because he didn't hold himself—as de Gaulle's aides used to say of their boss—'as if he had swallowed his sabre.' Nor was he exaggeratedly narrow, like the de Gaulle of those days; Flandin had already acquired the abdominal convexity that shows only in new photos of de Gaulle. His face was a mottled pink—amiable, slack, and reconciled to age, like that of a merchant of wines retired to the country. It was at once dignified, sly and tired, though he would have been only in his mid-fifties. I found it hard to imagine him thrusting his way back onto the international stage, or even rolling in from the wings with both Churchills pushing from behind. He wore the loose garments, made of a material that approaches mattress ticking, that drape the old-fashioned Algerian planter at home. Mme Flandin's head reached his shoulder; she was as tall for a woman as he was for a man. She was one of those massive, square-shouldered Frenchwomen who have style without chic, and charm without seduction. *Monsieur le Fils* had told me, en route, that she was of a ranking family of the office-holding bourgeoisie; her brother had been French Ambassador to Poland at the beginning of the war. M. Flandin was of the same caste; his father had been a lawyer, a deputy, a professor of law, a judge, and, as the climax of his career, Resident-General in Tunisia from 1918 to 1920.

The Flandins were delightful hosts. There was nothing to do but talk, except for a bit of drinking, and it was soon clear that M. Flandin had no political plans that he wanted to impart to me. He must have been completely puzzled by my intrusion into his oenological retreat. I decided within the first hour of my visit that Churchill *père* had never heard of me and that his son had brought me along merely because he wanted company. M. Flandin must have set my presence down simply as a whim of the unpredictable *fils* of the *père* upon whose good will his safety depended—for Flandin clearly saw then, as could anybody with a tithe of his shrewdness, that the Allies would win the war.

. . . A few months before the Allies came to Africa, M. Flandin told me, the idea had occurred to him to move there, so he had traded an estate he had in Burgundy for the one near Philippeville. where he cultivated five hundred acres of vines. He was not the only French statesman to experience such an intimation; Darlan had arrived three days before the landing. For Flandin, no role in the provisional government of North Africa had yet been announced— and, as things turned out, none ever was to be. It is possible that Churchill *père* and Roosevelt planned a whole series of mild ameliorations of the alternative-to-de Gaulle regime, but the General forced their hand the next summer, and the moment for Flandin's entrance never came. He remained in the wings awaiting a cue that had been cut from the script.

After a long midday meal—a *dejeuner dinatoire*, as the French used to say long ago—M. Flandin took a siesta, and I went walking on the hillside that overlooked the bay. It was covered with a scrub growth that was as yet merely lush; in April and May it would be a jungle, in July and August sere and brown. The goat paths were easy to follow. There were wild boar on the mountain, but I could not distinguish their trails from the others. . . .

I scrambled about for an hour and returned to the house, with a virtuous feeling of having exercised, to find the Flandins sitting down to tea—an English custom they had adopted early in life, Madame said. Churchill had gone off to report to his commanding officer in the Commando camp on the austerity side of the cove. This gave me an opportunity to listen to somebody else, and I asked M. Flandin if he would have time, after tea, to tell me what he thought were the causes of the French débâcle. . . .

That evening, when Churchill had returned from his military service, we had a dinner liberally moistened with the produce of the vineyard, which was, as I remember it, barely promising. Neither the wines nor the vines themselves were old, the Flandins apologized, but there was a plenitude of cognac after the meal. One of the subjects that Churchill and I got on to was Sir Oswald Mosley, the leader of the prewar British Blackshirts who, with other British Fascists, was being held prisoner by *Monsieur son Père* under a wartime security clause known as 18-B. *Fils* was for turning him loose, because he no longer represented a threat to security, and holding him longer actually constituted punishment for his beliefs. I was for keeping him in, to show that we weren't condoning Fascism now that we had it licked. *Fils* then acted out a charade in which he impersonated the spirit of habeas corpus. 'Je suis l'esprit de habeas corpus,' he said, 'et cet homme-là est in jail.' He pointed to an imaginary presence in an empty chair. 'Moi, je kick him bloody well out.' And he kicked the chair. The Flandins maintained a polite fiction of interest and amusement.

Next morning, heavy with remorse for having imposed my presence on the Flandins, and also for having wasted four working days, I walked down to the Commando motor pool and looked up Corporal Williams, Churchill's driver. I told him that Captain Churchill had authorized him to drive me to Constantine in the Bedford, so that I could make a plane connection for our front. (I based this on what Churchill had said before we took off.) The Corporal was delighted. He said that he had to take the Bedford down to Constantine, where the Royal Army Service Corps had proper repair shops, in any case. 'We can't put her right here,' he said. 'There's something gone vitally wrong. Bloody shame, too, when we need transport so. Might I inquire, sir, if anything out of the way occurred on your journey up here?'

'Nothing at all,' I said. 'I expect the inspection in the works is lax in wartime.'

'I daresay, sir,' the Corporal said, 'but she do look as if she'd been knocked about frightful.'

We had a pleasant and uneventful forty-five-mile drive to Constantine in second gear.

'Prenez Garde! Je crois que c'est Randolph!'

(*From a* Daily Express *Pocket Cartoon by Osbert Lancaster.
Reproduced by courtesy of John Murray Ltd.*)

'Framed in the Prodigality of Nature'

by
Kenneth T. Downs

(American journalist: formerly Paris Bureau Chief for International News Service; Commander of O.S.S. Field Intelligence in the European Theatre during the war; President of Downs and Roosevelt, Inc.)

I met Randolph Churchill for the first time on the day King George VI was crowned in England, 12 May 1937. He was a special correspondent of the *Daily Mail*; I was Paris Bureau Chief of the old International News Service. We met head-on in a resounding clash, but from that unlikely beginning there grew a long and cherished friendship.

While the coronation ceremonies were proceeding with pomp and ceremony in London, I sat in a black Citroën on a country road half a mile below the Château de Candé, in the Tourraine country of France. The Duke of Windsor and Mrs Wallace Warfield Simpson were guests at Candé.

I had begun a vigil there early that bright spring morning on the chance of picking up some colour on Windsor who, as King Edward VIII, had given up his throne to his brother for Mrs Simpson, whom he was about to marry.

From my vantage point I commanded a clear view of the fifty-yard sweep between the château and a small guest house which I knew contained the only radio on the premises. Through my binoculars I watched Herman Rogers, the Duke's friend and acting host, Mrs Rogers and Mrs Simpson come and go between the château and the guest house. The Duke never appeared, and I knew that I had a story that might crowd in among the London datelines that day. I cabled a dispatch to I.N.S. saying that the Duke of Windsor had ignored the broadcast of his brother's coronation.

My story was a clean beat, and I received an enthusiastic message of congratulations from New York. I drove into Tours to enjoy a late lunch and the controversy among the other correspondents as to what had happened at the château, which was incommunicado.

Then Randolph Churchill arrived on the scene from London. I first learned of this from Dick MacMillan, the big Scot from British United Press. His face flushed with wine and his eyes rolling in mock terror, he said, 'Now, you're in for it, Ken Downs. Randolph Churchill is looking for you with blood in his eye. You'll be sorry you ever sent that story. Oh! oh! oh! I wouldn't want to be in your shoes.'

There was something of a mob scene back at the château that evening when Herman Rogers appeared for the Press conference held daily at 5 p.m. outside the main gate. Rogers refused to answer the storm of questions fired at him about activities in the château that day. The final question, as I recall it, went something like this, 'Can we take your refusal to deny the story that the Duke ignored the broadcast today as confirmation of it?'

Rogers said, 'No comment,' and departed back up the road to the château. As I started for my car, I noticed that a sort of *High Noon* hush fell over the scene, and I suddenly found myself confronted by a husky young man with a shock of golden blond hair, large blue eyes and an engaging smile.

'Churchill is my name,' he said. 'What's this nonsense I am told you have been sending I.N.S. today about the Duke of Windsor?'

The battle was joined. I told him why I knew my facts to be right, and what the hell did he know about it anyway? If I knew so much, Churchill wanted to know, where was the Duke of Windsor during the coronation broadcast?

'Maybe the Duke stood in bed,' said Bill Reed of Universal News.

There was irreverent laughter from the American correspondents, and Churchill looked somewhat bewildered and asked what was so funny.

The debate was continued that evening at dinner in Tours. Churchill was determined to torpedo my story before the correspondents for the American morning papers filed. He bet me £5 that Jim Lardner of the New York *Herald Tribune* would not use my story. He lost the bet and cheerfully paid up.

When Lardner had phoned in his story, we repaired to the Hôtel de l'Universe where a table stakes poker game went on every night. Randolph joined us.

It was a hilarious game. The balance of payments, which had been flowing steadily to the U.S. side, swelled to flood proportions. Churchill was the worst poker player I ever saw. It was a case of 'courage without cunning'. His curiosity kept him in every hand, and he paid more attention to the running verbal exchanges than to his cards. After losing one particularly big pot, he said, 'I appear to be doing something wrong. What should I have done that time?'

'I think you should have stood in bed,' said Lardner.

After the laugh which followed, Churchill held up the game.

'Should have stood in bed—what's so funny about that?' he demanded. 'It's the second time I've heard it today. Will somebody please explain.'

The action was suspended while the story was told of the little fight manager who, a few years before, at Madison Square Garden, had leapt up, hysterical with rage, when his gladiator was knocked out in the first round.

'The lousy bum,' he screamed. 'He shoulda stood in bed!'

Damon Runyon, Dan Parker and the other sports writers at the ringside chronicled his words, and they became part of the Broadway idiom.

'Hmm-m, I see,' said Randolph.

A few hands later Randolph lost another whopping pot.

'Well,' he said triumphantly, 'I seem to be standing up in bed again.'

That broke up the game.

Some years later, during the war, Bob Low sent me a private cable from the Middle East. The concluding four words of his message would have defied any cryptologist, friend or foe, and they baffled me for several hours before their meaning finally burst upon me. They were:

'BEDSTANDER HERE. SENDS REGARDS.'

Following the coronation, the date for the Windsor wedding was set for 3 June. Invitations were issued to a pool of correspondents representing the big wire services. Among our working Press quintet was Maurice Schumann, later to become Foreign Minister of France, who was then writing for the old Havas Agency.

A special invitation was sent to Randolph Churchill, not as a representative of the *Daily Mail*, but as a personal friend of the Duke.

For the three weeks following our belligerent introduction, Randolph and I were together almost constantly. He was curious about the working ways of the American Press and was both amused and fascinated by the ferocity of the competition among its correspondents.

Those three weeks, some of the most delightful I ever knew, were worth more than a year at any university for me. I was a graduate of the old Front Page school of journalism and rated as a star reporter at home. But I was new to the European scene, and my ignorance was vast. It was great good luck for me to meet this brilliant mind, generous spirit and mine of information at that time.

Randolph loved argument. He was a verbal brawler by nature. And he liked to lecture. Explaining why he had quit Oxford to go on a speaking tour in the United States, he once said:

'I felt it was more blessed to teach than to be taught.'

We had little work to do before the wedding because the château was still cut off to all except Randolph, who went out there for a dinner or visit every two or three days as a friend, not as a newspaperman. He wrote nothing of these visits and scrupulously refrained from repeating anything he heard there, but he passed on enough 'colour' to make my daily stint of reporting easy, giving us time to spend the days leisurely visiting the historic châteaux of the region and trying all the fine restaurants.

On our visits to such famed châteaux as Chambord and Chenonceaux, he was able to amplify the information from our *Baedekers* and *Guides Bleus*. He had an extraordinary, almost photographic memory, and could recite verbatim whole passages from classic works of history and literature.

During these fascinating days I learned much about what was going on in Europe and England, and about the great personalities of the day, especially Winston Churchill.

Randolph's love, adoration and respect for his father knew no bounds. His affection was fully reciprocated by Winston, and the relationship between this gifted pair was a thing of beauty in those days. Randolph telephoned him almost every evening to report on the gossip from Candé and Tours, and to receive the news from

London. He also made frequent calls to Lord Beaverbrook, the proprietor of the rival *Daily Express*, who had an insatiable appetite for gossip.

Randolph was not drinking in those days. He had no need for drink. He was exuberantly gay, vigorous and interested in everything. He required no artificial stimulation. But that was not the reason he was on the wagon. The reason was a bet of £1,000 apiece which he had made with Rothermere and Beaverbrook, the Press lords, and Churchill family friends, that he would not take a drink throughout 1937. £2,000 in those days were worth $10,000 and constituted a very respectable sum.

Late in that month of May, he was put to a test on the wager when Stanley Baldwin resigned as Prime Minister in London. Baldwin was anathema to the Churchills. Randolph was wildly exultant at news of the resignation. He immediately called his father. After an exchange of felicitations, Randolph said, 'Sir, I think this calls for a very special celebration. Do you think it would be improper for me to ask Max and Lord Rothermere for a one-day dispensation in my wager?'

Winston chuckled in appreciation and said he did not think such a request would be out of order. Randolph then called Beaverbrook and Rothermere. Both were amused at his request and graciously granted the one-day dispensation.

Plans for the celebration were launched with loving care.

'We must start out slowly, so that we don't spoil it for the wine,' he said. 'We must have a fine dinner. Let's see. Who shall we have? Jim Lardner and Bill Reed. That ought to do it. Maybe one more. We'll just slowly sip a whisky now, and then one more before dinner.'

There were several whiskies before it was time for dinner. There followed a fine selection of vintage château wines with the meal, especially his favourite clarets, then champagne, then port, then cognac, then some final whiskies. Then oblivion. He was back on the wagon the next day.

One of the things that astonished me most in our early talks was the Churchills' dislike for Franklin D. Roosevelt in those days. We had long and strenuous arguments on this subject. The New Deal was a fraud and a sham. F.D.R. was a hypocrite. Roosevelt's ultimate aim was to soak the rich in the U.S. until their fortunes reached the level of the Roosevelt fortune. After that they would be safe.

I was sure they did not really believe all this. But there was no doubt about their conviction in those days that F.D.R. was a political faker. My knowledge of this was to increase my awe of Winston Churchill when later he was able to banish these prejudices completely and become a genuine friend and working partner with the 'Distinguished Naval Person' during the war.

Politics were Randolph's consuming passion. At that time he was mainly interested in promoting his father's career. He was certain that Winston would become Prime Minister. But he hoped some day to attain the prize himself.

He regarded journalism as a temporary phase of his career, though he was destined to be in and out of it most of his life. Had he made it his chief interest, he would have been one of the greatest newspaper men who ever lived. He wrote beautifully and effortlessly. He had a keenly analytical mind, a strong instinct for the real truth, and, of course, matchless access to high sources of information. He was in on the inner circuit of history in the making.

He preferred to dictate his material, otherwise he resorted to longhand, because he never mastered the typewriter. He had one formidable problem in journalism—the publishers. He would brook no tampering with his copy, and whenever one of his stories was refused, especially if the reason was timidity, he went wild with anger.

I saw the first example of this during the Windsor wedding story. Randolph did not bother with day-to-day reporting, which was handled by other reporters for the *Daily Mail*. Apart from covering the wedding itself, he planned only one big story, a friendly exposition on the position of the Duke of Windsor, based on his private conversations at the château.

He composed this paper with great care and it was a good one. He read it over the phone to Winston, who suggested a change here and there, including a reduction in the number of mentions of 'the woman he loves'.

'That phrase is getting a little shopworn over here,' Winston said. 'You know, when the plumber is late these days, it is because of the woman he loves.'

But the conservative *Daily Mail* developed cold feet about using a story so friendly to Windsor and decided not to publish it. Randolph raged at one editor after another, and appealed all the way to Rothermere. When he failed there, he telephoned Lord Beaverbrook of the rival *Daily Express*, read him the story and asked if he cared to use it. The canny Beaver expressed surprise that the *Daily Mail* would not use such a fine story and, why sure, he would be glad to print it, and he did.

I have never seen a son less affected by the greatness, or the sudden improvement in fortune, of a father. When Winston arrived at his goal of 10 Downing Street, and the centre of the world stage as well, there was not the slightest discernible change in the attitudes or behaviour of Randolph. There was never a hint of stuffiness; he was incapable of that. And he never traded on his father's name or position.

This impressed me very much during the last seven months of 1941, when I spent a great deal of time with him in Cairo. The Second World War was then almost two years old. Winston was at the peak of his glory as the embattled war leader. Randolph was a lieutenant in the Commandos.

The officers of the Commando group based in Egypt had been drawn from various famous regiments and included the cream of British aristocracy. They were a rake-hell lot who performed incredible feats in action. When idle, they were given to high-stakes gambling, drinking and other activities which made them the despair of the military establishment in the Middle East, whom the Commandos dubbed 'The Gabardine Swine'.

One of these high-spirited officers was a particular headache. During idle time in Cairo, his pranks kept him in trouble and at times occupied the nervous attention of the M.P.s. A sigh of relief went up at G.H.Q. the day that orders arrived from London summoning him home.

Randolph knew the inside reason for the recall and it filled him with glee. It seemed the young man, the last living male of his line, had no heir. His mother and some ladies in high court circles, pulling the necessary strings, were able to arrange to have him ordered home to repair this situation.

Randolph went out to the desert to take his parachute training that summer. Jumping out of aeroplanes was not so commonplace in those days. I asked him if he had been nervous before his first jump.

'Not at all,' he said. 'I have no imagination, so action doesn't bother me in advance. But when I was in the plane, the horrible thought occurred to me: what if I should freeze when I look down the hole? So I slipped five quid to the sergeant who was next in line behind me and told him to give me a shove if I showed the slightest hesitation. It wasn't necessary. When the time came, old Randolph hopped right out.'

There was one officer among the Commandos who particularly commanded Randolph's admiration. He was Lieutenant-Colonel Robert Leacock, who will be mentioned here later.

In early summer, Randolph's tour with the Commandos ended. He was promoted from lieutenant to major in one jump and given a key position in the public information and censorship section. It was a smart move on the part of the Army. Randolph took with him to G.H.Q. another Commando officer, Captain Robin Campbell, a gifted writer and son of Ambassador Sir Ronald Campbell. With almost ferocious energy and great skill, he began to transform the inept information section into the most efficient operation of its sort that I saw throughout the war. His experience in journalism and his personal acquaintance with the correspondents, particularly the Americans, paid off handsomely.

I asked Randolph as a special favour to keep his eye out for a big Commando operation and deal me in on it. He promised to do this.

In June I met the fabulous Colonel Desmond Young and went off with him to the Fifth Indian Brigade for the invasion of Syria. While accompanying a patrol I was captured by the Vichy French in an ambush at the outskirts of Damascus, and was later expelled to Turkey.

Upon my return late in September, I met Randolph for lunch at Shepheard's. He suggested going to my room before lunch as he had an interesting letter to read to me privately.

It was a handwritten letter of six or seven pages from Winston telling of the historic meeting with President Roosevelt aboard the *Prince of Wales* in mid-Atlantic on 14 August, which resulted in the Atlantic Charter.

Most of the letter was personal, written in high good humour and full of little 'in' jokes about incidents on the voyage to the meeting and observations about various V.I.P.s But there was a serious paragraph at the end which burned itself into my memory. I cannot quote it verbatim, but it went essentially as follows:

> I feel that this is the beginning of a great and lasting friendship. The President is a great man, without any doubt. But there is something about him that troubles me deeply. It is his concern about public opinion. He tends to follow public opinion rather than to form it and lead it. I must say that our greatest single preoccupation today is with how the United States is to be brought boldly and honourably into the war.

In November I went out to the Western Desert to cover the grand offensive designed to crush Rommel but which turned into one of his greatest triumphs over the Eighth Army.

Early in the battle, I ran across Randolph and joined him in his desert-equipped Ford station wagon. It was one of the wildest days I have ever known. With our 'soft' vehicle, we were in the midst of a series of swirling tank engagements from about 11 a.m. until dusk. Tanks were hit and burst into flames within fifty yards of us. Once a stick of bombs (from the R.A.F., of course) missed us so narrowly we couldn't hear for a couple of hours. There was nothing quite so exciting as this war of movement in the desert, and I never encountered anyone who enjoyed it more than Churchill. He was like a Packer fan at a game with the Bears. A Packer fan, that is, who could quote poetry, history or classical literature to fit any situation.

Pearl Harbor came and with it the end of journalism for me. I cabled my resignation to the United Press and prepared to go home and join the Army.

Then followed a maddening waiting period. Transportation out of Cairo was difficult and greatly overtaxed. Day after day I waited for a seat on a plane.

During this waiting period Randolph sadly told me, in confidence, about the fate of the big Commando expedition to which he had tried to have me assigned. It was a raid behind the lines on Rommel's headquarters near Sidi Rafa in Libya, with the mission of capturing or killing the Desert Fox. This incredible operation was carried out as planned, and Rommel would have been killed if he had been in his quarters. But Rommel's lucky star was at work; he had been absent that night, attending a birthday party, as it turned out. The Commando landing parties who had been put ashore by submarine were lost and their fate was unknown.

At last, word came one evening towards the end of December that I was assured of a place on a plane which would depart at 7 a.m. the next day.

I packed and at about 10 p.m. went down to the terrace of Shepheard's for a nightcap. I was sipping my drink when suddenly I thought I was losing my senses at the sight of an emaciated, bearded apparition in torn khaki shorts coming up from the street. It was Lieutenant-Colonel Bob Leacock. I took him up to my room and, while he bathed and had a drink, he told me the story of the raid. After the shoot-out in Rommel's house on 18 November he and an N.C.O. had struck off into the desert, hiding by day and travelling by night. He had just reached a British outpost late that evening and been flown to Cairo. He related how Lieutenant-Colonel Geoffrey Keyes, who was in command, had been killed. (Keyes later received a posthumous Victoria Cross.) Robin Campbell, who had asked to participate in the operation, had been shot down. But he didn't know the fate of most. Campbell survived, it was learned later, but lost a leg and spent the rest of the war in a P.O.W. camp.

I telephoned Randolph that Leacock was back and was with me at Shepheard's. He was elated and asked Leacock to meet him at Maud's [Maud Marriott, wife of the then Brigadier-General John Marriott] right away.

I had to catch that plane in the morning. But I asked Randolph if he would write the story of the raid for me and file it to U.P., when it could be cleared. He said he would.

The flight back home took days, down and across Africa and the South Atlantic, with stops in Brazil and the Caribbean, and we finally reached New York just after the first of the year.

When I arrived at the United Press offices on 42nd Street to pick up my pay, I was at once congratulated on my great story.

'Which one?' I asked modestly.

'The Rommel raid, of course. What a beat. We made page 1 of the *New York Times*.'

So I knew Randolph had come through again, above and beyond

the call of friendship. The story he wrote for me was one of the cleanest scoops and one of the best written ever sent out over my signature.

As an example of journalistic excellence, the story bears repeating. This is how it appeared in the *New York Times* on 31 December 1941:

By the United Press

CAIRO, Egypt, Dec. 30.—Colonel Geoffrey Keyes, son of the World War hero who organized Britain's black-shrouded Commandos, was killed leading thirty of them on a night raid on the headquarters of German General Erwin Rommel, commander of the Axis armies in Libya, it was revealed tonight.

The raid was made on the night the British Libyan offensive started, Nov. 18. The Commando party swooped down on General Rommel's headquarters, 200 miles behind the front line, and would have captured or killed him if he had not been away at a birthday party.

The full story of one of the most dramatic episodes of the desert campaign was brought here by a bearded young lieutenant colonel, who survived the raid and wandered forty-one days through the desert to reach safety.

Colonel Keyes, son of Admiral Sir Roger Keyes, who led British ships in the historic raid that blocked up the entrance to the German submarine base at Zeebrugge, Belgium, in the World War, was shot to death in the doorway of the German headquarters building.

Survivor Relates Story

The surviving officer gave this account of the adventure:

Three days before the desert campaign started the Commandos arrived near the Axis headquarters at Sidi Rafa. Their objective was the administrative headquarters of the 'Afrika Corps,' and for two days and nights they lay in a wadi (watercourse) near by, scouting the area and awaiting the 'zero hour' that would send the Imperial Army, strung out along the Egyptian border, into action.

On the night of Nov. 18 the Commandos went to work. Dressed in black uniforms, their faces and hands covered with burned cork, they approached the German headquarters building. The back door and the windows were locked, so the Commandos pounded on the front door.

Obligingly, a German sentry opened it. The Commandos began shooting. They killed the guard and burst open another door. There they found two German staff officers. These, the Lieutenant Colonel said, they 'dispatched' with pistols and 'tommy' guns.

The shooting aroused the entire headquarters. Groups of soldiers and officers who had been sleeping started downstairs shouting the German version of 'What the hell's going on here?'

A sergeant of the Royal Artillery let them have it with a 'tommy' gun.

Other Germans, who came running from other buildings around the headquarters, were driven off by two corporals with 'tommy' guns.

Keyes Killed in Doorway

While all that was going on Colonel Keyes, whose father only recently was relieved as head of the Commandos, was working with a captain and a sergeant.

They opened the door to a second room, which was dark. Although they could hear suppressed breathing inside, Colonel Keyes ran in firing his pistol. He was met with a volley of fire and fell in the doorway.

The sergeant climbed over Colonel Keyes's body and sprayed the room with gunfire. The Germans fired back. The British captain dashed into the room after the sergeant and yelled 'duck'. The captain then blew the room apart with two hand grenades.

The captain had slammed the door shut as he threw the grenades. He and the sergeant had carried Colonel Keyes's body outside before the explosions.

Other Commandos withdrew from the building and lobbed grenades through every window as they retreated. The captain, doubling around the building to supervise that activity, had his leg broken by a stray bullet.

A lull followed, during which the Commandos started making plans to get the injured captain home.

The captain, knowing that a rendezvous was to be made with the rest of his force which was nearly twenty miles away, handed his comrades his two remaining grenades and ordered them to finish the job by blowing up the electric light plant.

He then ordered the sergeant to leave him propped up against a tree. The sergeant gave the captain a morphine injection and carried out the orders. All the survivors later managed to join the main body.

Bad weather prevented the Commandos' evacuation and the following day—Nov. 19—a large party of Germans and Italians attacked them.

After a 'brisk engagement' which lasted about two hours, the Commandos were ordered to retreat east toward Jeb el Akhbar to await the advance British armored forces striking west from Egypt.

The Commandos broke up into a number of small parties. The lieutenant colonel, whose name cannot be revealed, found himself alone with the sergeant who had worked with Colonel Keyes.

The two survivors had iron rations, which, he said, they wisely kept for a real emergency.

The lieutenant colonel said the worst thing was a shortage of news and he would have given 'five years of my life' for a wireless set.

He said it was torture for a month, wondering how the battle was going and not knowing whether it was safe to venture into the open. They finally made their way to Cerene, between Benghazi and Derna, he said, and had a Christmas dinner of bully beef, which 'we wolfed down with a full pot of marmalade, after which we both were promptly sick.'*

I was in Claridge's Hotel in London when news broke of Hiroshima and the first atom bomb in August 1945. What now? How was the monster to be controlled? Would war with Russia be necessary? Inevitable? I began to hunt for my old source of solid, inside information. Finally, through White's Club, I located Randolph. He was in the country and told me to drive up for lunch.

He was with young Winston and Evelyn Waugh and his son, Auberon. To my astonishment, I found that Randolph could add nothing to what I knew. What did Winston think? He didn't know. Had he talked with him? Yes, of course, but nothing.

* Reprinted from the *New York Times* of 31 December 1941.

For the first time since I had known him, Randolph seemed apathetic. He agreed that it would be unthinkable, and possibly the eventual end of the human species, to allow proliferation. But he had no ideas as to what should or could be done.

We had one consolation, he said at one point, with a wry smile, and paraphrased one of his favourite verses from Siegfried Sassoon lampooning British jingoists of the Boer War era. Substituting 'atom bomb' for 'Gatling gun', he quoted:

> And don't forget
> That we have got
> The Atom Bomb,
> And they have not. . . .

As I left that day, I tried to realize how much the world had suddenly changed. The Churchills for the first time had had nothing to say because apparently there was nothing they could say. In world affairs we had relied on British brains, power and intelligence for a long time. Now we were on our own.

The last time I saw Randolph was on 25 April 1968. I went up to Stour for lunch with him on that beautiful spring day. I told him that I thought he looked better than when I had seen him last in Switzerland a couple of years before.

'Do you think so?' he said. 'I really am not at all well though.'

It was the only time I had ever heard him allude to his health.

He said that he was behind schedule on the third volume of the Churchill biography. For the first time, I had the impression that he knew he would not be able to finish the massive task he had set for himself. He walked out to the car with me when I left and thanked me for coming.

It was a sad trip back to London. I had the feeling I would not see him again. He died a few weeks later.

Kay Halle could not have chosen a better title for her book. No one could ever accuse Randolph of having been a pretender in any sense of the word.

Another Randolph Churchill is as unlikely as another Winston Churchill.

Fate was kinder to the father than to the son. Winston was the right man at the right place and time in history to realize his dreams and win immortality. Randolph had his dreams too, and he had the qualities to attain them. He was fearless, brilliant and truly 'framed in the prodigality of nature'. But history's clock was timed wrong for him.

He never complained though. In all the years I knew him, from the time he was a vital young man, full of the zest for life, until the end, I never once heard him complain about his well-being, his health, or his luck.

He was a true aristocrat, and he had the heart of a champion.

With Randolph in Darkest Africa and Elsewhere

by

Stephen Barber

(British journalist: Washington Bureau Chief for the Daily Telegraph; *author of* America in Retreat)

There is a saying that the world is divided into the sort of people you would be glad to go tiger-hunting with, and those you'd sooner not. So it was with Randolph. You either liked him or loathed him. If you liked him, you would put up with his villainous moods and sometimes deeply wounding rudeness, but you would gladly go hunting with him. Even at his most impossible, he was fun. And on the whole, I found the people he disliked eminently detestable and vice versa.

I remember once in Athens during the 'December events' of 1944, as they are still known in Greece, how he made an enemy for life but ended a rather tedious discussion on whether the British had been right in intervening in the civil war that had broken out between the Communist ELAS and the nationalists after the Germans withdrew from their country. We were at that time marooned in the Grande Bretagne Hotel, hemmed in on all sides by ELAS *andartes*, who, but for a small force of British paratroops, would have easily overrun the city. A certain amount of shooting was in progress. The electricity was cut off. It was bitterly cold. But we had ample stocks of brandy. Randolph, who had arrived on the scene mysteriously enough—he was supposed to be attached to Marshal Tito's Yugoslav Partisans at that time but had evidently felt impelled to take some local leave to find out what was afoot in Athens—soon got embroiled in the candlelit debate in the hotel bar.

There was a particularly pink brigadier-general with us who, as the night wore on, ventured some rather injudicious doubts about the Government's policy. This was, I recollect, largely due to the fact that he was somewhat infatuated by a female journalist of leftish views who was present. Randolph, of course, was stoutly loyal to the intervention. His father, the Prime Minister, was indeed already embattled at the time in the House of Commons on the subject. The Americans, strange to relate, were on the whole critical of Britain's action then in preserving Greece from ELAS take-over. Communists were not regarded automatically in those days as the enemy—far from it. But Sir Winston could see further ahead than many simple-minded souls in Washington at that time. So could Randolph.

He spoke with a certain passion. He crushed the brigadier.

Then suddenly up spoke a young public relations officer—a captain to Randolph's then rank of major. 'Look here, Churchill,' this fellow expostulated. 'You shouldn't talk like that to your superiors. You'd never get away with it if you were not your father's son!'

Randolph put down his glass deliberately. There was a hush. Then he said, quite gently: 'I don't see why you have to bring MY father into this discussion. I never would bring up *your* father, even if I knew him, which I don't. I can but assume you do . . .

'As a matter of fact,' he resumed after a brief reflective pause, 'I am bloody sure he's an utterly dreary, middle-class bore. . . .'

Of course, some say this proved Randolph to be a horrible snob. It certainly did not help matters that in this instance it was all too obvious that the captain's parent would certainly have lived up to the description.

Randolph tended, most days, to line up on the side of the underdogs of the world. While he was not notably sentimental about Africa's downtrodden blacks, for example, he was none the less contemptuous of those who thought themselves superior by virtue of the colour of their skins.

I remember once in the spring of 1960—early in what became known in Britain as 'Africa Year' because so much happened then in that continent—I found myself on a plane flying with Randolph from Salisbury, the capital of what was then the Rhodesian Federation, to Johannesburg.

There had just been an ugly police incident at a Transvaal township named Sharpeville. Afrikaner troopers had lost their heads and shot up a crowd of black Africans. Dr Verwoerd's government had told lies about it. Emergency laws had been proclaimed. It looked for a moment as if a massive native uprising against the Whites was about to begin. Randolph was heading down to South Africa to report for the *News of the World*, whose chief foreign affairs columnist he had become.

Soon after we took off, the stewardess came round handing out long immigration forms to fill up for the Johannesburg authorities. They asked many more questions than most and Randolph, who never cared much for bureaucratic nonsense of any sort, was soon showing exasperation. He was incensed over a question relating to his 'proposed means of financial support while in the Union of South Africa'. He wrote down: 'This is an impertinence but you may take it that I am most generously treated by my employer.'

Then came the question on race—the burning issue in a country where apartheid is strictly practised.

'Damned cheek!' said Randolph. He then began writing furiously across the form, filling up the small space allotted and spreading himself down the margins of the paper. 'They can try and make something of that!' he muttered.

Peering over his shoulder I read the following:

Race: human. But if, as I imagine is the case, the object of this enquiry is to determine whether I have coloured blood in my veins, I am most happy to be able to inform you that I do, indeed, so have. This is derived from one of my most revered ancestors, the Indian Princess Pocohontas, of whom you may not have heard, but who was married to a Jamestown settler named John Rolfe. . . .

The Afrikaner passport officers did not find any of this amusing. They impounded Randolph's passport at the airport. It was only after a great deal of argument that he was allowed to land temporarily in the custody of a South African friend who had motored out to fetch us. But this did not worry him much, since it was Friday night and he intended to write precisely one story next day for his Sunday paper and then fly home again.

The following morning, however, having engaged a stenographer to take dictation from him while he had a masseur pummel him on a trestle table he demanded and got from the astounded hotel management in the middle of the night, he made a big thing out of his encounter with Dr Verwoerd's immigration authorities. He was, at that time, going through a phase of calling all those with whom he disagreed 'silly-billies'. He asked me to edit his telegram for him before sending it off. In doing so, I remember deleting at least half a dozen 'silly-billies'.

'Now,' Randolph announced over lunch, 'we will go and interview Dr Verwoerd!'

The South African premier was not in a loving mood towards the British at that time. Nor was he anyone's pin-up in England. But he was making a speech at an Afrikaner township some distance across the veldt from Johannesburg and it seemed to Randolph both obvious and simple to climb into a taxi and demand to be taken thither. I tagged along, becoming increasingly alarmed at the enormous sum we soon began running up on the meter.

In due course, we got to the place. Verwoerd had made his speech and was riding slowly in stately triumph through dense crowds of tow-headed Afrikaners, surrounded by exceedingly tough-looking jack-booted bodyguards at the head of a motorcade. Randolph was dressed rather casually in a sloppy pair of grey flannels and a white shirt. It was hot and he was also sweating. He did not, in short, cut an awesome figure. But that did not prevent him from diving through the mob and reaching the premier's car —an open Ford convertible—to demand an interview. Verwoerd looked stunned, as well he might have been. But he quickly realized who Randolph was, which probably saved us both from being locked up, if not actually shot on the spot.

Randolph was very pleased by this journalistic enterprise. I must confess, I did not myself see where it had got him. The good doctor never did agree to see him. But it so happened a week later, by which time Randolph had reached Nairobi, the Kenyan capital, on his way back to London, that an eccentric Anglo-South African liberal confronted Verwoerd at a Johannesburg agricultural fair and shot him in the head with a .22 pistol.

Verwoerd survived. But Randolph felt totally vindicated. He was able to write a splendid column for the *News of the World* that weekend, telling his readers how he could have forewarned the South African leader that an assassination attempt was going to be made against him. During his Johannesburg visit, Randolph had heard a number of important people remark that it was high time someone shot Verwoerd. And he had not been impressed by the quality of local security arrangements. He illustrated this point by recounting how he had himself been able to accost the great man with the greatest of ease only the previous Saturday. I heard afterwards that a number of prominent members of Johannesburg society, who had been Randolph's recent hosts, endured some embarrassing moments after that column appeared, when they had to parry probing police questions as to the views they had so recklessly imparted during his visit.

Randolph was a splendidly free-wheeling, let-the-chips-fall-where-they-may journalist. Considering his capacity for indiscretion, it was astonishing that he retained so many sources of information. But he could be serious and his judgement was usually sound as to which faction was likely to emerge triumphant in any given intra-party political battle. On the other hand, I think, he really enjoyed the 'I was there' type of action reporting which is still more in vogue in Fleet Street than in America, where more prestige attaches to punditry.

Don Cook, the veteran European correspondent of the New York *Herald Tribune* and later of the Los Angeles *Times*, once remarked to me: 'Randolph is a secret vice for people like us. An evening with him is like living history. No matter how offensive he can be at times, if you get into an argument, it is worth it for the range he covers. He talks about Marlborough at Quatre-bras, and who was who when Churchill was at Omdurman, or Chamberlain was at Munich, just as if it had all happened yesterday.'

Don told me this one night in a singularly dreary hotel by the Tigris in Baghdad the day wisely foolish statesmen signed what was later to be known as the CENTO pact. We agreed then that this was not an act of statesmanship so much as of desperation. We had only just struck up an acquaintanceship when we found that we were both wishing Randolph was with us.

'Pity Randolph isn't here!' we agreed. He would have put the non-event into some sort of historical perspective, which it sadly lacked, and even had he been wholly mistaken in so doing, he would at least have been entertaining.

Baghdad was truly a very dull place.

Not long afterwards, of course, the mob made it duller still.

They murdered Nuri Said Pasha and his monarch—a creation of

ours—and this made nonsense of the Baghdad Pact concept, and also made that city, mercifully, quite unnecessary to visit.

I remember a fantastic series of adventures with Randolph in Algiers following the famous 13 May revolt in 1958 which led to the overthrow of the French republic and the installation of General de Gaulle as President. Randolph had contrived to get to Algiers via Switzerland, which was, as I recall, the same way that M. Jacques Soustelle smuggled himself from the Metropole to his beloved Algeria. Most of the rest of us flew in aboard an Air-Algérie passenger plane which an enterprising American radio correspondent had located at Orly and then wangled special permission for it to be released to return to its home base.

The big coup every reporter was out to make at that moment was to interview the shadowy M. Soustelle, who was obviously the grey eminence behind the whole Gaullist plot—although he was later to fall out with the General. Randolph was then representing the *Evening Standard*. I ran into him on the steps of the Aletti Hotel near the waterfront, where our tardily arriving crowd of journalists from Paris found themselves billeted. It was, by then, too late for me to file anything to my paper, so I proposed dinner. Randolph demurred. Then he gave me a crafty look and said: 'If you'll keep the others off my back, I'll fill you in on what I'm going to find out tonight. I am due to be picked up in a few minutes by a man who is going to take me to see Soustelle himself.' He then vanished.

Early next morning I was awoken by a telephone call to my room. It was Randolph. 'Come round and have breakfast,' he said. 'I need your help.'

A few moments later I was to find him sitting on his balcony overlooking the harbour. He was working on a curious meal of orange juice, fried eggs and Veuve Clicquot and insisted that I join him in his menu. But he was in an awkward bind. He had secured his interview with Soustelle. The great man had received him in the same Villa des Oliviers overlooking Algiers as that in which Sir Winston met Charles de Gaulle in 1943. Soustelle had been most informative. They had talked at length. And there had been a good deal to drink.

The only serious snag, Randolph at length admitted, was that not only had he neglected to take notes, but he could not remember a solitary thing Soustelle had said. What was more, at any moment a telephone call was due to come in from the Paris office of the *Evening Standard*. The editor knew he had achieved the splendid coup—a veritable scoop—of an interview with the top mystery man of the whole affair. What was Randolph going to say when he started demanding 'copy'?

We worked hard on the problem. I tried one idea after another to prod some recollection out of the recesses of Randolph's memory. What had he said about de Gaulle? What role were the generals—Massu and Salan—going to play in the future development of the drama? When was de Gaulle going to come to Algiers? —in fact, he came some days later.

It was hopeless.

Then suddenly the telephone rang. It was Paris. Randolph took the receiver and plopped down on the bed with it in his hand. And, all at once, a beatific smile came over his face. 'I've got it,' he chortled. 'Just you listen to this. . . .'

Whether or not anything really came back to him at that juncture I shall never know. All I do remember is that it went rather like this:

> Last night I had the privilege of meeting the grey eminence of the Algiers uprising. He is M. Jacques Soustelle. . . . We met in the handsome Villa des Oliviers, high in the hills above the city and looking out over the bay of Algiers. . . . It was at this self-same spot that Sir Winston Churchill conferred during an earlier French crisis with General Charles de Gaulle. . . .

He paused at this point and then went on:

> I wish I was at liberty to tell you exactly what M. Soustelle told me . . . but my lips are sealed. However, I think it fair for me to tell you what I told M. Soustelle. . . . I told him that I believed that civilians must always be in control of the military . . . while the reasons behind the May 13 rebellion could be understood and even approved . . . the sooner the supremacy of civil authority was re-established, the better.
>
> I think you may take it that M. Soustelle agreed with me. . . . There was a good deal more in this vein.

It was so highly thought of by Lord Beaverbrook, the owner of the *Evening Standard*, that he caused the whole article to be reprinted in the paper's morning stablemate, the *Daily Express*, next day—a rare honour indeed.

Frankly, I do not know whether Randolph had a sudden total recall of his conversation with M. Soustelle of the previous evening. I doubt if it matters. It was undoubtedly off the record anyway. And the story did have Randolph's competitors in a great rage of envy, which is really what the game is all about.

After that Randolph developed an alarming enthusiasm for chartering singularly dangerous-looking light aircraft in which to sally forth on further exploits. We flew one anxious dawn in a twin-engined five-seater of indeterminate ancestry across the Mediterranean to Ajaccio in Corsica, I remember, in order to get the story of how that island was seized by the rebels. The rebel chief who carried this out was Pascal Arrighi, a member of the Paris Chamber of Deputies who was, in due course, to fall foul of de Gaulle, like Soustelle, and escape to exile.

We were arrested by paratroops twice in a matter of hours, coming and going, but it never worried Randolph. While military policemen and bureaucrats sought either to impound our plane, arrest us or, finally and in desperation, expel us, my dear old friend never lost sight of the main objective. We had the knack of getting hold of the only telephone around that could be coaxed into reaching London or Paris to enable him to dictate copy.

What made this all the more remarkable was the fact that Randolph's French was, to say the least, rudimentary. That was my job—dealing with the natives. Yet somehow, when it came to my turn to have a go at reaching my paper on the same telephone that had just performed splendidly for Church-eel, the line went down abruptly.

Randolph in Korea

by
Ansel E. Talbert

(American journalist: military and aviation editor and Korean War Bureau Chief for the late New York Herald Tribune; former Lt-Colonel in the U.S. Air Force and assistant to the Military Attaché at the American Embassy in London)

Knowing Randolph Churchill for any length of time and being exposed to the many facets of his personality in either peace or war was like watching a kaleidoscope of many colours that rapidly changes designs.

You never knew what combination was going to turn up, but you knew that whatever did was likely to be interesting.

The first time I encountered Randolph during the Korean War was in the Tokyo Press Club at No. 1 Shimbun [Newspaper] Alley during the early war days before the Inchon landings.

Randolph had just arrived in the theatre and was playing the club's only $1 slot machine with great energy and concentration. He had the general air of a tactician concerned over the progress of a battle but not sure exactly how much he could influence its outcome.

Across the Sea of Japan and the Tsushima Strait, it was exactly at this time that the hard-pressed United Nations forces—then almost exclusively American and South Korean—were fighting desperately for a shrinking piece of real estate in south-east Korea. This action centred on Taegu, the temporary capital since the fall of Seoul and Pusan, the only remaining large port.

Randolph was barely nodding to friends and acquaintances. I then was neither, although I knew other members of the Churchill family and had just arranged to share a base office in Radio Tokyo separated by temporary partitions with him and Stephen Barber of the *News Chronicle*, and with Lindsay Parrott, the *New York Times* bureau chief.

The combat between British war correspondent and one-armed bandit for a $100 jackpot consumed the better part of an afternoon, evening, and the entire morning following, while spectators who happened to drop in watched with increasing fascination.

It was interrupted at intervals only long enough for Randolph to change a succession of British £5 notes into silver dollars, take occasional liquid refreshment and nourishment which was brought to him, and catch a few hours of sleep in a near-by leather chair. He was obviously determined to stay close to his investment. He surely must have fed many times the amount of the $100 jackpot into that slot-machine's maw.

But perseverance finally won out, and the machine's spinning cylinders finally turned up three identical symbols in a row, with the resulting loud clinking of a stream of U.S. silver dollars changing ownership.

Randolph was exultant, together with those spectators who had placed favourable side bets on the outcome. His detachment vanished instantly and he became the happiest and most friendly correspondent in Tokyo; for that matter, anywhere east of Suez.

He beamed on fellow members of the Press, their military guests and Japanese girlfriends, with the uncomplicated and genuine joy of a small boy who had just received a long-hoped-for but possibly unattainable Christmas present.

Champagne was ordered for all, including those he didn't know, as long as the $100 lasted. After that, the party continued, with Randolph still insisting on playing the host. To all offers of buying the next round, he would counter with: 'It's my victory celebration.'

That night, well fortified in mind and body for the rigours of Korea, he left for the front.

Randolph's first arrival on Korean soil came at a crucial moment in the war—in mid-August, 1950. Some 25,000 North Korean troops had just swept eastward across the Naktong River, which constituted the western flank and a major defensive line of the embattled American and South Korean forces.

They had, in fact, cut the main North Road up the Korean peninsula only fifteen miles from Taegu.

With other members of the Allied Press corps Randolph personally witnessed the almost miraculous turn in the tide within a three-day period, which he credited to the heroism of 'the tired U.S. 24th Division . . . in action longer than any other unit, fortified by elements of the U.S. Marine Brigade'. With some air support, they saved Taegu and probably the entire U.N. position on the Korean peninsula.

And Randolph walked into, and emerged with distinction from, the tragic aftermath of a land-mine explosion. This deprived the international Press corps covering the war of two of its most respected and best-liked members: Christopher Buckley, chief correspondent in the war theatre of the *Daily Telegraph*, the London newspaper for which Randolph wrote, and Ian Morrison, Far East correspondent of *The Times*.

Morrison, with an Indian Army colonel and a South Korean lieutenant acting as a guide, was killed instantly when their jeep ran over a land mine on a lonely road, while its occupants were attempting to follow the enemy retreat. Buckley, mangled by the explosion, died a few hours later, in an American Army hospital, without regaining consciousness.

Because of the complete lack then of any commercial wireless or other dependable communication facilities, Randolph had flown back to Tokyo by thumbing a ride on a returning U.S. Air Force cargo plane, to file in person his own story of the great Naktong victory.

When the gruesome details of the reporters' deaths reached Tokyo, there was an equally sudden lack of volunteers to break the news to Buckley's wife, who was in the city. Even the British Minister and members of the British diplomatic mission ducked the unpleasant task.

But Randolph, on instant impulse, performed the task with such warmth, tact and sincere sympathy that even his longtime friends, who were aware that such qualities existed beneath his flamboyant and argumentative exterior, were astonished. Randolph told me later that he was, too.

Perhaps he was instinctively reacting to advice he once told me his father, Sir Winston, gave him:

'Never fall below the level of events.'

However, to me, Randolph's act from the heart was typical of him.

On 25 August Randolph was again back in Korea. By odd

circumstance, in the company of an American correspondent named Frank Emery and some American G.I.s, he came uncomfortably close to duplicating the fate of Buckley and Morrison except in detail.

By now, the defeated North Korean Communist forces were clearly withdrawing in some disorder both north and west of Taegu, but, as usual, Randolph wanted to see for himself.

He and Emery—who represented the old International News Service and later was killed in the war—decided to accompany a crack reconnaissance unit of the U.S. First Cavalry Division on a night patrol across the Naktong. The patrol was being sent into what had been heavily defended enemy territory.

It was the dry season, the river was low, and the entire patrol waded across to the other side almost without incident. It then split into three parts, one remaining near the bank to guard the rear as an exit route, and the other two fanning out to look for Communists.

Randolph used to say that you never should go on patrol with anyone you wouldn't care to take tiger-hunting, and in this instance he probably regarded the two veteran American sergeants in charge as being in this category.

Although Randolph's bravery was so outstanding a characteristic as never to be questioned, his sense of doing the right thing at the right time was somewhat less unassailable. In the light of what happened, it is just possible that the sergeants might have chosen another tiger-hunting companion.

Eye-witness accounts differed somewhat, but there was a consensus that Randolph picked the trip across the Naktong to impart to his companions in a somewhat hushed but also penetrating voice a few of the lessons he had learned from Second World War patrols with Tito's Partisans in Yugoslavia.

Emery commented: 'Randolph really is a great guy but he just doesn't always know when to stop talking.'

One forward wing of the patrol discovered a slit trench still warm from recent human occupation, but the enemy, forewarned and possibly shaken by Randolph's voice in the night, had apparently gone elsewhere hurriedly. They turned up in force as the patrol began to pick its way back across the sandy bank of the Naktong, and the first warning of their presence was the 'whomp' of a series of mortar-shell explosions, much too close to the patrol members for comfort.

Randolph received a leg wound from one of the fragments, and two military members of the patrol were wounded, one seriously.

It was characteristic of Randolph that he insisted upon writing his story and arranging for it to be flown back before he would submit even to emergency repairs. As he lay on a litter waiting to be flown to Tokyo a G.I. inquired of him whether he was Winston Churchill's son. 'Well, I'm certainly not one of Clem Attlee's off-spring,' Randolph growled.

There were no complications, but the U.S. Army medics insisted that he take it easy for a few days and stay away from the front.

Randolph found this hard to do. In preference to another round with the $1 slot machine in Tokyo, he flew to Hong Kong to witness the arrival of the first sizeable United Kingdom reinforcements (other than British Navy personnel) to the U.N. contingent in Korea. These were the 1st Battalion of the Middlesex Regiment, and the 1st Battalion of the Argyll and Sutherland Highlanders.

It was in Hong Kong that Randolph's strong pro-Americanism (he would often remind those who referred to him as a 'Britisher' of his American ancestry) and his sense of loyalty to an ally came into full view, at an off-the-record diplomatic briefing. This was conducted by one of the top British diplomatic personnel in the Far East. This gentleman, however, was what might be called 'an old China hand' with a dim view of the military capabilities of 'Johnny Chinaman'—particularly those in the armies of Generalissimo Chiang Kai-shek.

General Douglas MacArthur, the U.N. commander, had been hinting that perhaps the presence of a couple of Nationalist divisions from Taiwan might be a good idea on the Korean front. The British Foreign Office's contribution to Far Eastern strategy thought otherwise. He predicted without qualification that they would immediately go over to the enemy.

On hearing this, Randolph struggled to contain himself. Finally he rose and interrupted the lecture by saying:

Your remarks, sir, are an insult to an old ally which over many years has helped to resist both Fascist and Communist aggression, and whose leaders refused to make a deal with the Japanese militarists at a time when it could have benefited them immensely and could have injured or destroyed the position of the democratic powers in the Pacific.

Then, recalling the strong resistance of Chiang's ill-equipped Nationalist forces to the initial Japanese invasion of China and the long epic retreat in good order of the Nationalist government and military forces to Chungking, Randolph concluded:

'General MacArthur is a better judge of these matters than you sir, and I suggest that out of common decency you refrain from criticizing his competence.'

The British diplomat probably wasn't convinced, but he hurriedly changed the subject.

Randolph went back to Korea from Hong Kong just before the dramatic Inchon landings of the United Nations forces under General MacArthur's command—which might have ended hostilities had the Chinese Communists stayed on their side of the Yalu—and he gave highly competent coverage to the recapture of Seoul and the reverse crossing of the 38th parallel.

Randolph returned to England with the original corps of correspondents in Korea, all utterly exhausted by their hardships in the field and the enormous difficulties of communications they had encountered.

When the Chinese unexpectedly entered the war, after a lull and supposed mopping-up of the defeated North Koreans by General MacArthur's forces, Randolph wasn't around to cover.

Seventeen of his fellow correspondents had been killed in the fighting or in flaming air crashes going to or from the front. Among the few veterans remaining to break in the new crop of fresh faces, it was agreed generally that Randolph, with his ever-optimistic and combative personality, was going to be missed.

The Meeting of Prime Minister Churchill and his son Randolph Churchill in Italy in August 1944

by
Lyman L. Lemnitzer

(*American soldier: Chief of Staff, U.S. Army, 1959–60; Chairman of the Joint Chiefs of Staff 1960–2; Supreme Allied Commander, Europe, 1963–9*

During the Italian campaign of the Second World War, I was the Deputy Chief of Staff to General (later Field-Marshal) Sir Harold Alexander, whose forces were known as the Allied Armies in Italy.

After the capture of Rome by General Alexander's Allied Armies on 4 June 1944, the Allied Forces advanced northward in hot pursuit of the Germans. During their withdrawal the Germans suffered heavy losses from Allied Army and Air Forces, particularly from the heavy air attacks of the Mediterranean Allied Tactical Air Forces (MATAF) on the German motorized columns as they moved north with little regard to dispersion or highway congestion.

In August of 1944 General Alexander's field headquarters were located on the shores of Lake Bolsena, approximately sixty miles north of Rome.

In mid-August we were informed that Winston Churchill would be coming to Italy to spend approximately one month with General Alexander. The purpose of his visit was to get a closer look at the operations of General Alexander's forces (the U.S. Fifth Army and the British Eighth Army) and concurrently to enjoy a few weeks of long-needed relaxation. We selected a small but comfortable villa in which the Prime Minister and the immediate members of his staff could live during this visit. It was located several miles from the headquarters of General Alexander.

During that summer of 1944 the Prime Minister's son Randolph was in Yugoslavia where he was maintaining close contact with the Partisan forces operating there. One day we were informed that Randolph wanted to come to Italy to confer with his father. Accordingly, arrangements were made with the Allied Air Forces to pick him up in Yugoslavia and transport him to an Allied airfield located near the city of Viterbo, a short distance from our headquarters. I was designated to meet Randolph at the airfield and bring him back. He arrived in the early evening and I brought him to our headquarters where he enjoyed a much-needed shave and bath and put on a fresh change of clothes.

In the meantime, General Alexander and the Chief of Staff, General Harding, had departed for the Prime Minister's villa, where they had been invited to dine with the Prime Minister that evening. They left instructions that we should come to the villa at approximately 11 p.m., presumably to join them for coffee and brandy. Accordingly, Randolph was invited to join us at dinner at General Alexander's mess at Lake Bolsena, following which I would escort him to the Prime Minister's villa.

Upon his arrival at our headquarters Randolph made it quite clear that he was pretty well 'fed up' with slivovitz, the traditional Balkan liqueur, and was interested in getting some proper Scotch and brandy for a change. We did our best to accommodate him. By the end of the meal he was in a mellow mood. After dinner I accompanied him to the Prime Minister's villa, arriving there at the desired time. I was interested in what the reaction of the two would be when they met. I did not have very long to wait. As Randolph entered the dining-room, he promptly became furiously engaged in a heated argument with his father over the policies being carried out by the Allies towards the Partisan forces in Yugoslavia.

It was a time when the fortunes of Mihailovitch were waning and those of Marshal Tito were on the rise. The burning argument centred on the Allied shift in policy taking place at the time—father and son seemed to differ widely over the justification for the policy shift. Randolph also argued strenuously for greater Allied material support for Partisan activity in Yugoslavia, which was being provided from Italy by the 'Balkan Air Force', the cover name adopted by the Allies for those elements of the Allied Air Forces in Italy participating in that activity. Winston Churchill reminded Randolph of other priorities at this time when Yugoslavia was still almost completely held in the iron grip of the Nazis, and every piece of equipment had to be carefully rationed and dropped with extra care lest it should fall into German hands.

Following this meeting I discussed some of the details of the situation with several of the British officers at Headquarters. They told me they thought that Randolph was playing a most useful role in discussing face-to-face with his father with courageous candour and directness certain sensitive issues that government officials and members of the Prime Minister's own staff were frequently loth to raise with him.

I do not know what final results emerged from that particular animated and hotted-up policy debate between the Prime Minister and his son Randolph. But I do know that I had been a first-hand witness to a very courageous Randolph Churchill playing the role of 'devil's advocate' with cool-headed daring. This was not the first time that British officers had attributed to Randolph the important role of raising, presenting and discussing with his father the disagreement with certain features of Allied and governmental policy, that other officials and staff officers found almost impossible to express to the Prime Minister.

For this all could be grateful.

Before the Law

Sir John G. Foster

Randolph and the Law

by
John G. Foster

(British statesman and barrister-at-law: Fellow of All Souls; Recorder of Oxford 1938–51; Under-Secretary of State for Commonwealth Relations 1951–4)

Randolph was a successful litigant. He took a lot of trouble. 'Have we done our prep?' he would ask his legal advisers. John Sutro would be used for conducting a mock cross-examination, designed to make Randolph lose his temper. The reports of law cases would excite his interest in connexion with his own litigation. 'Have you seen what these idiot judges have decided? All lawyers are crooks and stupid.' However, the views of his solicitor and barrister on points of law were unequivocally accepted; on law only. Once his solicitor was referring to a paragraph in one of his articles that would not be in good taste. 'You advise on law,' he said, 'I am the judge of taste.' Again and again his lawyers were called up often as late as 3 a.m. Conferences would take place from midnight till dawn—often with great success. There was, for instance, his case against *Private Eye*, when Randolph obtained an *ex parte* mandatory injunction. This was a very rare achievement. It meant that he obtained a Court Order (an injunction), without the other side being present (i.e. *ex parte*), calling on *Private Eye* to expunge the libel on Randolph (i.e. mandatory, ordering positive action). 'No good having an apology in *Private Eye*,' he said, 'what we must have is a full-page advertisement in the *Evening Standard* withdrawing the libel and expressing regret,' and he got it.

When a Labour Party publication lifted several pages of his writings for political discredit of the Conservatives, Randolph called a conference lasting all night. His grasp of the essentials of the breach of copyright and his understanding of the legal formulation helped his lawyer to prepare the entire documentation and briefs in the night for the application to the High Court in the morning.

In the General Election of May 1955 Randolph wrote an article in the *Evening Standard*. Its main theme was that Cyril Lord, the then cotton magnate in Lancashire, was talking nonsense when he said that the Conservative Government would lose every seat in the area. Randolph called this 'loud-mouthed vapourings', the *People* newspaper reported the next Sunday in an article headed 'Voters Beware'. It characterized Randolph 'as the slightly comic son of our greatest statesman'. It included him in the ranks of 'paid hacks, paid to write biased accounts of the campaign'.

Randolph very astutely wrote a letter to the *People* pointing out that in his view the article contained untruths; in the subsequent case he was repeatedly to use the word 'lie' in connexion with the allegation that he had described as nonsense Mr Cyril Lord's opinion on the cotton industry. Only Lord's view that the Conservatives would lose all these seats was the subject of Randolph's criticisms. Randolph's letter finished by asking for a retraction, not an apology. Randolph told the editor that if the letter was published this would be the end of the matter. In fact the letter when published in the *People* was truncated. So Randolph sued for libel. He acquitted himself brilliantly in the evidence he gave to his Counsel and in his cross-examination:

> *Counsel*: So it was quite deliberate, was it, to say about Mr Attlee that he was a tardy little marionette?
>
> *Randolph*: One does not write by accident. I am not a monkey on a typewriter from whence the words come out by accident.

Challenged with the fact that in a speech he had called the editor of the *Sunday Dispatch* an old hack and therefore he should not object to being called a paid hack, Randolph answered that when referring to the editor as an old hack he was 'referring to a race of dark horses. . . . That is the sense in which I was using "hack", about a horse.'

The speech in which Randolph had used 'old hack' was in the context of comparing the various editors of Sunday papers and their proprietors as competing horses in a race for the post of Pornographer Royal and Criminologist Extraordinary. The race 'had set so fast a pace that old hacks had to look to their laurels'.

Randolph continued to point out in his cross-examination with great effect that a paid hack has nothing to do with horses.

The speech in 1953 at which Randolph had made these remarks on pornography was at a literary lunch given by Miss Foyle of the famous Foyle's bookshop which contains several million second-hand books. Mr Hugh Cudlipp was the guest of honour:

Counsel: The honorary guest was Mr Cudlipp, was he not?
Randolph: Honorary was not the word I used myself.
Counsel: The occasion was the publication of Mr Cudlipp's book *Publish and Be Damned.*
Randolph: I should explain perhaps in case you [Counsel] do not know that when I accepted to go and take the Chair I had not read the book.

As Randolph sought to ridicule and criticize Mr Cudlipp in his speech Counsel asked him: 'Did you think that if that was the position you might have said, "Well, I do not think I ought to be Chairman." '

Randolph: No. I did consider that very carefully and then I thought it would disappoint Miss Foyle and I did not want to do that. I might say she was delighted with the whole affair and thanked me most warmly. . . . I think she thought it was jolly good fun; I saw her laughing a lot.

Counsel for the defendant newspaper referred to the words 'as usual' in the context of the article including Randolph among 'those who (as usual) have not seen fit to fight openly for seats but prefer to be paid hacks'. Inevitably Counsel had to concede this went too far. Randolph had stood for Parliament in 1935, in 1936 and in 1945 and 1951. He was elected for Preston in 1940. On every occasion he had been defeated, except in 1940 when the election was uncontested under the wartime Party truce.

Counsel: As usual . . . it goes too far; I say that at once because it is not accurate.
Randolph: You may say it is not accurate, but it is not only not accurate it happens to be the reverse of the truth, in fact a lie.
Counsel: I thought I was trying to give you something . . . but never mind.

This capacity to parry Counsel's questions is again shown when Counsel was suggesting that Randolph's strictures on Mr Lord—the reference to Mr Lord's 'loud-mouthed vapourings'—were unnecessarily offensive.

Counsel: You see, Mr Churchill, you are a journalist. Why not simply say that 'I have tested the situation and in my opinion Mr Lord is wrong; I do not agree with him.'
Randolph: Well, I suppose if I had you to help me write my articles I might have written it like that, but I have to write them my own way, do I not?

On the same lines:

Counsel: Why not be reasonably polite to Mr Lord?
Randolph: Why not: well, Mr Paull, you must allow me to write my articles in my own way. It is too late for me to start taking lessons in journalism at my time of life.

Throughout Counsel was forced to be precise by Randolph:

Counsel: Why loud-mouthed vapourings? What you were intending to say was this—everything Mr Cyril Lord has been saying are loud-mouthed vapourings?
Randolph: No, everything he has been saying on this precise point. I was not aware of everything that Mr Lord said. This was the only thing on which I was informed as to Mr Lord's opinion.

Again the legal precision of Randolph:

Counsel: Is it criminal to call you a hack?
Randolph: I am not suggesting it is criminal; this is a civil action, Mr Paull.

Randolph waged a persistent campaign against the practice that one national newspaper never attacked or criticized another. Dog don't eat dog. When asked if he had not called the *People* newspaper 'the lowest mongrel cur in Fleet Street', he replied, 'That arose inevitably out of Dog don't eat Dog. If you use metaphors from the canine world you naturally use other metaphors drawn from the same world, otherwise you complicate the issue and do not carry your audience with you.'

Under cross-examination Randolph showed himself extremely

Randolph Churchill, aged nineteen.
(Photograph by Lenare, London)

2.   On active service.
(Photograph by courtesy of the Imperial War Museum)

With Anthony Eden at the Hague Conference, 1948.
(Photograph by courtesy of the Radio Times Hulton Picture Library)

4. At Stour, East Bergholt, Suffolk.
(Photograph by courtesy of the Sunday Telegraph*)*

At work on the biography of Sir Winston Churchill, with his father looking on.
(Photograph by Patrice Habans, reproduced by courtesy of Paris-Match*)*

With the pug Captain Boycott in the garden at Stour.

7. ' Could you come, please . . . '

(Photograph by Patrice Habans, reproduced by courtesy of Paris-Match*)*

After the ceremony at which he received, on behalf of his father, the Honorary American Citizenship conferred on Sir Winston by President John Kennedy. *(Photograph by courtesy of Abbie Rowe)*

At the White House with President Kennedy and the President's son John, to whom Randolph gave a set of first editions of his father's works.

10. Randolph Churchill, towards the end of his life.

quick-witted. One of the most difficult exercises when asked a question is for the witness to retain its exact formulation. The answer is apt to reflect the general impression of the question not its precise wording. Throughout he showed great accuracy in his treatment of words. As always, very articulate and precise, he revealed any ambiguity in the words used:

Counsel: That is a simple answer, is it not?

Randolph: It is not the complete answer. It is simple but it does not cover the full facts.

Counsel: If I suggest that you have been more concerned with publicity than anything else, would that be fair?

Randolph: I've never cared for personal publicity but of course as a publicist I do seek to obtain publicity for my opinions.

Counsel: Are you telling us that campaign was to try and raise the tone of public life?

Randolph: Not public life, the public press—certain sections of the public press.

Counsel: Tell me this—you enjoy a spot of malice?

Randolph: No, I would not put it like that. A spot of mischief perhaps, but I do not think I am a malicious person.

A campaign was conducted by Randolph against what he described as 'pornography' in the Sunday newspapers. Hence his attack on the *People* and the article in riposte which led to this libel action where Randolph was awarded £5,000 damages. In a speech in October 1953 he supplemented his attack by referring to Odham's, the publishers of the *People*, as the publishers 'who also published the *Horse and Hound*, the *Hairdressers' Journal*, the *Daily Herald* and *Debrett*'. Answering a criticism of Counsel on this score:

Randolph: I am sorry you do not think it funny but the people at the luncheon thought it quite funny and I got a little laugh which helped to ease the thing along.

Asked what his definition of pornography was, he said, 'The first and true meaning is writing for and about harlots.'

Randolph's quality of cutting through prejudicial matters, as in a law case, was exemplified in an interview on the B.B.C. The interview was dealing with Hochhuth's play *The Soldiers* and with the suggestion made during the interview that Sir Winston had tacitly acquiesced in the plan to murder Sikorski by causing the crash of his plane at Gibraltar. When Mr Kenneth Tynan, also present at the interview, was saying the allegation might be technically inaccurate Randolph exploded, 'It's not technically inaccurate, it's a bloody lie.'

Randolph pointed out that there was a strong possibility that the Germans had sabotaged the plane. Tynan then said that Hitler had nothing to gain from the death of Sikorski:

Randolph: He had a lot to gain from saying that my father had done it.

He further pointed out that the Germans had known suspiciously quickly of the air crash and had immediately made the accusation.

One factor that made Randolph such a fearless witness to cross-examine was his honesty. He knew also when to make admissions while separating the main point at issue. One of Hochhuth's so-called sinister elements is that Sir Winston Churchill never mentioned in his memoirs the fact of Sikorski's death. Randolph's explanation was, 'I think my father simply forgot. My father wrote the war as a free tale—as an old man remembered it.'

In the libel case he was asked who, either he or Mr Ainsworth, the Editor of the defendant newspaper, the *People*, had 'first tried to bring the other into public ridicule':

Randolph: I did. May I amplify that slightly?
Counsel: You may.
Randolph: Of course I would not have been able to do so unless he had afforded me such impressive material. He produced the material: he produced the material first and I drew attention to it.

Like his father, Randolph was magnanimous in victory. What he objected to were lies. He did not mind criticisms, hard knocks, or strong language. In the *People*'s case he was asked, 'Are you surprised that a newspaper which supported the other side wanted to say something in reply to that sort of attack on Mr Lord?' 'Well, nothing surprises me about the *People*,' was his reply. Later he said, 'It would not have surprised me to have criticism, but deliberate lies I think are rather surprising.'

Randolph often trailed his coat and wrote defamatory matter

about important people but he was seldom sued for libel. It would have been too dangerous. It was almost always fair comment. In other cases the language used was extravagant but humorous and a plaintiff would have looked ridiculous. Who could sue for the suggestion that he was perhaps suitable for appointment in Corona-tion Year as Pornographer Royal and Criminologist Extraordinary! Or, 'The portrait of a Fleet Street boss is not complete; he does not read, will not write and never stirs from his office chair except to creep up behind the Editor and crash a plank of balsa wood over his unsuspecting head.'

Counsel: When it came to Mr Bevan you said, 'Meanwhile Mr Bevan has saluted his return to the Labour fold by once more spitting in the face of his leading colleagues.' Is that the sort of language you used?

Randolph: Yes, in a perfectly fair electoral comment, I should have said that was.

As a litigant Randolph was courageous, articulate, quick and, unlike his usual nature, completely self-controlled. With his intelli-gence he understood the principles on which cases were fought. He pointed out to Counsel, who was complaining about certain articles referred to in opening by Randolph's Counsel: 'I do not think you objected at the time to us putting any of these papers in.' Randolph, when dealing with the law, showed up in his best light because he respected its rules, and the limitations imposed on him by the legal system. If he had recognized the even more important limitations sought to be imposed by society and fellow-human beings he would have been as successful in his life as he was in his contact with the law.

Colleagues of the Press

Henry Fairlie
Alan Brien
Lady Jean Campbell
Leonard Lyons
Clive Irving
Arthur Krock
Malcolm Muggeridge
Anonymous Profile in
The Observer
Philippe Barrès

Ho! Ho! Ho! and a Bottle of Printer's Ink

by
Henry Fairlie

(British journalist: Washington columnist for the Sunday Express; *author of* Politics and Politicians)

Think—it does not need much imagination—what Randolph Churchill, as a journalist, would have made of the student uprisings.

He would have demanded to cover them: he had the same impulse as his father to be where the action was. At perhaps four o'clock one morning, the editor of, say, the *Evening Standard* would have been woken by a telephone call. 'Ho! Ho! Ho!' the familiar voice would have shouted across the wire. 'Still abed at this hour, and you a servant of the Lord?' (Once, when he telephoned Lord Beaverbrook and was told by his butler, 'The Lord is out walking,' he answered, 'On the waters, I presume.') 'And gentlemen in England now abed,' he would have declaimed to his sleepy editor: he had a remarkable memory, and would use it, at whatever cost, even on a transatlantic telephone call, to recite his personal anthology of English literature, 'shall think themselves accurst they were not here; And hold their manhood cheap while any speaks that fought with us upon Saint Crispin's day.' It was 'time to do something' about the students, he would have said; and the editor, knowing at how many Agincourts he had suffered defeat before, would not have had the muscle to resist. 'O.K., Randolph, go,' he would have said: editors were a little like Dauphins to Randolph Churchill, and anyhow editors need to sleep.

He would have given the student rebels *a pasting*: taught them something, as he would no doubt have put it, 'which they would not forget in a hurry'. The master of the art of incivility would have given them his lesson. 'Apprentices, that is what they are,' he would have bawled late at night across a bar; 'has no one told them their place?'; and, within an hour or two, the same words would be in print.

The first quality of Randolph Churchill as a journalist was that he always sent back a story from the front. If there was no story to send back, then he would create it. By this, I do not mean that he would make one up—he did not play false—but that he would actually make a story happen. He had the good sense to know that *Hamlet* was not good journalism—'To be or not to be': how is *that* as an opening sentence?—and, if he found that it was *Hamlet* that was being played by the actors, he would himself leave the audience, march on to the stage, and turn the play into *Henry V*.

His arrival at the Conservative Party Conference at Blackpool in 1963, when Harold Macmillan had announced his retirement, was more than the arrival of a journalist. He had been in Washington—he had, in fact, been with President Kennedy—when the crisis was precipitated; a memorable occasion, by all accounts, not least by President Kennedy's own—and, commandeering the telephones and the airlines of two countries, he had flown immediately to Blackpool. I remember his arrival; I remember the lunch-time; I remember the bar. For two days, we had been trying to report *Hamlet*. The Conservative Party was paralysed, not least because R. A. Butler, the hapless Prince of Denmark who could never make a first night, was as usual acting out his part in his dressing-room, expecting his audience to hear him from there. In flew Randolph Churchill. 'Ho! Ho! Ho!' he said at that lunch-time drink, 'you are writing the wrong story.' In fact, we were not; he merely proceeded to make his own story happen. Nigel Birch was pulled into action, a proficient schemer; Christopher Soames was pushed to the front, and told to try to be a Churchill; with musket, fife, and drum, the entire platoon of the Old Guard of the Conservative Party was commanded to march, partly by its own instinct, but partly also by Randolph Churchill himself. He had made his own story. In his work, as in his life, he was actor and audience and reporter and critic.

The second quality of his journalism was that, finding or creating a story at the front which was worth sending back, he then sent it in the correct language. His best journalism reads like despatches, and any of us who was with him on a story knows that it was as despatches that he wrote it. Wherever he was, there were his field headquarters. As the hour approached when his despatch must be sent—and he postponed it as long as possible—whatever room or bar he was occupying became a command post: apparently disorganized, but legendarily efficient, not unlike one of the better regiments of the British Army. There was always a batman at his elbow, to whom he rapped, 'Take that down.' There were always messages arriving from further up the lines: 'From Second Lieutenant Soames, Sir, for Captain Churchill.' There always seemed to be an invisible walkie-talkie, through which he could hear the sound of the cannon and, if he could not hear it, issue the order for it to commence. At these moments, one always knew that Randolph Churchill might lose *his* battle, but he would win *his* war; and, sure enough, at some unearthly hour, when the smoke of the battle drifted greyly across the No-Man's Land to which he had reduced his surroundings, the despatch would be sent: *its own victory*.

The carnage, one must frankly admit, was dreadful. 'Throw in more men,' was the only way he knew in which to overcome the resistance which separated him from his story; and, again and again, apparently indestructible, but in the end not, he threw in himself. His best stories were all Passchendales; and, if one complained at the waste of the battle, the only retort one would be given would be Ole Bill's in the Bruce Bairnsfather cartoon: 'If you know of a better 'ole, go to it'. Oh! What a Lovely *War*: without it, he could not have written his despatches.

If his despatches were their own victories, what did they accomplish? Why did one wait for them impatiently; and, when they arrived, read them immediately? First, of course, because they told what was happening at the front. He was, quite simply, a marvellously good reporter. He might describe a single engagement— he could be brilliantly exact in doing so—but he always retained, and gave his readers, a sense of the whole battlefield. His invisible walkie-talkie always kept him in touch with his flanks. Secondly, because he wrote his despatches as a participant, and this did not, as some might expect, detract from the keenness of his observation, but added to it. His best stories were outstanding illustrations of the fact that a polemical journalist, by the very fact of his being polemical, can be an accurate and acute observer. Thirdly, because the man was there in his writing; and, just as there was nothing small, at his best, about the man, there was nothing small, at its best, about his journalism. Neither needs any false excuse: he could, in his journalism as in his life, stoop to conquer. But, more often than not, one found in his journalism a vivid impression of the remarkable qualities which, in his personal life, made it irrelevant for his friends to ask themselves if they could forgive him, because it was enough that they knew that they would not forget him. If he could not *find* a story, even if he could not *make* a story, his resources were still not exhausted: he was big enough to *be* his own story.

One evening in Nairobi in 1960, I went by myself to the game park. I had a guide and a jeep; and, as we approached the lions, which had killed the night before and were therefore placid and somnolent, I saw another jeep with another guide, and standing in it, with a cane, Randolph Churchill. He was shouting, at the top of his voice, at the inert beasts. 'Call yourself lions?' he accused them. 'Call yourself British lions?' Before his guide could prevent him, he jumped from his jeep, and strode towards the lions with his cane pointed at them, still accusing and abusing them. He did not stop until he stood over them, and one of them lifted its head. 'Do you know who my father is?' he shouted into its ear. 'He is a British lion. I know a British lion when I see one, and no self-respecting British lion lies down like you under attack. Get on your feet.' There may be those who say that such wanton courage is meaningless. I did not find it so in Randolph Churchill; and the final, the truest, reason why one enjoyed and was rewarded by his journalism at the time, and why one remembers and is still re-warded by the memories of it now, is that his courage was in it. 'Get up', he said to his words, 'on to your feet,' and, like self-respecting British lions, they did.

Great Contemporary*

by
Alan Brien

(*British journalist: diarist of the* Sunday Times; *columnist in the* New Statesman

From the moment I met Randolph Churchill in May 1953, I was never the same again. Before that I had been hollow-cheeked, resentful-eyed, resembling, I liked to think, Epstein's bronze bust of a Young Communist. I drank beer, ate at pub counters, scraped a passable living writing free-lance features for second-rate magazines. All I knew about the Establishment, I gathered from reading between the lines of *Who's Who*.

When I became employed as Randolph's assistant I was transported in an instant from the underworld of Graham Greene to the magic landscape of Evelyn Waugh. Weekending with him, I began to eat breakfasts for the first time since I was a boy. And what breakfasts—buttered kippers, rashers of bacon like the ears of a giant, kidneys that must have come from the entrails of mammoths, haddock kedgeree, liver steaks, poached eggs, volumes of toast rejected and replaced as soon as it was cool enough to hold in the bare fingers.

Like many plump Père Ubu figures, Randolph had unconsciously adapted his vision to suit the image he woke to view each morning. To himself, he was a trifle over-weight. I seemed by comparison a walking skeleton, a constant reproach to his hospitality and cuisine. Even when he didn't eat, he insisted that I did and took an almost voyeurist delight in watching me tuck in. It was with him that I learned to accept oysters, caviar, asparagus, artichokes, mounds of strawberries and cream, as normal ingredients of the ordinary man's diet. Champagne, almost invariably Pol Roger, was not regarded as booze but more like a superior mineral to be broached

* Reprinted from the *New Statesman* of 14 June 1968.

when the pause between drinks became too long. I took over his habit of the large whisky, dangerously diluted with water in a tall tumbler so that it seeped quicker into the bloodstream. Within six months, I had added an extra layer of blubber an inch thick all over me, and I have spent the last 10 years trying to reduce it by half an inch.

My working-class, Puritanical instinct that it was indecent to stuff yourself, unless you were sure there was enough for tomorrow, dissolved then and has never returned. It was a central impulse of his existence that you should live today as you hope to live in the future and somehow the ravens will provide. I began to see the ruling class of Britain as he saw it from inside—not as an impregnable, armour-plated citadel but as a papier-mâché stage-set to be shaken and shivered, and, if necessary, to be walked clean through like a mirage. He would have approved of McLuhan's definition of money as 'the poor man's credit card'—not that he would have stooped to use a plastic tab to prove his ability to pay. If your pocket was empty, you ran up a bigger bill as a sign of goodwill and added an extra percentage as a tip. Occasionally he would announce a minor retrenchment in the household but usually prove unable to find any luxury which was not also a necessity. I remember him slapping his hands and crowing: 'I have it. We'll stop taking the *News Chronicle*.' When I laughed, he was crestfallen. 'Well, you've got to begin somewhere,' he argued. But usually he quoted one of his favourite anecdotes about the duke whose trustees urged him to give up his second pastrycook.—'What! Mayn't a man have a biscuit?'

Many of his critics used to complain that it was easy for him to engineer journalistic scoops, to lock horns with press lords (was ever a better remark made about Beaverbrook than 'he has never espoused any cause which was both honourable *and* successful'?), to outwit learned counsel, to shout down cabinet ministers, to meet anybody and be invited anywhere he chose, because his father was Winston Churchill. But the world is full of the sons of famous men who even the greatest snobs and sycophants cannot pretend are worth knowing. His father's reputation was a hindrance rather than an advantage, until 1940, among many of the most powerful and privileged in the land. Even if Sir Winston had died before becoming Prime Minister, the psychological weight of such a parent, so mercurial, so demanding, so confident of destiny with its hand on his unbowable head, would have unmanned any lesser offspring.

It did, I think, give Randolph that streak of childishness, even infantilism, which was both attractive and unbearable, often in alternating moments. Sometimes he brought me nearer despair and apoplexy than I have ever been with any other human being. It was not so much that he would erupt late at night in lava-strewn blow-ups, calling me a communist coward, say, as that he would not allow me to insert one tiny word into the molten flow of rhetoric. 'Must I be interrupted in my own house?' he would trumpet. Or alternatively: 'Am I not your guest and entitled to courtesy?' I remember once deciding to leave the next morning, telling him that in all probability I should never speak to him again. He was amazed—'But how have you been offended? It surely could not have been anything that happened last night. I make it an inflexible rule not to remember anything that is said after midnight. The kidneys are particularly good today.'

In an odd way, his famous rudeness, his bellicose wit, his determination to say what oft was thought but ne'er so unforgivably expressed, his instant intoxication on his own 100-proof adrenalin, which cowed and frightened off many who would otherwise have been his friends and allies, stemmed not from arrogance but egalitarianism. He just could not believe that other people did not think as quickly as he did on his feet, did not enjoy swapping insults and marshalling arguments in public. He loved a dangerous enemy and hated nothing more than what he called 'flogging jellyfish'. He had no equal this century as a controversialist and proved himself the wittiest witness since Whistler. 'Never speak unless you have something to say,' he would advise me. 'Do your homework. Never write a letter you are afraid to see printed. Always keep one weapon in reserve.' In his various battles, he never trusted to luck. Many a night, barely able to keep one eye open, I have been forced to play the judge, the heckler, the Q.C., the editor, the politician, in some drama he was rehearsing, bombarding him with the most offensive and damaging missiles I could mount, until he had discovered a shield to deflect them and a spear to stab back a re-doubled blow.

He taught me not to think of antagonists in stereotypes—pointing out that fools were often better survivors than clever men, that cowards tried harder to escape than heroes, that no answer was better than a bad answer. He did not always follow his own prescriptions but many times when he appeared in an unattractive and untenable posture it was due to taking up a weak position out of loyalty to someone else. Once he rebuked me for not supporting him in some argument, and I said I had kept quiet because I knew he was wrong. 'Are you mad?' he demanded. 'If I had been in the right I would not have wanted help. It is when you are wrong you need a friend.'

Vanity and honesty were not incompatibles in his nature. His opinion of his own talents and qualities was sometimes higher than objectivity warranted—but only by about 10 per cent. He had few illusions about his own appearance, his own character, his own ambitions. The first time I met him, he was standing under the De Laszlo portrait of himself as a golden boy. The contrast was startling—as if Dorian Gray had changed places with his picture for one day of the year. 'Yes,' he said good-humouredly. 'It is hard to believe that was me, isn't it? I was a *joli garçon* in those days.' And he nodded at himself affectionately, as if at a favourite son. 'I expect you've heard some off-putting things about me. Fascist-beast, spoiled-brat, rude-to-waiters, bringing-his-old-father's-grey-hairs-in-sorrow-to-the-grave and all that sort of rot. I think you'll find it exaggerated. Not much, but exaggerated.'

Death itself did not frighten him. 'I'd like to go just like that—pop!' he said to me once. 'It can be tomorrow. I've enjoyed myself and I won't complain.' In hospital for the operation on his lung, it was a treat to see him refuse to be reduced to a vegetable, as most people are, ticking off the eminent surgeons for talking about doctor's orders ('I'm paying. It's my lung. I give the orders. I take advice but I give the orders') and instructing the formidable Matron in how to make a decent cup of tea. He insisted on seeing what had been removed before allowing it to be disposed of. 'It was rather nasty-looking, really,' he told me. 'Like a fat mutton chop you wouldn't even give to the dog. Well rid of that, I'd say.'

It is conventional to say that Randolph Churchill will live on in his books—but not for me. They are groundworks for future scholars rather than works of original scholarship in themselves. It is the person who cannot be forgotten, kind and cutting, generous and implacable, maddening but never dull, with marvellous sunbursts of gay, smiling charm which often resembled Franklin Roosevelt rather than Winston Churchill. When the telephone rings at three in the morning now, it can only be bad news. No one else would choose that time to retail a 'jolly tease' or to ask 'What's going on?' Though we rarely agreed on politics, or many other things, he remains a kind of minor Olympian deity in my household for, among the other changes he made in my life, he introduced me to my wife.

'Look, darling! Signs of spring!'

(*From a* Daily Express *Pocket Cartoon by Osbert Lancaster.
Reproduced by courtesy of John Murray Ltd.*)

*Visiting Randolph**

by
Lady Jean Campbell

*(Journalist: granddaughter of the late Lord Beaverbrook; a correspondent in
America for the* Evening Standard)

Noel Coward first hissed the words 30 years ago but they were
repeated a little too often, for a little too long, like some dirty ditty
nobody could quite forget: 'I'm so fond of Randolph; he is so
unspoiled by his great failure.'

Randolph is built on the heroic scale. He does not possess one
small fault or one small virtue. Loving, imperious, loyal, tormented
and tempestuous, he is too truthful for his friends' comfort—and
according to his wartime chief, Brigadier Sir Fitzroy Maclean, 'far
too brave.' Those wide blue Churchillian eyes used to look out on
a strange world which, like André Gide's early world, was a world
which pained him because it couldn't recognize by the look in his
eyes the work that was one day to come.

Now all that is over. Randolph at the age of 55 has presented a
solid body of work which no critic or historian can question as an
eminent and scholarly contribution to the history of mankind. The
first volume of his biography of his father, *Winston S. Churchill:
Youth, 1874–1900*, in 614 printed pages, has vindicated Randolph
Churchill and given him his lasting place in the *Dictionary of
National Biography*—for in the stern circle to which Randolph was
born, a man is bred and raised to dare, to fight, to rule and to write.

Has Randolph's first major success changed him? He tells me
that he loves and hates the same people and is loved and hated by
the same people. 'And I only care,' he explained, sipping a glass of
Dutch beer, the one drink he now allows himself, 'about the people

* Reprinted from the New York *World Journal Tribune* of 25 December 1966.

who have always loved me.' In America he has a goodly passel of
real friends: Kay Halle, Stewart Alsop, Dorothy Schiff, Frank
Conniff, Janet Rhinelander Stewart, the William Paleys and his own
first wife, Mrs Leland Hayward. However, in spite of Randolph's
assertions, I do believe his attitude to the outside world has changed.
He has a gentle and benign air today which is quite new. For instance, when Marquis Childs on *Meet the Press* questioned Randolph's objectivity in writing of his father, Randolph smiled and
answered with monklike calm, 'You are entitled to your doubt. I
an entitled to my faith.'

'We must meet,' mused Randolph, looking out of the ninth-floor
window of his bedroom in the Saint Regis hotel, 'with triumph and
disaster and treat the two imposters just the same.' Kipling, Belloc,
Mother Goose, Swift, Chesterton, Betjeman and Sir Winston's
speeches speckle his conversation. I was asking him whether he had
managed to sell the serial rights of his five volumes in the United
States. 'The magazines all refused me. They said they felt the
Churchill name belonged to *Life* and I answered that I certainly did
not belong to *Life*. No matter.'

'Dear boy,' he said, addressing his cherub-cheeked research
assistant, Andrew Kerr, 'is my five-hour interview aboard the
Queen Mary with Sir Isaac Wolfson typed up yet? Can we now
proceed to devote our attentions to Chapter 12? We are now working on the Irish Home Rule chapter of Volume Two and I try to
imagine myself living through the Irish troubles, and how I would
have felt had I been my father at that time. You see I try to live
with my father in the period we are working upon, forgetting all
about subsequent events such as World War One and Two. We
are working, as it were, at advanced headquarters, at the rate of
roughly 1,000 words a day. We keep in touch with our sources
though: I have just received letters pertaining to later volumes
from both Harold Macmillan and Roy Jenkins.' The telephone
rang. It was Bill Paley. 'What was that strange sketch of your wife
and I lunching together in the Woman's Underwear* newspaper?'
teased Randolph. 'They gave the idea that I attended President
Truman Capote's party. All I hear about in New York today is
President Truman Capote!' There was a knock at the door and a

* *Women's Wear Daily.*

slim dark man came in bearing a large black suitcase. 'Good evening,' said Randolph, 'pray prepare to tell me all you know about
the circumstances surrounding the publication of Manchester's
book on the assassination. You will not mind my recording your
statements on the tape recorder? Human memory is very fallible; I
know mine is, but it's getting better since I left off hard liquor.'

'Randolph,' I said, 'someone called you vain on a BBC program.
Do you think that is true?' 'No,' said Randolph, 'vain means
empty and caring for appearances. If I were vain, I should not be
wearing these baggy old clothes. Egotism, yes, I plead guilty to
that. I am even an egomaniac, but I am not vain.'

'Did your years of journalism help train your mind for writing
this biography?' I asked.

'Do stay still, dear girl, and stop fidgeting. Of course not.
Journalism did not train my mind for anything. But it did teach me
to string words together. Now kindly shut up and we shall proceed
to speak of the dissolution of parliament. Andrew, dear boy, are
you ready at the typewriter? Hope deferred maketh the heart sick.'

On December 23, Randolph left for the Barbados where he plans
to start work on Volume Three of the biography which covers the
period 1915 to 1922. Because of an original and orderly method of
assembling his material in advance learned by 'hours of trial and
error over Lord Derby's voluminous correspondence,' Randolph
can journey whereso'er he pleases over land and sea in the next
years and be confident that he can work at any speed he chooses,
with his raw material at hand.

All the raw material, his father's original and unpublished documents, have already been sorted, filed, assembled and photostated
in triplicate, and they are now being printed in galleys. Later this
raw material will be published in the form of companion volumes
for scholars and historians to peruse—the first two companion
volumes will be on sale in May. Randolph is justly proud of his
method. 'We have perfected our technique; it is almost an assembly
line,' he explains. The Chartwell Trust papers—Churchill's papers
—are housed in steel filing cabinets in Randolph's lovely 18th-
century house, Stour, in Suffolk. They are in the charge of five
researchers, an archivist and a team of secretaries. On the book
office wall is a large notice: 'Advice to Researchers: Seek and ye

shall find. Knock and it shall be opened unto you.' After the papers were sorted, filed and photostated, Randolph read all the material himself and decided where it must be supplemented by documents from other archives. Later the Royal Archives, the Admiralty and Home Office archives, the Asquith, Bonar Law, Beaverbrook and Lennoxlove papers were all tapped. ('I have had to piece the story together like an enormous jig saw puzzle, and sometimes I think the puzzle will never be solved.') Randolph, who has a boyish delight in order, showed me with great pride his beautiful manilla folders, each containing the raw material for a chapter—marked 'secret.'

'You will note,' he said, 'that like my father I insist on small page-size galleys with wide margins instead of those dreadful rolls of lavatory paper which your pencil and pen goes straight through.' Randolph's pen is a heavy one. It is gold, and was given to Sir Winston for his birthday on November 30, 1939, by Randolph and his first wife, Pamela. 'He signed all his wartime documents with it,' said Randolph, putting it carefully into his pocket.

Randolph, who has the Churchill acumen for getting at the truth and sending image makers to the devil, enjoys the sleuthing aspects of his work. His present passion is the missing Plowden letter. Sir Winston's first great love was Pamela Plowden, now the 92-year-old Dowager Countess of Lytton. 'She is like a little piece of Dresden china and still writes a beautiful hand. My father spent years trying to make Lytton viceroy of India, but he never succeeded.'

In 1900 Winston, who had just been elected to parliament, spent Christmas at government house in Ottawa with the governor general, Lord Minto. He wrote to his mother, 'Pamela was there, very pretty and apparently quite happy. We had no painful discussions, but there is no doubt in my mind that she is the only woman I could ever live happily with.'

While Randolph was being interviewed on English television, sitting in his rock garden at Stour, he happened to say that sadly enough very few of Pamela Plowden's letters seemed to have survived. A few days later, a letter arrived from the Channel Islands from an old lady who said that in 1943, during a visit to Toronto, she had read a letter addressed to Sir George Parkin, first secretary of the Rhodes Trust, from Pamela Plowden, dated 1900, explaining in detail all the reasons why she had decided not to marry Winston

Churchill! It appeared that Sir George, an older man, was a friend of the Plowden family and a close confidante of young Pamela's. When Randolph heard this exciting news he immediately wired to Ottawa and arranged to search the Parkin archives for the precious Plowden letter. It was missing; evidently the old lady had forgotten to put it back in its rightful place. In the meantime, another member of the Parkin family wrote to Randolph and said he well remembered the Plowden letter, as his mother used to read it aloud to the family after Sunday tea to illustrate how foolish young women could be in their judgments. To Randolph's glee, this gentleman remembered, in detail, why Pamela Plowden had refused Winston.

'What were the reasons, Randolph?' I asked.

'Ho, ho, ho, you silly-billy, just you wait for Volume Two! By the way, I have already written the last page of Volume Five. . . .'

Randolph lit a cigarette—he smokes continually—'We have no time to lose. Andrew, dear boy, where's our prep? We cannot brush Mr. Asquith aside, can we?' The telephone rang. It was a message from *Time* magazine saying that Mrs. Luce was in Phoenix and could not be disturbed as she was writing.

'Ho, ho, ho,' said Randolph, 'pray tell Mrs. Luce that Randolph Churchill can always be disturbed by his old friends, and he is a writer, too!'

Morsels from the Lyons Den*

by
Leonard Lyons

(American journalist: syndicated columnist for the New York Post)

When young Randolph Churchill was in Moscow in 1945, he was recognized in the stands during a Red Army parade and invited to make a speech. He made the speech, criticizing the U.S.S.R. and supporting his father's position. He was not arrested but asked by a Red Army officer to smoke a cigar and pose for a photograph showing resemblance to his father.

* * *

When Randolph was once arrested and fined for speeding, a press despatch reported that he was driving so fast that the speedometer couldn't record it. The traffic officer who issued the ticket asked if Randolph had any idea how fast he had been going. 'You wouldn't want me to dawdle, and obstruct traffic,' said Randolph. 'Young man,' said the policeman, 'that's one thing you're NOT going to be charged with.'

* * *

Italy's Communist leader, Togliatti, agreed to be interviewed by Randolph in a T.V. film short, one of a series to be made by Randolph and his brother-in-law, Anthony Beauchamp. Togliatti neither spoke nor understood English. Randolph, sitting beside the Red leader, turned towards the movie camera and microphone and introduced his guest: 'Here is the most dangerous Communist outside the Iron Curtain. Know Your Enemy—Signor Togliatti.'

* * *

* Excerpts from Leonard Lyons's columns in the *New York Post*.

On the day Sir Winston resigned as Prime Minister and was succeeded by Anthony Eden, his son Randolph went, as usual, to his London club—White's—in St. James's Street. On leaving, he saw an unusual sight—a policeman tagging a ticket on the car parked outside White's. 'The Eden terror has begun,' said Randolph.

* * *

Once when Randolph arrived in New York, he was halted at Customs. In his eagerness to cable a despatch to a London paper, he had forgotten to fill out a Customs declaration. The rule, however, was waived for him—as a tribute to one of his relatives. 'After all,' he was told, 'you're a cousin of Humphrey Jerome, who used to be with the U.S. Customs Division.'

* * *

Randolph was at the night club, El Morocco, where he was introduced to a tall young man, John Hemingway. They spoke of John's father, Ernest Hemingway, and then John said that he had met Churchill once before. It was in wartime Algiers, at the home of Duff Cooper, who was Britain's Ambassador to the French Provisional Government. 'You were my hero that day,' said Hemingway. 'You were just back from parachuting into Yugoslavia—and I was about to jump into France. You proved an important thing to me—that a man could jump and survive.'

* * *

Randolph usually stayed at the St Regis, explaining that, 'As the late Lord Birkenhead said of my father, "Mr Churchill is a man of very simple tastes. He is always prepared to put up with the best of everything".' . . .

Randolph referred to the many Rothschilds who were his friends as 'the Rothschildren' . . . Randolph once wrote a check on the back of a champagne label—and it cleared.

* * *

When Randolph was last in New York, he lunched with John Barkham at the Colony and ordered crumpets, only to discover they had none. 'No crumpets at the Colony?' Churchill sighed. 'Change and decay, change and decay . . .'

* * *

Young Winston Churchill, who collaborated with his father, Randolph, in the book on the Six-Day War, learned of an incident about his father that occurred after the Suez war in 1956, when Randolph was in Amman, Jordan. When he left the hotel, he lined up the entire hotel staff—and tipped them each in Israeli pounds.

*Randolph in Retrospect**

by

Clive Irving

(British journalist: former managing editor of the Sunday Times;
Director of London Weekend Television)

Randolph Churchill never knew anonymity. Not only did he possess, from a very early age, a profile of classical perfection, but also features which were indelibly Churchillian: the pugnacity of his father, the warmth of his mother. Thus was the standard set for him in his face, the Marlborough blood suddenly rekindled by that of his grandmother, the American Jennie Jerome, and the inescapable consummation of these fires in his father. Inescapable, all Randolph's life, was this lineage and its expectation of him, which he never could meet, for it was unattainable. As soon as he could comprehend, it must have been apparent that the very air he breathed was a challenge. Although it would be many years before his father reached his greatness, Randolph was, from very early on, living in the shadow of a figure who would always be larger than life. Randolph spent the best part of his life in that shadow, and his fidelity to it meant that there could be no escape.

I wondered once whether Randolph was ever explicitly asked by his father to be ready in the wings, or whether it remained an unstated apprenticeship. At a suitable moment, I asked Randolph. There was a time, he said, when his father was at the front line in the First World War, when he wrote home in a rare moment of vulnerability and said 'if anything should happen to me, Randolph will carry the torch'. It was nearly fifty years later, while Randolph was sorting through his father's papers, that he came across this letter. Nothing so specific had been said to him by his father. In the event, the need never arose. The torch was never passed on.

* Reprinted from *20th Century Magazine*, Vol. 177, September 1968.

Randolph's early life, which he described entertainingly but sketchily in his slim volume '21 Years', was lived among those who largely shared his own fate of having to try to live up to their fathers. There were dinner parties at which the sons would be called upon, in the presence of possibly the world's most exacting audience, their fathers, to make political speeches. Randolph's own style of public speaking, never boring but seldom inspired, was for the rest of his life paced by the metronome set at those dinners, trying to feel by the heat on the back of his neck whether he was making the grade. This form of test was employed to celebrate Randolph's twenty-first birthday, in the company of the young Quintin Hogg, the young Lord Birkenhead and the young Mr. Esmond Harmsworth, now Lord Rothermere, among others. Winston's comment on his son's performance was, as it turned out, prophetic: 'a fine machine-gun, and it is to be hoped he will accumulate a big dump of ammunition and learn to hit the target'. Randolph's ammunition dump never ran out. His fire-power increased from machine gun. But all his life, he was like a battle-ship running amok, scattering shells indiscriminately, often bombarding the innocent, defenceless and uncomprehending. Sometimes a direct hit was scored on the enemy's magazine, but only by divine intervention on behalf of a random shot. Randolph never learned properly how to hit the target.

I think the most striking thing about him was the eyes. They concealed nothing. Since my friendship with him began only in 1963, the younger Randolph existed for me only in legend and on paper. But I suspect those eyes were unchanging, except for their accumulated sorrow, which they sometimes showed. They were an early warning system to his companions. The sudden switch from the calm to the combative registered first in the eyes, to be followed almost at once by the verbal barrage. At other times, they signalled pleasure, wit and careful scrutiny. No wool was ever pulled over them.

I have known Fleet Street editors, skins hardened by a thousand proprietorial insults and consciences intact after an equal number of assassinations, to whom warning from the switchboard that Mr. Randolph Churchill wished to speak to them would despatch them, uncontactable, to the Press Club bar more quickly than even a missed edition. Randolph's calls came at all hours, and from all places. Their purpose could range from questioning the syntax of a freshly minted editorial, to providing a tip-off of an impending political drama, and editors had to risk the wrath of one in order not to forgo the value of the other. The Randolph legend was already well known to me from colleagues who, at various times, had been researchers in his migrant labour force. So when a call came from him to visit his home at East Bergholt in Suffolk, the invitation was simultaneously irresistible and slightly alarming. He phoned me at the Sunday Times about a book which I had written with two colleagues about the Profumo affair. He said 'I'm going to give your book a rave review in the "News of the World", but you've made a few mistakes and I want to make sure you'll correct them in the second edition. You'd better come down.' No wise man ever spurns a rave review in the News of the World, and so the journey was undertaken. Looking back now, in sadness, it's hard to understand why so many strong hearts could quake on exposure to Randolph.

It is true that the few years in which I knew him were his most mellow. It is true, also, that even during that time he could be, and often was, intolerably boorish and rude, and sometimes very silly. But as a host he was unexcelled in generosity and unrivalled as a political raconteur. And to somebody of my generation, he was more than that. He was a living link with figures, emotions and standards which have passed forever from our public life—ideas and attitudes which Randolph himself embraced and which made him an increasingly incongruous figure so long as he pursued, in vain, his own political ambitions. Sitting by his fire, as the logs spat and burned through the night and often well beyond sunrise, the room would fill with Thespian figures, walking again through Randolph's memory in the interplay of power, all of them dominated by the central figure of his father, and all of them seen through the double vision of his own and his father's eyes, the handed down assessment mixed with his own, and sometimes the mimicry of his father's voice, which he did better than any of the professionals. By that fire there were two very deep armchairs, one each side, and a pouff in the middle, possession of which was frequently fought for by a gaggle of pugs, and usually held by the favoured Boycott. All night long Randolph and guest would sip the large and misleadingly diluted glasses of White Horse and water. Occasionally, Randolph would rise to seek a reference in the library, or to produce the manuscript of a coming article, or papers from his file . . . more to elaborate than to prompt, for he had a remarkable gift for total recall. At other times we would be jerked back to the present by a bout of his telephone calls. There was sadistic pleasure at being at the right end of those calls. The local operators were hardened to nocturnal demands for immediate connection with this number in Washington, with that number in Paris. But the bombast paid off. Randolph's calls to the United States went through a good thirty minutes faster than any other I knew.

By this time, Randolph had withdrawn from London, alienated by every manifestation of the present, and mourning the receding past. Apart from occasional skirmishes—a nostalgic call to the bar at White's; an appearance on television, a family dinner—he relied on the telephone to keep him in touch, and he elevated its use as a political intelligence system and provocative weapon to that of a fine art: his one acceptance of electronic aids. It cost him a fortune in phone bills—£400 a quarter at 1964 prices. He had two lines at East Bergholt, controlled from a push-button system which he kept by the fireside chair; quite often one cabinet minister would be held on one line while another was being interrogated on the other. I wondered how it was that they always talked to him, even if it was only to pass the time of day. Partly it was that all of us are particularly vulnerable to the telephone, the absolute violator of privacy, when even a receiver left off the hook invokes some ghastly pitch of protest from the exchange. But in the case of Randolph's calls, another reason was that all the usual filters proved impotent. Secretaries and personal assistants quailed. Press secretaries dissolved in fright. But another reason, and probably the decisive one, was that whatever the perils of talking to Randolph, there was often a useful piece of gossip to be picked up. Whatever the reasons, people did answer the phone to Randolph, and at any hour, as I saw in a set piece demonstration of his technique during the scheming for the leadership of the Conservative Party after Harold Macmillan's fall in 1964. Randolph had been waging a misguided and foredoomed campaign on behalf of Lord Hailsham, the putative Quintin Hogg. This, as Mr. Hogg must have realized, was the kiss of death. Although Randolph's support was well meant and robust it was, in the current jargon, counter-productive to a disastrous degree. Having flown back overnight from America on the news of Macmillan's illness, Randolph had made a characteristic public intervention at the Tory conference at Blackpool, stalking the unwary at the Winter Gardens and the Imperial Hotel. The following week, as the unseemly struggle went discreetly underground, Randolph, too, withdrew back to the East Bergholt command post, and deployed the telephone. One night he got word that the pro-Hailsham lobby was disintegrating. At about 12.50 a.m. Randolph rang Mr. Selwyn Lloyd, said to be wavering. The somnolent Mr. Lloyd was instructed to remain 'steady on parade'. Next on the list was Mr. Iain Macleod, one of the few people who knew how to cope with and despatch Randolph's calls. His response was short and expletive. Other leaderless Tories were pursued, and the last name on the list was that of Lord Home. Randolph reached him at about 1.30 a.m. The phone rang, and an understandingly distant peer replied. But Randolph was taken aback. It was, he felt, a terrible sign of the attrition of the aristocracy's living standards that Lord Home had himself answered directly. Without bothering to reply at once, he put his hand over the speaker and said: 'Goodness, how sad. They live like bloody coolies, these days.' He then opened the conversation. 'Is that you, Alec? Randolph. Look here, I hope you're advising the monarch that it should be Quintin. It is being said that you might yourself be in the ring. I trust that that is not so . . .' Lord Home, three days later to become prime minister, was remarkably polite and patient, and utterly enigmatic.

That was one rare occasion when Randolph's political antennae let him down; but since every other commentator was backing the wrong horse it was, perhaps, forgiveable. His greatest political scoop was a previous struggle for the leadership of the Conservatives. For the Evening Standard he correctly predicted that Harold Macmillan would succeed Anthony Eden. That result, like the succession of Lord Home later, thwarted the hopes of R. A. Butler, and if ever there was one person to whom Randolph could be less than generous, and on occasion vindictive, it was Rab. Randolph bore a grudge against Rab, and never attained the magnanimity to drop it. This was, of course, rooted in the Munich period. Randolph knew, very well, the despair and bitterness which his father felt during his years in the wilderness. At one point, this despair became so acute that Winston Churchill considered abandoning politics altogether. Randolph told me of a discussion between his father and Bernard Baruch, whose advice on the change he was seeking. Fortunately, Baruch told Churchill that he would be hopeless as a businessman.

While in Randolph's heart the feud with Rab never died, his relationship with Macmillan intensified during the last few years. 'I love that man' Randolph told me six months before he died. The journey between Randolph's home, Stour, at East Bergholt in Suffolk, and Macmillan's seat at Birch Grove in Sussex was an inconvenient one for both men. As with his use of the telephone, Randolph once again harnessed a modern aid to overcome this: he hired a helicopter for the journeys he made. The two biographers, finding more in common among the past than they could when viewing the present, must have relished the encounters. Macmillan was, I suspect, Randolph's kind of Tory—the opportunist with humble roots not too far distant who had married into and surmounted the Tory establishment. I asked Randolph once about his concept of Conservatism—how did he reconcile his party loyalty to his predilection for playing the rogue elephant? 'I don't really consider myself a member of the Tory Party,' he replied. 'I'm a buttress rather than a pillar. I don't admire everything about the Conservative Party. I don't admire all their leaders. But I do think they're a very much better lot than the other side.' This simplistic view of politics, using the prep school concept of one 'lot' against the other, drawn in black and white rather than subtler shades . . . this was a childish streak in Randolph which made a lot of his political writing too unsophisticated. He was quite shameless about talking this way: his columns abounded in 'silly billies', 'all that rot', 'blackamoors' and all the other jargon which belonged to Greyfriars School. It was one of the irritating paradoxes of the man that analysis which was often shrewd came to be expressed in a language which devalued his writing. This was Randolph the clown, a role which he enjoyed too much. And yet this was the same man whose life of Lord Derby demonstrated that scholarship, judgment and readability were there to be summoned if he chose.

When he died, Randolph had completed only two and a half of the five planned volumes of his father's biography. The reviews of the first two were mixed. But whatever the reviewers' feelings, they were all pleasantly surprised by one thing: Randolph's un-characteristic restraint in the narrative. Realizing that he had the most comprehensive collection of papers covering the life of any statesman, Randolph had been content to organize, explain where necessary, provide continuity and apart from that, to shut up. It was the shrewdest decision he ever made, and protected him from the otherwise inevitable charges of filial subjectivity. From early in the nineteen sixties, the preparation of these books required, and got, a scale of effort which transformed Stour into a cottage industry. There were relays of research assistants, from journalism or the universities, who came not only to share the excitement of ploughing through the vast store of papers, but also, no doubt, to have their steel case-hardened in the fire of Randolph's devoted supervision. Some failed this test, and dissolved into the night, neither physically nor intellectually robust enough to endure the task. It was sweated labour. Sleep of the normal pattern did not suit Randolph's mercurial metabolism. He worked in sustained bouts, extending often at one stretch for 36 hours or more, to be followed by repose of equally unpredictable periods. As well as the re-searchers, there was a specially bred race of lady secretaries, stoic, patient and extremely pale. They, too, would be summoned at any hour. At one or two in the morning, as the inspiration came, I have seen Randolph summon one of these ladies and stride the study dictating, as they battled with insomnia and myopia. And when the dictating was done, it often had to be read back, and interpolations incorporated.

In spite of this treatment, his secretarial staff seemed remarkably stable . . . unlike his cooks, the turnover of which was rapid, except for occasional stalwarts who outstayed the average. Once or twice, I arrived between cooks. What followed then was either a journey to the inn at Dedham, across the valley from East Berg-holt, or inspired improvisation from the remaining staff. Randolph liked gourmet gadgets. In the summer, a barbecue burned often on the terrace; and one of his last kitchen devices was a smoking box for producing kippers. On one occasion, a departing cook, stung beyond endurance, administered an effective reprisal before she left by switching off a refrigerator containing one of her master's favourite desserts: cherry ice cream. It was not until she was well clear that the sorry remains were discovered.

This last decade of his life, at Stour, was probably his happiest. He had, by then, conceded the futility of his political ambition. With his telephone, he was able to follow the vocation of, as he put it, quoting Beaverbrook, 'being an old concièrge', picking up the gossip and spreading more. He loved his family, his dogs, his books, his garden, America, and the sound of his own voice. He reviled cowardice, Communism, fools, the G.P.O., Sir William Haley's Times and the shift of power from the bar at White's. He was a patriot.

Sometimes, he became very lonely. He hated seeing his guests go. He contrived, with childish stratagems, to make them miss their trains so that they should stay a little longer. He drank too much, but he could hold vast amounts of liquor, and his tongue thrived on it, if his health did not. He had an oversize ego but knew that even that was overpowered by the legend of his father. He was, he said, 'the small sapling, living under the shadow of the great oak tree'. He was old-fashioned, far-sighted when looking back, puzzled when looking forwards. Towards the end, he weakened in body but never in spirit.

More of his father's biography might have been completed, but for his journalistic impulses. He took to producing his 'contemporary chronicles'—one, 'The Struggle for the Tory Leadership', in 1964, another last year, with his son Winston, on the Arab–Israeli war. Between, the slim volume on his early life, an eccentric and scholarly investigation into the distribution in England of tulip trees, and his intervention on behalf of Mrs. Jacqueline Kennedy in the dispute over William Manchester's book. These diversions were inevitable, but a pity in that they slowed down the major valedictory task. He was never himself certain of finishing it. To make sure, at least, of the final judgment, he had secretly written the final page of the last volume. I hope his successor lets it stand.

Randolph—Without the Boast of Heraldry, the Pomp of Pow'r

by
Arthur Krock

(*American journalist: former Editor and Washington correspondent of the*
New York Times)

The sons of famous men labour under the special difficulty that they are expected to live up to their immediate heredity. Sometimes, endeavouring to do this in the same pursuits, they have become inferior and often ludicrous caricatures of their progenitors.

Not so Randolph Churchill. He was a genuine individual with gifts of his own, and these he developed by allowing full play to the promptings of his bold personality.

Hence, though he, too, was a good professional journalist and he, too, exploited this talent for political preferment at an early age, the parallel ended there. Winston Churchill, despite a half-century of frustration in his persistent reach for ultimate political power, continued to major in that trade, employing his pen as holdfast and breadwinner in the intervals between success and failure. Randolph Churchill reversed the procedure. Equally following the indices of what destiny equipped him best to be, he concentrated his active career on daily journalism.

Both father and son spaced journalism with the lucrative writing of histories and biographies. But while the splendours of Winston Churchill's prose in this branch of literature were not matched by those of his son (or of anyone else in the elder's time), for Randolph they more definitely reflected a hope to earn him permanent professional rating in the field illuminated by Hume, Gibbon, Green and Macaulay.

Whenever his restless journalistic travels took him to a place where I was similarly engaged—principally Washington—he was at once on the telephone seeking information on what was current at the time. I never knew a more searching reporter. When he had extracted from me whatever contribution to his news commentaries I was able to make, off he went to question those in office who lived at the heart of the matter. And by knowing the right questions to ask of the right people he met the basic marks of the competent reporter and commentator.

Often, though Randolph knew the right questions to pose to the right people, their doors were closed to him—the price of tough-minded reporting. But this never embarrassed him or impelled him to cease knocking at the closed doors, as it might have a more sensitive journalist. And this persistence and indifference to personal slights was rooted, I think, in a canon of heredity—that what would be resented by the lesser castes as an insult could not reach an authentic member of the ducal aristocracy.

In this context I recall an occasion when after Randolph had repeatedly mixed cruel personalities with attacks in print on Anthony Eden, he took passage on the same ship that bore Eden to the United States. Though rebuffed in efforts to interview Eden, Churchill continued in this vain endeavour until the ship docked in New York and throughout Eden's stay in Washington. To Randolph this brush-off was merely an amusing experience. In true English understatement he remarked only that he found Eden's conduct 'rather odd'!

He was enormously courageous, physically and professionally. In the latter activity he attacked not only those in office but the newspaper proprietors who supplied him with the forum to do this.

With equal cheerfulness he engaged in indulgence of the pleasures of the table and the bottle, and accepted the subsequent denial of both that was the consequence of excess. He was a good listener, and courteous up to the point, short or long, where he lost interest or wanted to take over the floor. Now and then Randolph's interruptions were delivered in a tone of annoying loftiness or phrased in language so harsh that the person to whom they were addressed was justly offended or outraged. But unless the issue was one in which Randolph's passions were deeply engaged, he was quick to apologize. On one occasion he accompanied this act of penitence by saying, 'Really, I ought not to be allowed out in private.'

He mumbled his words, swallowed his terminals—all made more unintelligible to American auditors by the tongue-entangling accent that Kipling described as the '*eu* of the upper class'. But in the larger sphere of personal relations Randolph was a loyal and devoted friend, if an exacting one. He sought company at times convenient to him that were distinctly not so to friends whose schedules for work and play were set by the clock, who could not or would not talk all night and sleep until the sun crossed the yard-arm. Yet, though he found it difficult to understand how regular habits could comport with a happy or even a tolerable life, he adjusted to those who followed such time-tables with a meekness unknown to his father.

For some who may read these lines and never saw Randolph Churchill in person and by video, a brief word-portrait might be ventured. In stature he was above the middle height. In physique he was sturdy until the waste of illness began. His eyes were very blue. His complexion was the pink-blond of the Blenheim breed with the fair hair that attends this pigmentation. His voice was pleasant though progressively inclined to hoarseness.

His quartering of American blood was not discernible. Instead, he was the archetype of the Saxon–Norman Englishman who had attended a good public school, an ancient university and has the 'U' of the privileged class implanted on him like a birthmark.

Being the descendant of dukes, and bred to fame, he exuded a sense of superiority; but social snobbery was unknown to him. He was indeed a climber, but Mt Parnassus was his goal. When Winston Churchill made it plain he was uninterested in the tender of a dukedom that was his for the taking, I asked Randolph if he was disappointed he would never wear the strawberry coronet. 'Hell, no,' he said. 'A horde of British mums with marriageable daughters would set their sights on me, regardless of my poor record in that department. And to be born Churchill, the son of Winston, is a heritage that no title in the Peerage can match.'

In Defence of Randolph Churchill*

by
Malcolm Muggeridge

(British journalist and writer: Deputy Editor of the Daily Telegraph *1950–2; Editor of* Punch *1953–7; author of* The Earnest Atheist, London à la Mode, Jesus Discovered, *and other works)*

It is by no means true that the major figures of history are the most interesting. Indeed, in a sense, the opposite is true. Those who take the leading roles in the world of action are often so obvious that there is really nothing to say about them, and vice versa. Thus, for instance, Benjamin Constant is (as Sir Harold Nicolson has so admirably shown) inherently more interesting than Napoleon; and I myself, if I had to choose between undertaking a biography of Sir Winston or of Mr. Randolph Churchill, would unhesitatingly choose the latter.

To some this may seem a whimsical judgment. Sir Winston, they will contend, belongs to history, and will be remembered as long as the English-speaking peoples, etc., etc.; whereas his son has been, in politics, a non-starter, in letters, no more than a privateer journalist, in society, a turbulent nuisance—an embarrassment to his friends, a gift to his enemies, and a brawling bore to neutralist or uncommitted associates. Yet I still contend that, objectively considered, he is, in Lermontov's sense, an authentic hero of our time. At first sight, he might seem something of an anachronism—a pinchbeck Marlborough in the century of the common man, who for a consideration is prepared to allow the public to look round his views and prejudices in much the same way that his distinguished kinsman allows them to look round Blenheim; an ageing *enfant terrible* whose pranks and teases become ever more dated.

This, however, would, in my opinion, be a very superficial view.

* Reprinted from *The New Statesman and Nation* of 28 April 1956.

Mr. Churchill belongs essentially to this age, and his clowning and outrageous sallies are the measure, not of his obsolescence, but rather of his contemporaneousness. Like Cyrano de Bergerac, the secret of his appeal lies in the fact that everything about him, including his appearance, is somehow out of focus. The edges are blurred. He puts into the causes he champions (for instance, his crusade against newspaper pornography) more than they can rightly contain. It is a case of old wine in new bottles. Considered as a political warship, he carries a lot of antique artillery, but the shells fall in unexpected places—here, there and everywhere, but rarely on the enemy. And quite often the guns misfire or backfire, to the great disconcertment of any who have been foolhardy enough to associate themselves with him.

At the same time, how preferable this is to the sort of career which seemed to offer so surely when he was young, handsome, eloquent, and in the full enjoyment of the *réclame* which his name effortlessly bestowed. Surely, one thought in those days, he will soon be in parliament, soon on the Treasury Bench. It was the first Lord Rothermere, I think, who called him England's young man of destiny—a scarcely original epithet which would, admittedly, have been more impressive from another source, but still heady enough for someone in Mr. Churchill's situation.

Who would have thought in those days that Conservative Party constituency selection committees thirsting for knighthoods would one day turn palely away when his name was put forward as a possible candidate? That even Bournemouth, which had meekly, if coldly, taken Brendan Bracken to its bosom, would indicate unmistakably that it did not want him? That the vast wash of Churchillian influence, capable, among other extraordinary feats, of translating a Professor Lindemann into a Lord Cherwell, would quite fail to translate its most natural, its most obvious, beneficiary into anything at all?

Dealt an incomparable hand, that is to say, Mr. Churchill has scarcely taken a single trick. Why? The answer doubtless lies embedded in his curious and contradictory temperament; in some *farouche* strain which induces him to kick over the table just at the moment when he seems to be about to play his aces, or (what really amounts to the same thing) in a propensity to self-pity which can dissolve away in a moment his seeming resolution and pugnacity, leaving him to be counted out before anything in the nature of a knock-out blow has been delivered.

Nonetheless, it would be quite mistaken to regard him as a total failure. If one of his brothers-in-law has, so far, comfortably held his ministerial position even after Sir Winston's retirement, and another has now got his foot on the lower rungs of preferment, Mr. Churchill has made far more noise in the world than they have, or are ever likely to make. Hostesses on both sides of the Atlantic may grow pale at the prospect of one of his visitations, but they know that, as a topic of conversation, he is inexhaustibly diverting. Everyone has an anecdote to contribute, wounds to display, bizarre episodes to recount. As a conversationalist himself he is often as devastating as one of those hurricanes which sweep away whole towns in their train; as a stimulant, *in absentia*, of other conversationalists, he is in the very top class.

It is, of course, true that his lack of success in conventional (as distinct from atomic) politics has been a bitter disappointment to him; but there is always White's bar, whose proceedings, like those of the House of Commons, quite often get reported in the press, and whose frequenters (particularly as the afternoon wears on) provide on the whole a more lively and appreciative audience than members of parliament. There is also the telephone—an instrument peculiarly suited to Mr. Churchill's particular brand of declamation. Night and day, it is always available, and the receiving end is liable, as the pips sound with monotonous regularity, to accept, rather than reject or question, spirited polemics, whether impromptu or read from a prepared manuscript.

As a journalist Mr. Churchill has lately enjoyed a kind of Indian summer. By concentrating his fire on press lords and Sir Anthony Eden, he has overcome the faults of diffuseness and imprecision which marred many of his previous productions. His most persistent detractors cannot but admit that some of his recent pieces (notably those he sent from Washington on the occasion of the recent visit there of the Prime Minister and the Foreign Secretary) have, as Johnson said of Garrick, increased the public stock of harmless pleasure, while his denunciations of newspapers and their proprietors have been, by comparison with the feeble and meandering efforts of the Press Council, as red biddy is to ginger ale.

In this connection, it may seem a little disappointing that one press lord, and he not the least vulnerable—I mean, of course, Lord Beaverbrook—should have become, as it were, immunized to the Randolph Churchill virus. But there it is. One has to write somewhere and be paid by someone. And anyway Mr. Churchill has used the platform Lord Beaverbrook has provided to assail Lord Beaverbrook's current favourite, Sir Anthony Eden. This must be counted to him for virtue. He might perfectly well have swelled the Beaverbrookian chorus of praise of his father's chosen successor. To judge from past experience, it is also probably true that, by employing Mr. Churchill, Lord Beaverbrook is preparing a rod for his own back. Other newspaper proprietors have likewise employed him, and look what has happened to them!

For myself, I would not have him otherwise. Like the sirens in the blitz, his arrival at any social gathering sends everyone scampering for cover; produces that slight shiver and tautening of the nerves which presages danger and excitement. When the 'all clear' sounds and he departs, there is a corresponding sense of relief, but the intervening experience (as long as one has not been personally involved in the explosion) is exhilarating, or at any rate memorable. Society needs its scourges. What more suitable one in this strange twilit time than a displaced Churchill—uproarious, unexpected; above all, uninhibited?

The Irrepressible Randolph Churchill*

Anonymous

No one can set the adrenalin flowing simply by the rumour of his approach as Randolph Churchill can. At the news that he has arrived at a party, at a press conference, at a railway station, hearts pump more madly, temperatures rise, lips tighten, voices sharpen. It is like the day war was declared.

Why is it that Randolph (after his grandfather, the fiery Lord Randolph) Frederick (after his godfather, the vitriolic Lord Birkenhead) Edward (after his godfather, Lord Edward Grey) Spencer Churchill (after his ancestor, the first Duke of Marlborough) is personally disliked by more people who have never met him than any other public figure in Britain today? And why is it that he should also manage to be personally disliked by a great many who have?

Both groups agree that he presents the same unforgettable unnerving image—a sort of scarlet Michelin-tyre man, dangerously overinflated with hot air, bursting with ruderies, strained around the seams with egoism, self-sealing against the tin tacks of opposition and criticism.

But the first group is unlikely ever to alter its picture of Randolph Churchill as a forty-nine-year-old ogre on the prowl.

The second group tries hard to preserve its original hostility. But when its members do get close to the monster, many cannot help succumbing, at least in fits and starts, to the charm of the other Randolph.

Charm would seem to be the last, least likely secret weapon of Randolph Churchill. He himself is as unconscious of it as his

*Reprinted from *The Observer* of 30 October 1960.

enemies are. He assumes that the world will take sides for or against him simply on the basis of the correctness of his opinions. He finds it hard to understand that people would be so childish as to oppose him just because he has called them, say, 'jumped-up Communists'. Is the phrase accurate or not? he demands. If not, where is the evidence to disprove it? If it is so unfair, why do they not issue a writ for defamation?

This is why he has the shocking habit of denouncing and rebuking men and women in public at parties and dinners. He gives them all credit for thinking before they speak and immediately interrupts and contradicts them for the sake of his version of the truth. It never occurs to him that anyone can be defenceless in an argument.

This is also why he upbraids waiters, browbeats porters, contradicts taxi drivers. He cannot imagine that this could ever appear to be bullying. After all, he also upbraids millionaires, browbeats press lords, contradicts Cabinet Ministers.

Randolph Churchill thinks on his feet. As an arguer he is in the light heavyweight class, nimble and yet powerful, The sound of his own voice never rings embarrassingly in his ears. Indeed, it is to him the most cheerful and comforting noise in the world. It shows that someone is talking sense.

He is very much of an actor, or rather a theatrical old-style advocate. Much of his anger and indignation is simulated for effect. Not that he does not feel strongly and deeply about the subjects of his arias. But while his brain is coolly sorting out arguments and quietly sifting evidence, he realizes that nothing unnerves an opponent more than a display of furious emotion. This is why, after denouncing a group of opponents as 'blanks' in an Old Testament falsetto, he will pause and say in normal conversational tones. 'No, I take that back. Not blanks. In fact, honourable, intelligent, sane chaps. But on this particular issue'—voice rising in fury again—'on this particular issue, *absolute blanks*!'

Randolph Churchill has never had any kind of stage fright in his life. His stomach never sinks, except through dieting. He is willing to step forward at a press conference or before a television camera or at a crowded party with the same boundless self-confidence that most people could display only in front of the bathroom mirror. This is why he is so brilliant in the witness box; if he had produced nothing else in his life but his answers in court during his libel action against the *People*, he would deserve to be remembered as the wittiest witness since Whistler.

COMMENTATOR OR CREATOR?

The secret of this lies partly in his careful rehearsal and repetition of his opinions. His strongest condemnation of any public figure is to say he 'hasn't done his prep'. He rarely plunges out of his depths, and in private he is almost embarrassingly insistent on his deficiencies as a writer or a thinker.

The trouble is that almost no place where Randolph Churchill appears *is* private. It is only down on the farm, at the registered office of Country Bumpkins Ltd in Suffolk, where his windows frame a Constable landscape, that a mild, gay, relaxed persona can peep out from behind the mask of the professional angry middle-aged manic. Many an unfriendly journalist has been lured there, only to leave a converted ally. (Also, many an old friend has fled on a Saturday afternoon vowing never to return.)

Journalists, as a group, are hostile to Randolph Churchill. They are made uneasy by the ambiguity of his position in the profession. Is he a news commentator or a news creator? Is he an opponent or a pet of the newspaper proprietors? They complain that he is not a real pro.

Yet, though he has a small private income, modest by White's Club standards, he has earned his living for more than twenty years by journalism. And he cannot resist biting the hand that feeds him; there is scarcely a press lord in Fleet Street who has not a finger or two missing to prove it.

Churchill's personality seems fuelled by an apparently endless flow of truculence. He dares not dodge a fight or ignore a challenge, just in case it might be remotely thought to seem pusillanimous. The only son of a father who has bubbled over with a natural, unthinking courage from his earliest days and courted danger like a lover, Randolph Churchill has always known that many an unfriendly eye would be watching for any weakening of the standard, any dilution of the fighting blood. Compulsive pugnacity was the quickest escape route from Sir Winston's giant shadow. This bottled aggression may explain his bitter vendetta against Sir Anthony Eden, which has often embarrassed even some of his most sympathetic partisans. It could be analysed as an unconscious rivalry directed against pretenders to his father's throne.

But it must also be remembered that, even in the thirties, Randolph regarded Eden as a vain man kept afloat by a certain anaemic charm. Before, during, and after Eden's premiership, he never spared Eden. His admiration for other lieutenants of Sir Winston—a Macmillan, or a Sandys, or even a Soames—is often gushingly effusive.

Though probably not physically daring by nature (he tends to jump at sudden noises and rear at an angry gesture), he forced himself not only into the front lines but behind the enemy lines during the war. He was parachuted into Yugoslavia to fight with the Partisans. He took part in the long-range desert raids into the German camps in North Africa. He was wounded as a war correspondent in Korea.

Randolph Churchill's war record cannot be ignored by even his bitterest enemies, though they are likely to suggest, unfairly, that sometimes he appeared to be almost as much of a nuisance to the Allied High Command as he was to the German High Command. Even in war—perhaps especially in war—it was hard for Randolph Churchill to believe that there could be generals so short-sighted as to turn down an opportunity to listen to his advice.

Politically, Randolph Churchill is a Tory, because he believes that the Tories are more intelligent, mature, efficient, and gentlemanly than the Socialists—and besides, in one of his favourite phrases, he has 'known them all my life'. By 'Tories', he means the top Tories. He passionately believes that it is the duty of the undeserving rich to support the deserving poor, of whom he will often elect himself the articulate representative.

The central tenet of his political philosophy is that the class with power should be kept in power, but only as long as it proves itself morally superior to any alternative.

BOTTOMLESS WELL OF ANECDOTES

His conversation has far more liveliness and vivacity and imaginative wit than his writing. He is probably best as a monologuist, and he can spout for hours from a bottomless well of anecdotes, quotations, epigrams, rumours and theories. His quotations are usually from middlebrow authors—Kipling, Saki, Belloc, Nash, Betjeman—or from solid sonorous classics—Gibbon, Macaulay, Walpole. He has a photographic memory for the authors who impressed him in his youth.

He is fond of the rumour as a genre. When he reaches out by telephone to his friends at three a.m., he always begins cheerily: 'Well, what's going on?' It is inconceivable to him that there is a time of day or night when people are not plotting and planning and making fools of themselves.

Randolph Churchill might have been the original man about whom the child asked, 'Mummy, what is that gentleman *for?*' Nobody, least of all Randolph Churchill, has yet discovered the answer. When he left Oxford, it seemed to him impossible that he would not be in the House of Commons before he was twenty-five. He sat for Preston in the political truce during the war, but he has never won any election he has fought.

As a writer, except when moved to passion or fury, his prose can be dull and ponderous in an empty Augustan manner, though it often has subtleties which are easily overlooked and the structure of the argument is strong and formidable. As a journalist, he is at his best when he is taking us on a guided tour of leading Tory minds. As a news reporter, he has only rarely been successful because he combines the instincts of a press lord with the equipment of a gossip columnist.

What, then, is he for? Perhaps he is here to express those frustrated furies we all feel but are too self-conscious to express—fury at bad railway food, at grammatical howlers in *The Times*, at clumsy waiters, at monopoly in Fleet Street, at stupidity in parliamentary speeches, and a hundred other assorted provocations.

He believes that power is least corrupting, and democracy best preserved, when the power is shared among competing blocs. It is his task to see that blocs do compete and quarrel. Perhaps, most of all, he is here simply to keep us on our toes.

*Randolph**

by
Philippe Barrès

(Editor, journalist, author, son of Maurice Barrès: Editor of Le Matin
1935; Editor of Paris-Soir *1939; founder of the pro-Gaullist French
newspaper* Paris-Presse. *A Gaullist deputy from Lorraine, then a Muni-
cipal Counsellor for Paris, he resigned from de Gaulle's party in 1962 over
the Algerian question)*

Randolph Churchill—the son of Winston Churchill—who died
at the age of fifty-seven, was a splendid example of an English
aristocrat—full of indomitable passions in the ordinary course of
his life but brave and inflexible on his chosen battlefields. I have
spent many hours with him during our careers as journalists in the
hot spots of the world. Especially in Berlin between 1931 and 1939,
during the dark years when Hitler was growing in strength without
awakening either England or France from their lethargy. Germany,
then in an explosive state, constituted a splendid testing-ground for
judging the character of a man.

Randolph and I agreed about the danger that threatened our two
nations and we saw no salvation except through our determination.
Not surprising when you think of our fathers. We were agreed on
this, except that Randolph, less versed in German affairs than a
Frenchman, vainly shouted himself hoarse castigating Hitler in the
name of democracy, at a time when we were already on the road
to war.

Democrat he surely was, this son of the Marlboroughs. A democrat as Lord Byron was a liberal; this was due to providential
circumstances, and without, for a second, dreaming of comparing
himself to someone or trying to live like anyone else. I still laugh
when I recall this daring golden-haired young man with the leonine
head dressed as if he were going off to play golf; rumpled as if he

* First published (in French) in *Le Figaro* of 14 June 1968.

had spent the night before in bars; casual and superb. Kicking open the doors of the sacrosanct offices of the Wilhelmstrasse; breaking through police cordons without seeing them; euphoric with whisky and moreover protected by the prestige of a resounding name.

I have compared him to Byron. He had something of the same allure—a free spirit informed by pride. Once in Berlin, when he was staying with me at 22 Regenstrasse, near the Tiergarten, he rang me up at three in the morning from some nightclub, in extreme agitation. 'Tell me about the customs of this country. There is a lady here who interests me but her boss does not want her to leave before closing time. Do I knock him out or pay him?'

Another time at Nuremberg, during the National Socialist Congress, Randolph perched himself on the top of a column, towering over the crowds while we were waiting along with some hundred thousands of Nazis for the arrival of the Führer. But the Gestapo hated this show of fantasy that might easily lead to an attempt on his life. Twenty policemen shouted at him, '*Herunter! Herunter!* (Down! Down!)' But protected by the mass of the crowd he did not deign to listen to them. Finally an S.S. colonel, fuming with rage, made his way up to ask him for his '*Ausweis*' (pass). Randolph answered in English: 'I see. You want my invitation card?'

Underneath this detached manner, Randolph concealed a great sense of honour and, I believe, a nostalgic desire to preserve not only his father's memory—whose biography he was writing—but also the England that Winston Churchill represented, loved and defended with such glory.

At least this is how I explain the crusade to which he devoted himself in his last years towards raising the moral level of the London press by protesting against the exploitation of scandals, the abuse of the sensational and pornographic which prevails in every country. He, the journalist who had everything to lose by attacking the dreaded proprietors, did not hesitate to name them as he accused them. What is astonishing is that his campaign enjoyed a certain degree of success.

The deference shown by the great to the bearer of a great name who lectured them without correcting his own ways is so typically British! The nature of the affection which linked the illustrious

Winston to his faithful son—in spite of their temporary differences in which each asserted himself without restraint—also seemed to me to be British. This tempestuous but united race of the Churchills reminds me a bit of our Mirabeau.

'With the Prime Minister in Scotland, Lord Hailsham, Mr Heathcoat Amory, Sir David Eccles and Mr Maudling in Canada, the Foreign Secretary going to New York, Dr Hill in the East, and Mr Butler departing for Africa, I am in the happy position to tell you exactly where the Government stands . . .'

(*From an* Evening Standard *Vicky cartoon. Reproduced by courtesy of London Express News and Feature Services.*)

In Politics

The Rt. Hon. Julian Amery
Michael Foot
The Rt. Hon. Iain Macleod

Electioneering with Randolph

by
Julian Amery

(British statesman, journalist and writer: Parliamentary Under-Secretary of State and Financial Secretary, War Office 1957–8; Under-Secretary of State, Colonial Office 1958–60; Minister of Aviation 1962–4; Minister of Housing and Construction 1970–)

One morning, in the autumn of 1943, I walked into the bar of the Mohammed Ali Club in Cairo. A familiar, bulky figure in Army uniform was sitting in a corner alone. It was Randolph. On the table in front of him was a pile of letters. He handed one of them to me. It was from the chairman of the Preston Conservative Association, for Randolph, at this time, was one of the two Members of Parliament for Preston. The letter stated that the other member disapproved of Randolph so strongly 'on personal and public grounds' that he was not prepared to run again for Preston in harness with Randolph. The chairman went on to explain that the Association would accordingly have to select another candidate. They were naturally anxious to avoid further quarrels. Could Randolph think of anyone with whom he could work in harness and in harmony?

'Would you like to have a go?' Randolph asked. My mind, at the time, was wholly concentrated on the war in the Balkans. The General Election seemed a long way off and I was not very sure where Preston was. Randolph, however, was at his most persuasive —and he could charm birds off trees, when he wanted to—and so, rather light-heartedly, I agreed.

A few weeks later Randolph left for Yugoslavia with Fitzroy Maclean. Not long afterwards I jumped into Albania. I had heard nothing from Preston and concluded that Randolph had forgotten to write or that the Preston people had chosen someone else.

In September 1944, when I was on the run in Albania, we received a parachute drop of explosives and other supplies from

Bari. These included a packet of mail. In this was a letter from the chairman of the Preston Conservative Association, inviting me to stand as their candidate along with Randolph. It was nearly ten months old, and had been misdirected round most of the Mediterranean.

It is easy enough to drop mail by parachute but there is no equivalent method of catapulting back replies. Two months later, however, I was back in Italy and presently accepted the invitation.

Many friends had warned me against the perils of trying to work in harness with Randolph. They told me that I would find him quarrelsome, overbearing and selfish. They begged me to stand almost anywhere but Preston. I am very glad I did not believe them.

I had liked Randolph from the moment of our first meeting at the Oxford Union, and we had become friends during the war. He had a very quick intelligence and an astonishing memory, and his provocative views and uninhibited curiosity made him the most stimulating of companions. He liked to have his say at some length, and resented interruption; but I soon discovered that, provided you first let him talk himself out, he was perfectly ready to listen to you afterwards. He liked a conversation to be a series of speeches, like a debate in Parliament, rather than a rally of comments and interruptions. But, if his method seemed a trifle ponderous, he was, in fact, very quick to see a new idea and had no hesitation in changing his mind if once convinced of strong reasons for doing so.

I had feared a quarrel with him over the election address to which, as always to the written word, we both attached perhaps excessive importance. In fact, he was very conciliatory, and cheerfully accepted several points I wanted to make but with which he did not altogether agree.

He was very keen, I remember, that we should have a campaign song, and for some reason believed that *Lily of Laguna* was a Lancashire tune. We accordingly asked a friend to write some suitable lyrics. This was the result:

> Churchill and Amery,
> We're backing Churchill and Amery,
> They're the pair that Preston needs today,
> They're the pair we'll vote for on Polling Day

Our votes they won't lack,
We want them both back,
We'll get them both back.

Good old Winston wants them with him—
And that's what Preston wants today!

Winston for Premier,
We're backing Winston for Premier.
He's the one to make a Conference go
He's the one who's known to Uncle Joe.

A true friend of Truman.
D'you want a new man?
Some Laski crew man?
No! We want Winston for our Premier—
That's what Preston wants today!

We had gramophone records made of it, and played it both in the streets and at evening meetings. Some of our supporters thought it in bad taste. The tune is admittedly rather dreary, but the general public seemed to enjoy it. At any rate, it helped to raise the temperature.

In the course of the election we only had one cross word. I had never spoken on a public platform before and my speech at our adoption meeting had been very carefully prepared. I read it out word for word from a typescript, and was relieved when Randolph turned to me, at the end, and said to the amusement of the audience —he had forgotten the microphone was still on—'Well, at least you can speak.' I accordingly prepared my speech for our next meeting in exactly the same way. Just before the meeting Randolph asked if he might look at it. I took the text from my pocket and handed it to him. He tore it up, explaining that platform speeches were far more effective if made without notes. We were in a crowded hotel bar full of constituents, otherwise I would certainly have struck him. But he was, of course, quite right, and from then on I spoke only from the briefest notes or from none at all.

I shall always be grateful that I fought my first election with Randolph. Most candidates have no one with experience to guide them during a campaign. Agents and chairmen may have views but they have never done the thing themselves. They are critics not authors, producers not actors. Randolph had made a close study of electioneering techniques and had plenty of electioneering experience. He was bold in canvassing, stopping people in the street and making himself known to them. He was also very skilful at handling deputations. When he knew that he could not hope to satisfy them, as with the doctors* in the 1945 campaign, he had an uncanny way of luring them into quarrelling among themselves and then sending them away to try and reach an agreed view. He was an outstanding platform speaker and, if the meat he served up was sometimes a bit strong for the floating voter, his supporters revelled in it. When booed in a meeting, he would often boo back which usually brought the house down. He had, besides, a great gift of phrase and was adept at thinking out a point to catch the headlines. Above all, he had absorbed most of his father's and his grandfather's political maxims; and, since politics are continually repeating themselves, he was seldom at a loss for a formula for dealing with any challenge, however unexpected.

Winston Churchill once said to me: 'Randolph has big guns but not enough ammunition.' There was some truth in this. But his most dangerous gift was his facility for speech and writing. Winston Churchill achieved literary and rhetorical triumphs only by immense labour. Randolph could dictate a good article in twenty minutes and make a good speech wholly unprepared. But, just because of this facility, he seldom took enough pains to make his articles or speeches very good. It was a case, with him, of the good being the enemy of the best.

People often said that Randolph was overshadowed by his father. I do not believe that this was so. His difficulty, psychologically, was that the world did not accept him at his father's valuation. Churchill had taken Randolph into his confidence and treated him as a colleague from the time he went to Oxford. So, perforce, had Churchill's intimate circle. Randolph had learnt much in the process but as he grew older, he found it increasingly difficult to speak his mind freely at home to the greatest Englishman of his time and yet to show proper respect out of doors for the views of lesser mortals

* The future of the Health Service was a controversial issue at the election, and one on which the medical profession was itself very divided.

who were nevertheless his elders and, in the eyes of the world at least, his 'betters'. He knew that his father thought this or that Commander-in-Chief or Minister a 'booby' and, though only a junior officer and backbencher M.P. himself, could not restrain himself from saying so, loud and clear, if he happened to share his father's view!

My father, too, had taken me into his confidence early; but I was several years younger than Randolph and my experience in the Secret Service had taught me to live my life in compartments. I might spend the evening planning a *coup d'état* in Belgrade but in the office next morning I was careful to be only the keen, young assistant press attaché. Randolph's experience had been the opposite. He had made a name as a journalist largely by saying in public exactly what he thought in private. With years the habit grew on him and by the time of the 1945 General Election he said what he thought quite bluntly without regard for the self-esteem of the great or, indeed, the self-respect of the lowly. This made him enemies.

This lack of self-restraint emerged at an early stage of the campaign. Randolph decided that there was too much apathy among the voters and that we must do something to raise the temperature. We discussed different ways of doing this, but there were powerful objections to each. Then suddenly he hit on an idea. He and I would parade down the main street on two elephants. Our *howdahs* could be draped with placards or party favours and we could address the passers-by through loud-hailers as the pachyderms ambled along. Someone raised the question of cost. He accepted this as a valid point and at once got on to the Manchester Zoo to find that elephants could be hired for only £20 each a day. He warmed to the idea and duly booked the elephants for three days later. It was, I still think, a good idea but it had an exotic quality which shocked the officers of our association. 'We don't like stunts in Preston,' they said, and went on to argue that we could not afford the money. Randolph as a concession offered to make do with one elephant. He and I would share it. What could be a more reasonable compromise? But, when this too was refused, he became very angry and told the committee that they were narrow-minded, middle-class provincials with no imagination and no guts. They never forgave him.

Our campaign reached its climax with the end of June. I was exhausted but exhilarated. The weather was fine. It was all new to me. There was real enthusiasm on our side and as far as we could judge, very little on the other. We took a theatre for the eve of Poll; and when the curtain went up, Randolph and I marched on to the platform, through a Moorish arch, to the strains of *Land of Hope and Glory*. There were nearly 3,000 people present, and the stage effects and lights helped to convince the audience that they had come there to enjoy themselves. They cheered our speeches to the echo. Then when the meeting was over we were literally carried off by our supporters, who chaired us—no easy task where Randolph was concerned—from the theatre down the main street to the Conservative Club.

On polling day, we drove in a cortège of open cars preceded by a loudspeaker van which blared out slogans and played our campaign song. Our reception was lyrical. People cheered and waved their handkerchiefs. Even our opponents smiled. In the centre of town, barmaids came out into the streets with welcome trays of drinks for us, and were duly rewarded with a kiss from Randolph. At almost every polling station the officers and constables on duty wished us good luck. As the stations closed, everyone forecast an easy victory for the 'lively lads' or 'terrible twins' as we were variously known. In fact we were soundly defeated.

On the evening after our defeat, we went round the Conservative Clubs to thank our supporters for their work. There were half a dozen such meetings, and, at each, the chairman made a short speech, mostly in praise of Randolph and myself. But there was one chairman who hated Randolph and regarded me as an interloper. In his speech he expressed regret at the defeat of our party, and talked of the country's ingratitude to the Prime Minister. But he made no reference at all to Randolph's efforts or my own. Randolph replied for both of us. I did not take a note of his speech, but it was on the following lines:

> I have been more touched than I can well say, and so I'm sure has Julian by the glowing tribute which Mr X has just paid to our work at this Election. What he said about our eloquence was far too generous. What he said about our assiduity in canvassing touched me to the heart. What he said about the punctuality

with which we discharged our many obligations was something I can never forget. I know how bitterly he shares our disappointment at our personal defeat, but the memory of his loyalty to me and to Julian is one that will encourage us both through the years ahead.

The poor man flushed crimson. The audience roared their heads off with laughter; and, for a moment, the bitterness of defeat was forgotten in the universal mirth.

It was hard to fault Randolph in public; and at meetings or with deputations he was invariably courteous. But his private relations with his supporters were too often marred by bitter altercation. He had a theory that anyone admitted to his private company must expect him to say just what he thought and accept just how he felt like saying it. One day, coming away from some angry confrontation with our chairman, he turned to me and said with an endearing smile: 'You know, Julian, I ought never to be allowed out in private.'

It was a true saying and in some ways an epitaph on the failure of his political career. He never got back into Parliament and showed no judgement in his own political undertakings. And yet his advice to others was, in my experience at least, invariably sound and usually cautious. He was the best of advisers as well as the most loyal of friends.

As an author he was good though in his biographies almost too restrained. But it was as a letter writer and still more as a conversationalist that he excelled. Here he was in the class of Horace Walpole and Dr Johnson. I only hope there was a Boswell somewhere to record his words.

Randolph's father and mine were colleagues at Harrow, in journalism, in Parliament, and in the Cabinet 'in often varying relations', as Churchill once wrote, 'but enduring friendship'. Randolph taught me much about politics, and we were friends and comrades in many battles besides the election here described. His son has just joined my present office. In due course, perhaps, my son may join him.

Untamable, Outrageous, Unforgettable*

by
Michael Foot

(British politician, journalist and writer: political columnist for the late Daily Herald 1944–64; Editor of Tribune 1948–52; author of Brendan and Beverley, The Pen and the Sword, and other works)

Randolph Churchill and I would wake up every morning, for several weeks on end, polishing the thunderbolts which each hoped to unloose on the unbowed head of the other before the night was done.

I was the Labour candidate for Devonport, dourly defending my home town against a Churchillian carpet-bagger.

He bustled in like something not merely from another world, but another century, talking as if the place belonged to him, as the Churchills have often done, from the great Marlborough and his Duchess onwards.

The brilliant cascade of abuse poured forth in all directions, sometimes drenching his own supporters.

They say that the joists and beams of Conservative clubs in Devonport still quiver at the name of Randolph.

Then suddenly, when he learned that he had lost, in the agonizing seconds which only parliamentary candidates can appreciate, the storm subsided and all was sweetness and charm.

'I thought you took that marvellously,' I felt compelled to acknowledge. 'Yes,' he replied, 'I've had plenty of practice.'

He had, indeed.

He lost all the parliamentary contests he ever fought.

(When he actually got in he was unopposed.)

Considering his boast at the age of 20, that he might emulate William Pitt and become Prime Minister at 24, considering the

* Reprinted from the *Evening Standard* of 7 June 1968.

family background and the expectations of his doting father, his whole political life might be seen as a crushing defeat.

He did not bury his talents; rather he scattered them in a riot of political profligacy.

Way back in the early 1930s he tried to batter his path into Parliament *against* the massed power of the Conservative Party machine.

He turned up at a famous by-election in Wavertree, Liverpool, as an Independent Conservative.

I happened to be present at one of his packed meetings when, mimicking his father, he perorated on the menace of Baldwin's India policy to the Lancashire cotton trade.

The periods soared until he was shot down in mid-flight.

'And who is responsible for putting Liverpool where she is today?' he cried, whereupon a voice from the back recalled the devastating blow inflicted upon the city on the previous Saturday: 'Blackburn Rovers!'

It almost seemed that the campaign floundered from that moment. But Randolph's achievement was truly amazing. He collected 10,000 Independent votes in a few days and handed the seat on a platter to the Labour Party.

And the machine never forgot or forgave, even when his father had helped lead the nation and, more especially, the Conservative Party, cowering beneath his shield, through the Valley of the Shadow of Death.

Not that Randolph never contributed to his own misfortunes, the ostracism, the constantly repeated thud of blackballs; no one could ever say *that*.

At Eton he was beaten for some crime he had never committed. When he protested his innocence with customary volubility, the Captain of Games refused to relent: 'Anyway, you have been bloody awful all round—bend down, you're going to have six up.'

The words have an authentic ring. 'Bloody awful all round,' is the kind of comprehensive verdict which others who had dealings with him were always searching for—politicians, newspaper proprietors, editors, reporters, TV interviewers and, alas, some less able to answer back.

Often in Fleet Street I have heard a fellow-journalist, still reeling from the impact, recall how Randolph had set the Thames, the Hudson, the Tiber or the Danube on fire with his boiling, intoxicant invective.

In how many places, in how many hemispheres, I wonder, did he stand there, unterrified and untamable, while the insults and the champagne bottles hurtled all around?

There were those days in 1938 and 1939, at Beaverbrook's house, when he metaphorically coshed any Munichite Minister whom his host had been ill-advised enough to invite to the party.

Or the splendid occasion when he turned the Foyle's luncheon table at the Dorchester upside-down, knocked Hugh Cudlipp's and Lord Rothermere's heads together, gave his own award to the Pornographer Royal, and launched a one-man campaign to stop newspaper bosses from selling the equivalent of filthy postcards on the street corner.

Sunday journalism has never quite been the same since.

Invective was his strongest suit, but he had real wit, too. When a previous editor of the *Evening Standard* held out one of his articles on the grounds that it was 'obscure', Randolph replied: 'To the obscure all things are obscure.' When Lord Beaverbrook's valet, who normally referred to his master as 'The Lord', informed Randolph that 'The Lord was walking in St. James's Park,' he insisted: 'On the water, I presume?'

Then there was the early-hours session in the startled salon in the Marrakesh Hotel when, half-dead, he poured scorn on all the bronzed weaklings who escaped from his entrancing monologue to their beds.

A couple of days later, after his operation in London for the removal of part of a lung, my wife found him sitting up, smoking, drinking and protesting to one of the most eminent physicians in the land, 'Stop treating me like an invalid.'

Somehow it is such incidents, senseless or grotesque, which stick in the memory.

Somehow his *character* compensates for all offences and explosions.

One feels it was his own work, achieved against hopeless odds: the spoilt child, the staggeringly handsome adolescent; the illusion that this Adonis could also talk as sparklingly as his father's beloved F. E. Smith, or write as readily as his father's model, Macaulay.

By the age of 30 or earlier all his juvenile ambitions were shattered.

Every time he attempted a political comeback he met fresh rebuffs.

Every way he turned he faced the jibe that when nature makes a genius she breaks the mould.

But he would not be beaten.

He would retire to the garden he loved.

He made himself a most formidable journalist, the trade he had never bothered to learn before.

He made himself the biographer of his father and set the style for a great book; the father with whom he could quarrel but whose political cause he served with selfless loyalty.

He was outrageous and endearing, impossible and unforgettable, a Churchill who scarcely ever tasted victory, and what super Churchillian courage that must have called for.

Along with his honesty ('Lies are so dull,' he would say) and his streaks of kindness, it was this reckless courage which shone most brightly.

It could make him magnificent in political controversy, as he had once shown himself on the battlefield.

Friends and enemies would look on, admiring or aghast. Both enjoyed the witticism when someone said that he was the kind of person who should not be allowed out in private.

But it is the private Randolph I remember now that he is sadly and prematurely dead.

He was a friend and enemy worth having.

"I'M NOT SOLICITING OR LOITERING, OFFICER! JUST WAITING FOR A CALL . . ."

(An unpublished Vicky cartoon. Reproduced by courtesy of London Express News and Feature Services.)

The Riddle of Randolph

by

Iain Macleod

(British statesman and editor: Minister of Health 1952–5; Minister of Labour and National Service 1955–9; Secretary of State for the Colonies 1959–61; Chancellor of the Duchy of Lancaster and Leader of the House of Commons 1961–3; Chancellor of the Exchequer 1970; Editor of the Spectator 1963–5. Died in 1970)

I can only remember one occasion when I hoped I would not see Randolph Churchill, and of course I did. It was in March 1960 and I as Secretary of State for the Colonies had planned a journey to Rhodesia and then to Nyasaland (now Malawi). I had determined to release Dr Banda then a prisoner at Gwelo about ninety miles from Salisbury, and to bring the state of emergency to an end. I knew first I would have to face fierce opposition from the Federal Cabinet and from the Government of Southern Rhodesia. They had already sent me blood-curdling prophecies of the massacres that would in their view be the inevitable consequence of Dr Banda's release. It seemed to me vital to spirit Dr Banda out of Gwelo under the noses of the journalists who haunted its gates: then to persuade Dr Banda—whom I had never met—to appeal for peace over the radio before the news of his release was widely known. A dozen journalists, in the belief that I was en route for Gwelo, were on my plane. The last thing I wanted was to have Randolph's genius for uncovering secrets added to my worries. He had told me he intended to come, but there was no sign of him at London Airport. The flight number was called: still no Randolph. We emplaned, fastened our seat-belts and the plane taxied to the runway: still no Randolph and I breathed again. Then nothing happened, and we waited and waited. Finally after a small commotion Randolph appeared through the pilot's cabin. Brushing aside my papers and my civil servants Randolph seated himself beside me. 'Ho!' he said. 'I suppose you thought I'd missed it?' 'No,' I said, 'I just hoped.'

We then had to wait while Randolph's not inconsiderable weight in petrol was siphoned off. In the end all was well. For once Randolph's news sense failed him, and by the time Dr Banda was finally released before dawn one morning Randolph had lost interest and disappeared to South Africa in search of new news. It remained an amiable point of grievance that I had let him go without a hint of what was afoot.

On another and even more dramatic occasion Randolph had the best of it. In October 1963, when Harold Macmillan's sudden illness and resignation as Prime Minister shattered the opening of the Conservative conference at Blackpool, I was Chairman of the Conservative Party. We were in deep political trouble, but all seemed fairly peaceful as I left the Tuesday Cabinet to head for Blackpool. Certainly Macmillan was far from well but it still looked a sure bet that he would lead us at the General Election then a year away. I held a press conference and then left for the Conservative Agents' dinner. Half way through I was called to the telephone to talk to the Prime Minister's principal Private Secretary, and absorbed the news of the operation which was being released in an hour or so. I had hardly returned to my seat when I had to answer the telephone again. It was Randolph calling from Washington. It was in fact pure coincidence that he telephoned just at that moment. Randolph's telephone bill wherever he was was always of monumental proportions as he 'kept in touch' with his friends all over the world. I greeted him, apologized for not being able to talk at length to him, and rang off. With Randolph in Washington, I thought the news was safe for at least an hour. I underestimated him. Randolph was immediately suspicious and concluded from my reluctance to exchange gossip with him that something was going on. He promptly made two more transatlantic calls to London, and put together what he was told. He then rang the British Embassy in Washington and President Kennedy and gave them a complete account of what was afoot before the official news was released. He was a great if somewhat unpredictable journalist.

When a month or two later, and partly in consequence of Macmillan's resignation, I became editor of the *Spectator* I turned at once to Randolph. I did not much mind what he wrote so long as he wrote for me and in the end we agreed that he should write a weekly Press Column. Most editors as part of their contract with Randolph had to pay his telephone bill. We could not afford to and our fees to him must have been swamped by the cost to him of the column. It was an excellent piece of journalism and we had as editor and columnist a stormy and affectionate relationship which exactly mirrored our attitude to each other. The end was inevitable but pleasantly long delayed. One week I cut a couple of lines or so from his copy not in any spirit of literary criticism but simply to make it fit the page. Next week no copy arrived. I had forgotten the small excision and Randolph's fury burst on my unfortunate secretary who had rung to remind him. I made no attempt to get him back. We were both much too pig-headed to apologize. We never did to each other. So that particular episode ended without so far as I can recall having the slightest effect on our friendship.

It is a hopeless task trying to explain to people who did not know him how overwhelming was Randolph's charm, and there is no need to those who knew him. I used to love arguing with him and sometimes the sheer joy of verbal conflict carried us both away. I remember once at a dinner party at his lovely country home in the Constable country at East Bergholt, becoming involved in an argument *à deux*. It became more and more heated, more and more thunderous until suddenly we noticed that we were alone. All the other guests had retired either bored or outraged or tired. Randolph looked round. 'Damn fools,' he remarked dispassionately and then resumed his diatribe at full volume. One evening particularly stays in my memory. We were dining alone (and in relative peace) and later we retired to his study. We both had formidable memories for poetry and a great store of favourites. We went on for hours reciting Shakespeare and Chesterton, Belloc and Kipling sometimes in turn sometimes together and always at the top of our voices.

Randolph had in full measure the courage that is so typical of his family. I believe with Sir James Barrie that 'Courage is the thing. All goes if courage goes.' I did not know Randolph until after the war, but his courage was of a reckless cavalier type equally suited, as his father showed, to war and to politics. And yet in politics he must I suppose be accounted a failure. He was Member of Parliament for Preston in the war years 1940–45, but he was of course away nearly all the time on service. He fought unsuccessfully three by-elections before the war and two general elections afterwards, but he never won a contested election. Perhaps he lived too much in the shadow of his father and his grandfather to be accepted in his own right, perhaps he was simply too arrogant for the selection committees that he deigned to notice. He rarely spoke to me of what must have been bitterly disappointing to him. No doubt his true and deserved success as a biographer was some consolation. So also was the beauty of his garden. But to a Churchill the true stage is the House of Commons and I doubt if Randolph found lasting satisfaction in any alternative setting.

I suppose he knew, as his friends knew in the last year or two of his life, that he had not long to live. I remember going to see him in hospital the night before he had a major lung operation. As usual there was uproar. A nurse was in tears because Randolph had been bellowing at her about the proper cooling of his champagne. The surgeon had just left before I arrived—'been giving him a quick run over the course,' said Randolph to me. Next day everything went well and a bulletin announced that the tissue removed had not been malignant. Perhaps he never fully recovered and he was in any event an impossible patient. Some people found him impossible as a person. Those who knew him best loved him most. One cannot explain rationally how it was that a man who was unforgivably rude was so much loved. It is no service to his memory to pretend that he was anything other than arrogant and overbearing. He did not even follow the accepted rules of rudeness. They say one should never be rude to servants, but Randolph was. One should never be rude to people who cannot retaliate, but Randolph was. One should only be rude when one means to be, but Randolph was often quite unconscious that he was being intolerant. The riddle of Randolph can only be understood if one accepts his failings and makes no attempt to explain them away. And then wait and all the picture begins to make sense.

Early in June 1968 I returned from a short holiday in Spain. I had seen no English papers for some days. A hired car met me and I asked the driver what had been happening. He brought me up to date with the cricket scores, and the political situation and added: 'Mr Randolph Churchill died.' The news was expected and yet unexpected and the sense of loss overwhelming. I remembered Edna St Vincent Millay's lovely sonnet, which starts:

> If I should learn, in some quite casual way,
> That you were gone, not to return again—

And I stared out of the window at the passing traffic. Randolph was dead. No one can take his place, he was irreplaceable.

A Sahara Mouse Hunt

Miggs Pomeroy and
Catherine Collins

The Great Sahara Mouse Hunt*

by

Miggs Pomeroy and Catherine Collins

(A diary of the safari of fourteen people, including Randolph Churchill and his son Winston, crossing the Sahara from Benghazi in Libya to the most inaccessible mountain ranges in the world—the Tibesti—looking for mice)

11TH MARCH

We are due to leave for a six- to eight-week trek into the Sahara tomorrow and everyone suspects everyone else of being disorganized. . . . Only the Churchills are in order.

This morning I go to help the Churchills with their list of supplies, in case they have forgotten something or need help with their shopping. At 9.30 a.m. Randolph is in a shirt without trousers or shoes. He shows me his neat packages of clothes and equipment, and insists that Winston put out a camp-bed so that I can be zipped up in one of their new mummy-style sleeping-bags. He is proud of his cooler—his Magical Box, as he calls it—which he says will be kept perpetually full of ice to chill his pâté de foie gras. Ice in mid-Sahara is a novel idea, but Randolph, if anyone can, surely will manage it. Over breakfast, which Winston† ate but Randolph drank, we discuss supplies and Winston decides that all he needs is deodorant. Father explodes that he's been seeing too much television, but Winston and I go shopping and buy two jars. We also buy ten kilos of charcoal for camp-fires.

'We shall,' Randolph says, 'sit around a jolly camp-fire and talk.' As he is a great conversationalist, we shall more likely sit around a camp-fire and listen. The first contretemps has reared its ugly head. Randolph insists that the 'other ranks' will have their own little cook-fire elsewhere. When Catherine and I protest at both the unfriendliness and inefficiency of this system Randolph's voice rises two full octaves of irritated authority.

* Reprinted from *The Great Sahara Mouse Hunt*, London: Hutchinson & Co., 1962.   † *Editor's Note:* Randolph's son.

'Don't you women go mucking up the British Army,' he cries. 'We've got a jolly good army and we don't want any American women interfering with it.'

The tense moment passes as Randolph cajoles us. 'The soldiers won't understand our jokes, you know, and we shan't enjoy their language. Let them have their own camp-fire. Every now and then we'll send them jolly little presents and converse.' . . . There is so much to be done and I am getting very lopsided. The halls are stacked with packing-cases; the children, multiplied by hordes of friends, run in and out pilfering casually from cases of chocolate or biscuits and scattering anything left in their path. The men are busy checking the cars, spare parts, sand-tracks and jerry-cans. Threading their way through the halls at meal-times, they complain loudly that there is no room in the cars for all of the stuff we are bringing. Catherine reluctantly eliminates a case of fruit juice and one of minute rice. Everyone is to regret this bit of austerity. Winston is tinkering with the Churchill Land Rover, installing a radio.

'The boy can take one of these cars apart,' his father says proudly. He ambles between cases occasionally picking up something he feels he might need. 'Just get yourself another,' he says grandly, and then, putting his arm about one of us, he coaxes, 'Come into a quieter room, dear child, and let us have a little conversation,' or, 'I must read you the jolliest little poem by Hilaire Belloc, marvellous chap.' He reads from *The Modern Traveller*. Amusing, and we think a delightful parallel to our trip. He reads beautifully. Altogether a gifted man who should have been spanked more frequently in childhood.

We cannot possibly get off tomorrow and have set Monday the thirteenth. Randolph is wild. 'We limeys,' he thunders, 'are steady on parade; but you bloody Americans . . .' He says (a) he is going back to England to watch his tulips grow, and (b) he is starting out ahead of us. His affairs are in order. His Land Rover is tickety-boo! He roars off, singing loudly, 'When the roll is called up yonder I'll be there!'

12TH MARCH

Randolph and Winston did in fact take off at dawn for Agedabia, where they have promised to wait for us. Agedabia is the jumping-off place for the desert. We'll see our last petrol-pump and our last road there. The packing-up is going forward and the extra day has given us time for detail. Alan has acquired viper and scorpion serum from the Pasteur Institute in Paris. This is supposed to be kept on ice, which despite Randolph's 'Magical Box' we are not so naive as to think possible . . . the French in Chad told us that the bite of a horned viper will kill you if the serum is not administered immediately in small doses every few minutes in a ring around the bite. However, Liv has brought home a batch of hypo needles and some extra-powerful vitamins for Randolph. His way of not eating his meals is worrying and we don't want him breaking out with scurvy, or whatever people get when they don't eat (aside from good figures). . . . Today the Governor gave Alan a beautiful document to all his local authorities, the Mudirs and Mutaserif, asking that they help us and make us welcome to their diocese. Personally I think that anyone who can write Arabic is by nature an artist. With schools in every town and most oases, a vast population of artists is on its way. Literally translated for us, this lovely flowing script reads:

NAZARAT OF INTERIOR

The Nazir's Office
March 11th, 1961

To whom it may concern
Departing this week, group of Mr. and Mrs. Alan C. Collins from the United States of America, Dr. Henry W. Setzer of the National Museum, Smithsonian Institute, Mr. R. S. Churchill and his son Winston. R. Churchill is the son of ex-Britain Prime Minister and the well-known journalist. Mr. and Mrs. Robert L. Pomeroy the Director of the American Cultural Centre in Benghazi, Lt. Francis Gibb and six others from the British Army.

The group with their six cars are leaving this week for touring through Gialo and Cofra from there to Chad. The purpose of the trip is visiting, studying and adventure.

It is requested from the departments concerned that to give all the assistance needed by the above mentioned and also any facilities which they may require during their trip to the Sahara.

(Signed) Mahmoud Abu Shraida,
Nazir of Interior.
(The Nazara Stamp)

13TH MARCH

Somehow we get packed up and loaded. The take-off looks more like a gymkhana than a well-mannered expedition. . . . The hard-surface coastal road streaks like an arrow from Benghazi to Agedabia. We scarcely know what we will find at the rendezvous with the Churchills. And if we had guessed at either place or condition we would have been wrong. Ahead of us, first a dot on the horizon and then looming as a road block, is a Land Rover mounted with a great six-foot flag; white, emblazoned with a blue U.N. In the middle of the road, at a formica-topped card-table, sits Randolph with refreshments laid out. Winston stands beside him with a gun at the alert. They both wear white tin helmets on which have been painted blue bands and large U.N.s.

'Stopping all cars,' Randolph shouts as the five of us brake up. 'I've been sent up from the Congo to investigate. The U.N. is worried about conditions in North Africa. Come, come, identify yourselves.'

Assisting the Churchills in their manœuvre are two amiable Dutchmen whom they had found at a near-by oil rig and impressed into amusing—Randolph—duty. Everyone is pleasantly intoxicated and we are all in a mood to join them. A party of Libyans, travelling their humdrum way from Tripoli to Benghazi, ogle as they squeeze by, their expressions setting us all into a gale of laughter. . . .

Everyone who heard of our expedition wanted to know where we were going and why. The first question was a matter of maps, not always accurate, and routes, sometimes never before travelled. The why had as many answers as there were members of the expedition. . . .

Randolph Churchill was one of the charter members of our expedition, for he had asked to be counted in a good year before we got down to serious preparations. There is a saying that he who drinks from the Nile must always return to Egypt, so perhaps whoever gets an eyeful of Sahara sand is also for ever drawn back to the desert. Randolph had his first taste of the Libyan sands during the war when he took part in one of the most ambitious and daring British raids behind the Axis lines. The time was 1942, the goal to mine ships anchored in Benghazi harbour. The raid was carried out by the famous Long Range Desert Group which had proved its worth in many seemingly impossible runs across hundreds of miles of trackless desert to strike the Axis far behind its lines. The operation was a well-planned and smoothly carried-out fiasco. The British got their truck past the German and Italian road blocks and into the city of Benghazi, where Randolph had charge of camouflaging and guarding it while the sappers made their way into the port area with rubber boats and demolitions. But the long bumpy ride across the desert had proved too much for their boats, which were so damaged by chafing in the back of the truck that they could no longer be inflated.

Now the old war-horse has come back to the desert, perhaps to see whether he can still stand up to it, perhaps for sentimental reasons, or to show it to his son Winston; but more than anything, I think, he has come back to taste the tranquillity and quiet strength of this, his 'vast desaart'. Randolph is a big man with a round head and brooding eyes. For a man who says that he likes things straight and simple, he seems to have made a very interesting job of his own personality. He says that he prefers his flower garden in Suffolk to any of these outlandish places, and yet the mere mention of a distant horizon is enough to set him packing his bags. Like some allegorical beast, he combines the dragon and the teddy bear; unable to turn his back on a challenge, he is as brave and heedless as the first when confronted, or sweet as the second when he thinks that no one is looking. Winston, who is twenty, is the youthful figure of a one-day sizable man. He has that pink-and-white British complexion, with big eyebrows which give him an authoritative air. . . . The truth of the matter is that no one seems anxious to tote for anyone in this group. If anything we are travelling with men who might adopt as their own the saying of Randolph's little daughter, 'Papa likes to see women work.' . . .

From Tekro, a desert outpost, we will make our way to Faya-Largeau, Zouar, Bardai, exploring the Tibesti and then through the Kourizo Pass northward into Libya again, to Sebha and back to Agedabia. These are our plans. We are on our way and Randolph is sitting in the middle of the highway passing the time of day. We join him in a toast to the success of our expedition; gather him, Winston and the two Dutch oil men whom Randolph has invited for dinner, and find a camp site in a eucalyptus grove near Agedabia.

Randolph claims the right to cook the first dinner. As we have brought along a cold roast of beef, potato salad, tomatoes, bread and butter and a Bel Paese cheese, we think it will not be too strenuous for him, and having laid out our provender Catherine and I drape ourselves about the grove and wait.

Randolph calls first for his table, his two chairs and some light refreshment. Then he sits down and orders Winston to open the pâté de foie gras and to put on the lobster bisque from Fortnum and Mason. The pâté is delicious, but when we try to find a Dutchman to feed they have both disappeared. Randolph has objected to their hovering helpfully about the women, who were only too obviously delighted with their good looks and charming manners. 'Leave the women alone,' he'd shouted. 'Bugger off'—and they had.

The moment came when 'the women' have to undrape themselves from the grove and rescue the bisque which Randolph shrieks is being ruined. It is a superb soup, but Randolph pouts that the 'white ladies' have ruined it and refuses to eat. I don't think he intended to eat, anyway. However he has endeared himself to me by presenting me with his hot-water bottle which has a velveteen cover decorated with his initials. 'For your poor little arm,' he says. (It has been broken and was in a cast.) I have forgiven him the banished Dutchmen.

14TH MARCH

The stars were bright and the night cold and we awaken in the morning to find ourselves covered with pools of icy dew. Boiling tea brings the blood back to our hearts and we attack our 'compo', sausages and hash hotted up over the primus, with appetite. Little boys from nearby Agedabia gather round to watch and Hank gives one of them the first discard of his twenty pairs of socks. Randolph complains that I had promised to look after him and where the hell are the bacon and eggs. So I carefully cook him two eggs which Winston eats, because the tea is gone and Randolph says he cannot stomach eggs without tea. It is a test and proves what I feared: he has no appetite. I even try to give him a vitamin pill, but Winston is right in saying he won't take those either. Catherine says he's going to develop a divine figure, and how do you lose your appetite? . . .

At last we turn away from the coast on a bumpy track through scrub and sage brush. The sand is rubbly and red. After a few kilometres we have trouble with the radio vehicle. Everyone climbs under it except Alan who photographs the workers and advisers in action, and the Churchills who with flag flying disappear southwards. . . .

While we make camp Hank and Liv set out a string of fifty mouse-traps in some nearby clumps of grass and stunted palms. Somewhere along the line we have picked up Randolph and Winston again and they have delved into the lovely Fortnum and Mason surprise box and produced petit pois à la Française which are *ravissants*. Randolph has been having little generalship meetings with Liv and Francis ('Just a word with you, dear boy') about the track, about travel procedure, about sending the little car back. He talks late into the night. . . .

15TH MARCH

I scramble eggs for breakfast which everyone pronounces delicious except Randolph. 'My dear girl,' he says despairingly, 'you've obviously never read Escoffier. It is essential to beat the eggs well first, then add the seasoning. Don't just *throw* a hunk of butter into a frying-pan full of unbeaten eggs.' . . .

We are without our navigator today as he is of course on his way back to Agedabia while we are on the south track racing towards Gialo. Liv is navigating by intuition, having done this leg of the journey before. The hummocks and land formations are gone now as are the sage and gorse. Here the world seems to be a platter rather than a globe. Nothing—a complete disc of nothingness. We feel the ancients were not so wrong, the edge of the earth is in sight and at the speed we are going we shall pop over it in no time. And again we think that this is Dali land. We would not be surprised to see a clock, a limp telephone and a lone eyeball appear before us on this pale blond canvas we are crossing. The Churchills' car continues to career off in maverick fashion seeking new routes to the south. When they have given us sufficient lead they stop, and get out the card-table and chairs. Randolph passes the time of day with his philosophy while Winston scouts the terrain or naps under the car.

Late in the day Randolph decides to play at being lost. He flags down Alan and Hank who are riding together and calls for a little conference. The other cars, all unaware, disappear over the horizon.

'We have over-shot Gialo. We must instigate rescue procedure,' he says firmly.

Hank, who is an old desert hand, says: 'Well, yes, but let's just follow Pomeroy. We're not in any danger.'

Alan, who has had no desert experience but has a built-in bump of direction, agrees with both of them. 'We're lost, but let's get on with it. We just waste time sitting around here. Give me a drink, Randolph, and let's catch up with Liv. If he doesn't discover his mistake we can always tell him.'

But Randolph will not be out-generalled. 'Goody!' he says. 'We will have a little drink. Get the table,' he orders Winston, 'and get me the binoculars.' Hank and Alan grin and Alan wonders wistfully if any of his three sons could ever be counted on to give him the cheerful service that Winston gives his father, and decides not. Of Alan's sons, Philip is married and not at hand. Duff, who is Winston's age, when home from college, is always just on his way out of the house, and Pom, aged nine, is at the 'in-just-a-minute' stage, which precedes the on-the-way-out stage. . . .

Numbers have been painted on the doors of all the cars excepting Randolph's. He does not want to mar his for future sale. However, the spectacular flagstaff identifies the Churchill car readily. Our car is No. 1, the Collinses' 2 and the army cars are 4 and 5. When the flag car and No. 2 are missed a halt is called. . . . One car will remain and he will go back to look for the stray sheep. And so are Randolph and Co. rescued, but fierce in denial that it is they who have strayed. Another little conference is held and Randolph declares that he is beetling off westward on his own. . . .

Randolph has a homing instinct. Without a brush or clump to guide himself with he has found Gialo which he has entered, conversing with the school-teacher and drinking tea with the Mudir. He has also found the seismic camp where he has delighted the men and outraged the manager. He has invited ten men to dine with us tomorrow night and instructed them to bring ice and four loaves of toast, hot and crisp, to serve with his pâté. He has also found his way to our own camp on the Gialo–Kufra track. The tent is pitched and the bed-rolls are out. Liv and Hank have gone to the oasis to set traps. Randolph and Winston give us the news and race off for an evening with the geologists. On our own we have a quiet supper, and as darkness falls we assume the Churchills to be dining at the rig, and pack away the kitchen. Late in the night the flag car roars into camp and we are berated for not having hot soup ready in language Randolph's Nanny never taught him. So the kitchen is unpacked, and Winston and I cook up a second supper. We have a difficult passenger in this great creature with his commanding presence, his brilliant wit and rough manners. It has reached the point where we relish the peaceful moments when he is sleeping and yet we all recognize his sweetness and find that he can be amusing and companionable. In the midst of the bruha-ha tonight he takes me aside in one of his 'may-I-have-a-tiny-word-with-you' confidences, walks into the darkness and tells me that he'd been touched by my concern for his health, and that he is enjoying the trip and already feels better.

'But pills,' he says, 'what an impossible, American idea. I never take pills.'

16TH MARCH

. . . The oil people have offered hospitality to Alan and Randolph, who says that since pâté and caviar are finished he may as well go home. A supply plane is due at the rig Monday and will fly them back to Benghazi. Winston will keep the Churchill Land Rover and come along with us.

'He's a good boy,' says Randolph. 'He's steady on parade. But I spent sixty pounds on tulips this year. It would be a waste not to see them come up. Besides, my little spaniel is in whelp. Very irresponsible of me to go away from home for six weeks.'

Only five of the oil men come for dinner. Randolph has countermanded the other invitations saying firmly, 'Five is enough and bring your own plates and forks.'

At least he did not put off bearded André whom we all love. André has taken care of the men and their problems, invited the women to bathe and conversed fearlessly with Randolph. We don't know what they conversed about, for Randolph set up his two camp-chairs in the desert well away from camp and the two big men sat there, on the shore of a mirage of blue water, a bottle of Scotch and one of Drambuie on the sand beside them. Even from a distance it was apparent that André was no mere listener. André is a Frenchman, from the Pyrenees. He told us that he commanded a battery of horse artillery during the last war and was taken prisoner on horseback. We think it must have been a singular honour.

The last of Randolph's pâté is delectable served with the crisp toast which our guests have brought us. For dinner we have green turtle soup, also from Fortnum and Mason. It is flavoured with sherry and we tell Randolph that he is a great gourmet, with which he readily agrees. We also have tamales, hot chili beans, beet salad and whisky. André holds a lantern for the women to do the dishes and Randolph complains that American women demand too much attention and that Frenchmen give them too much. An Englishman, now, knows how to treat women! Catherine thinks she has earned the Victoria Cross for not throwing the dish-water at him.

Late in the night our guests climb into their Rover, packing in Alan and Randolph and their gear. Randolph has kissed both of us and promised me a spaniel pup. Catherine watches the lights of the car as it draws away. Nothing diminishes in the desert, but suddenly disappears. . . .

18TH MARCH

. . . We find weird palm-fronds and decorate the breakfast table, thinking nostalgically of Randolph, who had complained at the lack of flowers on that first breakfast table. He does not like things to be ordinary, and pinning us with his brooding eyes he'd say: 'This is the age of the common man and the commoner woman. You should put flowers on the table.'

A Friend of Israel

Eliahu Elath

Randolph

by

Eliahu Elath

(Israeli diplomat, administrator and writer: first ambassador from Israel to the United States 1948–50; ambassador to Great Britain 1950–9; President Emeritus of the Hebrew University in Jerusalem; author of The Bedouins, Their Life and Customs, Israel and Her Neighbours, *and other works)*

I met Randolph in 1950, soon after my arrival in London as Ambassador from Israel to the Court of St James. I had carried with me a few personal letters of introduction to Mr Churchill from some of his friends in the United States, where I had served as Israel's first Ambassador before my transfer to London. But my friendship with Randolph was independent of my relationship with Sir Winston and it remained so for the rest of my tour of duty in London and beyond that when I returned to Israel.

Randolph and I met through Julian Amery, a mutual friend and a strong supporter of Zionism and Israel. It was Randolph who, at our first meeting, gave me an impassioned picture of what I could expect as Israel's envoy to a country where the Balfour Declaration was less remembered than Chamberlain's White Paper; and where Bevin represents most of what at present is associated with the British attitude towards the new State of Israel.

One must remember that Randolph was brought up in an atmosphere friendly to the Zionist cause. His father supported Zionism from the early days of the Balfour Declaration and fought both in the House of Commons and in the press restrictions imposed upon the National Home by Chamberlain's and later Attlee's Governments. In a letter to me, on 9 April 1951 in reply to an invitation to visit Israel in order to attend the opening of the Weizmann Forest, Sir Winston Churchill wrote:

As a Zionist since the days of the Balfour Declaration I am much complimented to receive this invitation from so great a world statesman as Dr Weizmann, whose son fell in the cause of freedom which we now all labour to defend. It is with much regret therefore that I do not find it possible to come to the ceremony which signifies another stage in reclaiming the desert of so many centuries into a fertile home for the Jewish people.

Sir Winston has always shown great interest in the state of Israel. In a conversation with me in October 1950 he called Israel's creation 'one of the great events of all times in human history', and said that he was proud of his contribution to the Zionist cause. He also said to me on that occasion that Israel had no better friend than Britain. In his view British romantic realists deeply respected and admired determination and courage. Israel's independence, he said, also achieved great historical significance by the restoration of a free Jewish nation after centuries of persecution. On another occasion he stressed to me the importance of a strong Israel in the Middle East for her own and democracy's sake. That was the attitude of Randolph's father which has undoubtedly also influenced his son's and grandson's views and attitudes towards Zionism and Israel.

At that first meeting Randolph explained that Israel had a solid and influential group of friends, mainly in Tory and Liberal circles; and some in the ruling Labour Party. He suggested that it would require much patience and work on my part to contribute to the restoration of Israeli–British relations and thus bring them to the desirable level of mutual trust and understanding that our friends would like them to be. He gave me a very vivid picture of those who were 'friends' of Israel and those who were against us and could not be trusted.

The picture Randolph painted for me on that memorable occasion was rather impressionistic, with strong and perhaps exaggerated colours in typical Randolphian style. But basically his was one of the most realistic and true evaluations of the situation which I could only later properly appreciate and fully understand.

During ten years as ambassador in Great Britain I profited many times from Randolph's analyses of events and situations. With time and my close relationship with him I learned a bit about his ways of presenting ideas and how he dealt with people. In many ways he was a radical who played flat-out, with no desire to compromise, or to be the pragmatist who 'sees all sides of the question'.

He used to be very critical of the Middle East experts in the Foreign Office, who operated, in his opinion, more on prejudices and formulae of the past than on a realistic and penetrating examination of the existing situation and trends in that area. Pan-Arabism was to him more an invention of the British romantics of the old Lawrence school than a movement with its roots in reality. He attributed most of the mistakes of British policy in the Arab world to the support of the Arab League by Eden and his experts, who created a Frankenstein to turn against the British themselves as well as against Israel, the only genuine friend of Britain in the area, a free and democratic nation respecting human liberty and the rights of the individual. Randolph was also one of the first to understand the militaristic and autocratic character of Nasser's revolution and did not believe in a settlement between Britain and Egypt under Nasser's regime, any more than such a settlement would have been possible between Britain and Nazi Germany. He was very critical of Eden's failure to resolve the Suez war despite American and Russian opposition and difficulties at home. 'Father might not have started the operations, but having commenced them he would not have abandoned them before achieving the objectives,' he told me soon after the fiasco of 1957.

Events on many occasions proved his Cassandra-like predictions right. One such presentiment concerned trends in Soviet policy—that to stabilize their position in Europe, and in view of the importance Africa was acquiring in world affairs, the Russians would turn to the Middle East in order to penetrate from that end into the Mediterranean and so open a door for themselves into the Black continent. He also prophesied the possible *rapprochement* between the dictatorial regimes in the Arab world and Russia, like that between Stalin and Hitler. He was critical of the Western Powers, including Britain, for not helping Israel, not only for the sake of Israel's existence but for that of democracy itself.

Randolph was a most loyal friend and could always be trusted and relied upon. Hypocrisy he could not endure and he would often, to his great disadvantage, express his views in a most undiplomatic manner both in his personal and public conversations.

This of course harmed his opportunities in public life. But I believe he minded that far less than winning some desired goal through methods he repudiated on moral and public grounds.

On one occasion in my office at the embassy in London he clashed with another visitor during a discussion on Labour policy and Attlee's and Bevin's attitude towards Zionism and Israel. It so happened that the visitor was Hugh Dalton, one of the few Labour leaders who objected to the anti-Zionist and anti-Semitic attitude of Bevin towards Jewish aspirations in Palestine. But Randolph would not make any concessions to Dalton. He made the point that members of the Labour Government who objected to Bevin's stand should have left the Government rather than be party to a policy which meant not only an end to British commitment to the Balfour Declaration, but also a terrible threat to the Jewish community in Palestine and the end of its monumental efforts after 2,000 years of exile. In fact, neither Dalton nor any other member of the Attlee Cabinet resigned from the Government as Eden, Duff Cooper and others had done as a result of their disagreements with Chamberlain's policy of appeasement.

Randolph considered his visits to Israel great events. He would return full of faith in the country and her future. On occasion he would publish his impressions of those visits, but above all he would talk to his influential friends in London about the importance of British help to Israel. As Sir Winston undoubtedly had an influence on Randolph's attitude towards Zionism and Israel, so Randolph had a similar one on his son. The two, father and son, produced one of the best descriptions of the Six-Day War. It was a magnificent co-operation of spirit as well as of human and political attitudes. Both are true friends of Israel and of what she stands for.

Randolph was first and foremost a person of faith, with faith both in his objectives and in his methods of achieving those goals. The ways in which he went after what he wanted often did not conform to the methods commonly employed for public and political advancement in a society that respects the virtues of compromise.

My wife and I last saw Randolph when we spent a night with him in his country home in Suffolk. Though he was then a very ill man, there was no other occasion during the years that I knew him when we found him more noble in his conversation concerning history, its great issues and the people involved in them. He was living at that time with his father—not actually of course—but immersed in his great biography of Sir Winston, and was at the early, adventurous period of his work. He spoke to us about the biography, which to him meant everything at that period of his life, a life that was coming so rapidly to its close.

There was something spiritual in the way he was dealing with the great biography—both as a son and an historian. What he dreamed of accomplishing was immensely difficult to achieve without an inner conflict between emotion and intellectual honesty. I believe he accomplished the almost impossible; even to a greater degree than his father achieved in his noted biography of his father, Lord Randolph Churchill.

Randolph passionately loved his country and countrymen. But he loved and dedicated his best efforts to objectives he considered true and worth while for other countries. Israel was one of them. He will always be honoured by those of my countrymen who knew him for the deep concern he shared with his father and, yes, his own son Winston, for the survival of our state and the progress and well-being of her people.

A Neighbour

Viscount Blakenham

Randolph as a Neighbour

by
Viscount Blakenham

(British statesman: Minister of State for Colonial Affairs 1955–6; Secretary of State for War 1956–8; Minister of Agriculture, Fisheries and Food 1958–60; Minister of Labour 1960–3; Chairman of the Conservative Party Organization 1963–5)

Randolph and I were in the same class during our last year at Eton. Our teacher was a considerable character called Tuppy Headlam. His object was to inspire in us a liking for the classics. His method was to run through the *Iliad* or the *Odyssey* at great speed with the aid of an English crib. Both of us enjoyed this. For the first time, one was able to grasp something of the story as a whole and the wearisome process of translating these epics word by word and line by line which both of us had endured from the start of our schooling was joyfully abandoned.

Randolph was quick-witted, aggressive, handsome and somewhat unpopular. He longed to be away from the discipline of school and become involved in the outer world. I found him an interesting and stimulating companion. He went up to Oxford and I departed for America to take a job as an office boy in a New York merchant banking firm. The year was 1929.

To my surprise, a year later he telephoned me in New York saying that he was on vacation and was embarked on a lucrative lecture tour of the U.S.A. Would I please come and have a drink with him that night in his suite at the Waldorf Astoria. I duly appeared, to find him surrounded by a number of glamorous friends of both sexes. A glass of champagne and a large cigar were produced for my benefit. He then proceeded to harangue me on my folly and lack of enterprise in following such a dreary career. He was arrogant, self-assured and most eloquent. He meant well but I was not amused.

During the next few years, I saw him occasionally but he did not really come back into my life until he suddenly appeared from nowhere at the end of November 1942, just outside Mejez-el-Bab, some twenty-five miles from Tunis. I was with the 78th Division of the First Army and my divisional commander had decided that the push to capture Tunis was impossible owing to lack of air superiority and to the foul weather of the Tunisian winter. Randolph soundly berated General Eveleigh and indeed all with whom he came into contact. His criticisms only just fell short of accusations of cowardice. Frankly, he was a bore and a considerable nuisance as the General was right and he was wrong. By then his character had developed into what it was to become in his later years: utter courage, both physical and moral; a vast enthusiasm for any cause in which he had become involved; a total lack of the ability to know how far to go in furthering his projects; real generosity but accompanied by unreasoning intolerance. A strange mixture which made him unlike anyone I have ever known.

The years rolled on. Suddenly, in about 1954, he rang me up in Suffolk and informed me that he was about to buy a house at East Bergholt, a village near by. My feelings were definitely mixed. I had always retained my affection for him in spite of his infinite capacity to wound those near to him. I knew that life from now on would be less peaceable but was sure it would be more interesting. I was right. In those last years, we were to see much of each other. My wife and children became greatly attached to him and he was constantly in our house at weekends. But woe betide if those visits were not returned so that we could admire the latest development in the new lay-out of the garden, or some new piece of furniture to adorn the house which he had come to love.

Once I had become a member of the Government, this increased my interest to Randolph. He, of course, was by then a leading and controversial political journalist as well as the author of *Lord Derby* and about to be launched on the huge task of the biography of his father. His thirst for information was unquenchable. During the six years I was to be a member of the Cabinet, I was a sitting target. He made no effort to spare me. The telephone rang continuously. Why had Eden decided to retire from Suez? Why had Macmillan sacked Lord Salisbury? Why this and why that? The questions rained down day by day, year by year. They were always pertinent and interesting. But, not surprisingly, they were seldom of the kind on which I wished to make any comment. So a number of years passed during which I endeavoured to switch the conversation to gardening, in which both he and I were developing an absorbing interest. But late at night, this ruse was of little avail and because I refused to talk on the telephone, it was often my dear wife who had to take the brunt of the offensive because I was too tired and perhaps too impatient to cope with Randolph.

Two incidents of this period occur to me. The first was when I was made a peer on becoming chairman of the Conservative Party. He immediately nicknamed me 'Lord Clam of Claydon' (another neighbouring village). This, perhaps, was the greatest compliment he ever paid me.

The second incident was about a year later, when he decided to write a short book about the events leading to Sir Alec Home's selection to succeed Mr Macmillan as Prime Minister. He sent me the proofs of this book, which I smartly returned to him, having flatly refused to read them, explaining that as a rugged individualist he must surely need no endorsement from the chairman of the Conservative Party. He was livid with rage. When the book appeared, he had dedicated it to me. I was speechless but impotent.

Sadly, his years were now drawing to an end. Much of the Randolph we knew began to disappear. He lost his will to attack. He had been lonely for some time and was only at ease with his children, one or two very intimate friends and with the brilliant team of young men including his marvellously loyal secretary, Miss Twigg, who were helping him in his great work on his father's life which he longed to finish.

This was not to be. In the last eighteen months, he almost dreaded seeing people who were not very close to him. He made a great effort and came over to us for the wedding of my youngest daughter, Joanna, of whom he was fond. I used to go over to see him at East Bergholt as often as I could. There was no self-pity and a complete refusal to talk in any detail about his health, which was obviously deteriorating rapidly as each day passed.

He died on a Thursday. As it happened, I was driving from London to my home on the Thursday before and, perhaps from some premonition, telephoned him and invited myself to luncheon. It was a lovely day but rather cold. He insisted on eating outside.

Although he ate next to nothing, he was as usual most concerned about the quality of the food and wine which Andrew Kerr, one of the collaborators on the Winston book, and I were consuming with obvious relish. We retired indoors for a short talk, in which he merely said that he was tired, and that he was saddened by the fact he was not giving enough energy to the book on his father.

His courage remained to the end. It was the sort of courage which his father, whom he so dearly loved, would have saluted with pride. As for me, I mourn this neighbour and friend who, despite the tribulations and irritations which he imposed on others throughout his life, certainly gave much more than he took.

As Biographer

Martin Gilbert
Franklin R. Gannon
Barbara Twigg
Michael Wolff

Randolph and the Great Work

by
Martin Gilbert

(*Fellow of Merton College, Oxford; a research assistant for R.S.C.'s multi-volume Life of Sir Winston Churchill, he was appointed to succeed R.S.C. as official biographer of the remaining volumes; author of* The European Powers, Britain and Germany Between the Wars, *and other works*)

'The only thing that interests me is the *truth*.' At two in the morning, in the midst of an intricate discussion about the confused diplomacy of 1938, this dogmatic assertion seemed somewhat out of place. I began once more to explain the obscure point on which I had rather foolishly embarked. Once again Randolph exploded: 'In this house we are only interested in the *truth*.'

I first met Randolph after he had begun to write his father's Life. Perhaps he had had an earlier career or two, as a pugnacious young man fighting to enter politics, as a journalist in search of a story, or as a soldier in search of war; but if he had really been any of these things, then they belonged, in Hindu fashion, to a previous existence. Few Oxford historians were ever as single-minded as he was about history. At night when the rest of mankind was asleep, or at weekends when the world was relaxing, Randolph was at work. He had never taken a university degree or written a graduate thesis; yet in less than seven years he produced two volumes of narrative and five volumes of documents, nearly 5,000 pages in all, and a life's monument for most writers. Much of this was done during his declining years, while his enormous energies were already slipping away.

Sometimes the slow pace of research vexed him. At such times he found relief in weekly articles, first for the *News of the World*, later for the *Spectator*, in 'rotting the press', in libel actions, and in two privately-printed pamphlets attacking press lords, which were published under his own 'Country Bumpkins' imprint. Sometimes he allowed his attention to be captured by other literary activities—his own autobiography *Twenty-One Years*, and two 'quickies', *The Fight for the Tory Leadership* and, with his son Winston, *The Six Day War*. But each of these books took less time to write than an ordinary historian's summer holiday; and, as all his research assistants were turned on to them, they served as a 'change of air' after which the Boss and the Team would return, physically exhausted but mentally refreshed, to the Great Work.

Would Randolph really stick to his new profession? Did he still, in 1961, hanker after a political career, once the Great Work was done? 'You will make a fine show for yourself about the book,' his father said to him early that year, 'but don't give up politics.' To which Randolph replied: 'Well I am happy with the book and my garden, and we might let politics skip a generation. Perhaps Winston might get interested.' After 1961 politics took second place —so did the garden. A politician might still be rebuked on the telephone for failing to 'stand up and be counted' on some current issue; but it was just as likely that the aim of the call was to seek out a brother's archive or an uncle's diary. Randolph sent off hundreds of letters from East Bergholt in search of new material. He interviewed his father's contemporaries, even the girlfriends of pre-Boer War days. History became his task and his inspiration.

Randolph set about writing his father's Life with the same thoroughness and enthusiasm which his father used to show on entering a new Ministry. With both *The Rise and Fall of Sir Anthony Eden* and *Lord Derby: 'King of Lancashire'* behind him, Randolph was no novice at driving a team. Terse administrative notes were always being drawn up to explain the organization of the work. An effective system soon emerged, buttressed by a considerable collection of *aides-mémoires* and memoranda, the first of these being Ian Coulter's 'Points for Consideration' drawn up in January 1961. Randolph's own 'Directive Number 1' was signed by him on 1 February 1961. It read:

THE BOOK

1. Mr Michael Wolff today assumes control of the organization, research and preparation of all the documents and books necessary for the accomplishment of the enterprise.
2. Mr Ian Coulter will act as his second-in-command and will

execute the plans made by M.W. and approved by Mr. Churchill.

3. M.W. will prepare a short-term, flexible plan covering the next twelve months.

4. It is already agreed that everything connected with the book shall be kept in the Book Office on the top floor.

5. Anything that R.S.C. dictates on to the tape or to Miss Gibson will be transcribed, submitted to R.S.C. and then sent upstairs, where it will be collated by I.C. and Miss Harryman.

6. Miss Gibson will be in charge of the downstairs office, which will regulate everything else. Any correspondence or documents that should come in to her office should immediately be sent upstairs to the Book Office.

7. When Miss Gibson is off duty or away, Miss Harryman will look after the downstairs office without derogation to her duties in the Book Office.

8. At the end of six months M.W. will submit a report of progress and will recommend whether a further amended directive should be issued.

RANDOLPH S. CHURCHILL

Many more directives followed. Chronology books were begun, tracing Churchill's movements month by month—his travels, speeches, political activities and social life. Files were opened for quotations which would act as chapter headings, and with transcripts of the interviews with Sir Winston's contemporaries. Randolph began to record his own reminiscences. The 'Book Office' in which the research assistants worked was established in the upstairs region of the house, guarded over by Miss Eileen Harryman, and replete with Churchill's own press cutting books and *Hansards*. 'Office Instructions Number 1', issued on 2 February 1961, was followed by three more sets of instructions within two days. An intricate system was needed in order to deal as smoothly as possible with over fifteen tons of material—in Churchill's archive alone. When Hugh Trevor-Roper described volume one in *Book Week* as 'a triumph of organization', Randolph was delighted. The growing team of researchers, the directives, the box files, the manila folders, the treasury tags, the duplicate copies, the Xerox machine—all seemed justified.

Although Randolph was impatient of complex arguments and the minutiae of historical evidence, he took his responsibilities seriously. He had no intention of rehashing his father's own works, or glossing over episodes in which his father seemed to have been in the wrong. For more than seven years his ever-growing band of cohorts were sent on a hundred searches for 'the truth'. When he told his father of these efforts, Sir Winston said nervously: 'I hope you'll not waste your time in searching out complicated meticulous facts about me.' To which Randolph replied: 'I hope you don't want us to get these facts wrong.'

On my first visit to East Bergholt in May 1962 I was informed at once that the Great Work was to be written 'warts and all'. Of course, what many readers would regard as warts, Randolph considered beauty spots. But he never suppressed awkward evidence or muted just criticism. Indeed, in Volume One he drew the reader's attention to his father's 'egocentricity which was to become such a predominant characteristic, and to which must be attributed alike his blunders and his triumphant successes'. A. J. P. Taylor quoted this passage in his review in *The Observer* and praised Randolph's 'courageous frankness'.

But of greater encouragement to Randolph than all the reviews was Robert Kennedy's invitation to him to write the biography of John F. Kennedy as soon as the Great Work was complete. 'This is the greatest compliment I have ever been paid,' he told me; and plans for 'Project K' were discussed around the fire at Stour late into many nights. Randolph envisaged a two-volume work, the first on Kennedy's rise to power, the second on his Presidency. At one stage he hoped to begin 'Project K' in 1969, while nearing the end of the fifth and last volume of *Winston S. Churchill*.

As Randolph progressed with the Great Work, it seemed to some that he was criticizing his father less and less. But this was no lapse into filial forgetfulness. Rather, it was a result of the evidence which his assistants found, not only among Churchill's own papers but in the scattered archives of twenty or thirty contemporaries, which showed the extent to which, particularly before 1914, his father had held pugnacious, progressive, radical, and at times almost revolutionary opinions in advance of his time. Nor were the research assistants deliberately setting out to find only pro-Churchill material; by a strange irony the majority of Randolph's 'Young Gentlemen' whose task was to search through the archives were initially quite ill-disposed towards his father, some even hostile. Indeed, I believe that an actual majority of Randolph's team were Labour voters in 1964. It therefore surprised them as much as it surprised Randolph to see how often Churchill had been on the side of the underdog. Whenever a new discovery was brought to him, Randolph purred like a kitten. The document would be read aloud to all callers from the upright 'Disraeli desk' which had belonged to both Disraeli and Sir Winston. Even St Matthew was called upon to supplement Randolph's own exhortations, and in the Book Office he had caused to be displayed 'Advice for a researcher' in a gilt frame: 'Ask, and it shall be given you; seek, and ye shall find . . .'

Despite the many discoveries of Volumes One and Two, Randolph fretted to move on to the period which he himself could remember. Already, in these first two volumes, there had been several comments which showed the extent to which he was straining to get ahead. Typical of many reviewers, Cyrus Sulzberger criticized the 'irritating asides' and Asa Briggs was unhappy about 'too many peeps around the corner into the future'. But these were Randolph's own link with the past. In the early volumes they were no more than amusing marginalia. But in the volume which was to cover the wilderness years from 1929 to 1939 they would have been central. During those ten years Randolph had seen more of his father and shared more of his experiences than anyone else. He had edited a volume of his father's speeches, *Arms and the Covenant*. He knew by instinct facts which a research scholar must grub for in dusty archives, and might still perhaps miss. It was this intimate personal link with his father which would have given Randolph a head start over all other write s when dealing with these years. 'WE START GRUBBING TOO' he once telegraphed to me from on board ship, as he began to scratch the surface of his memory; at such times we Young Gentlemen could only look on in awe. However eager, efficient and inexhaustible we were, he was the Boss, in the historical sense as well. He had done m ore than admire his father and echo his opinions; he had lived th rough the period and had held strong opinions of his own. Nor ha d he lacked confidence in his abilities. For example, in August

1929, having tried to persuade his father that spontaneous speeches were superior to prepared ones, he wrote in his diary: 'I think Papa is gradually coming round to my point of view and is relying less and less upon notes.'

Randolph's historical interests reached their greatest intensity at the time of Munich. His outspokenness, which affected both his friendships and his future, would certainly have dominated the biography. The Men of Munich were his foes. No attack on them could be too severe. As he told Clive Irving in an interview published in *The Sunday Times* in 1964: 'I insulted everybody who was taking what I conceived to be a defeatist view. I dare say this was rather embarrassing to my father because though he fought these issues very stoutly he was always very careful to maintain urbane relations with people of all views. But I rather charged out in every way, and was apt to attack people on any favourable occasion. . . .' Randolph's bias might not have pleased the reviewers, but it would certainly have made explosive reading.

It was of the Munich period that Randolph spoke with the most vivid recollections and the fiercest passion. The last Country Bumpkin pamphlet on which he worked in earnest was a collection of documents intended to 'expose' the activities of the Under-Secretary of State for Foreign Affairs, R. A. Butler, between 1938 and 1940. Randolph believed that when the truth was told it would damn appeasement even more than historians had already done, and would cast his father's behaviour into contrasting brightness. His attitude towards 'the appeasers' had already edged its way into Volume Two, as, for example, when he wrote of Lord Esher (who died in 1930): 'Some may think him an embryo of those busy-bodies . . . who as members of the Cliveden set did our country so much harm between the two wars, barging about in every field with high-minded irresponsibility.' Such was his devotion to anti-appeasement that Randolph was always rather put out by evidence of his father's appeals for Anglo-German co-operation before the First World War.

In his review of Volume Two in the *Daily Telegraph*, Julian Amery hoped that in later volumes Randolph would 'share his conclusions on men and events more fully with the reader'. He would certainly have done so once he had reached the 1930s. Some of the great dramas at Stour centred on appeasement. On one occasion the editor of a national newspaper arrived with his wife for dinner. Before we had been five minutes at table the editor revealed that he had served on the editorial staff of *The Times* during the appeasement period, and, to the horror of the research assistants present, expressed his opinion that Geoffrey Dawson had been right to shorten the despatches of his Berlin correspondent. 'Surely you couldn't have approved of that?' Randolph asked in amazement; 'that was censorship of the worst sort. Dawson was a traitor to his country . . .' and so on for nearly five minutes, with increasing fury. When the tirade was over the editor, quite unabashed, replied calmly that he had not only approved of the cuts, but actually advised them. With a shaking and trembling of his whole mass, Randolph rose from the table, brandished his knife at the editor, and bellowed more savagely than any of us had heard before: 'Men like you should have been shot by my father in 1940.' Then, turning from the table, the knife still held high, he left the room. The editor and his wife had both turned white. On the following morning they breakfasted alone and left the house.

Randolph believed that the Men of Munich, however honourable, were totally misguided, and his criticisms of their action was constant, fierce and well-informed. His loyalty to their opponents was equally impressive. After *The Times* had published a hostile obituary notice of Duff Cooper in January 1954 Randolph helped to assemble in booklet form all the other obituary notices which appeared, all laudatory, some written as direct answers to *The Times*, and a few produced at Randolph's own prompting. Before presenting me with this 'rare work' (on my first evening as a research assistant) he made me read the obituaries aloud, chortling at Brendan Bracken's description of *The Times* as 'a newspaper with a disgraceful record of pandering to Ribbentrop', and moved to tears by his own contribution in *Truth*. He was always urging me to publish various 'Rolls of Honour' concerning this period: a list of all those who had written to congratulate Duff Cooper on his resignation; another list of all who had spoken against Munich between October 1938 and the coming of war; and a list of all those Conservative M.P.s who had courageously voted against Chamberlain in May 1940, including, as he would often point out, his own friends Quintin Hogg, Harold Macmillan and John Profumo, and, somewhat surprisingly, Nancy Astor. When dealing with his father's attitude towards Bolshevik Russia or Indian independence or the abdication of Edward VIII, he would have been as critical of his father as the facts required; indeed he intended to be quite severe. But in the Munich chapters we would have had the passionate appraisal of a partisan; for in his own way Randolph was as active, as enraged, and as 'sound' as his subject.

Randolph was often impatient with the earlier periods of his father's life; but he did not intend to neglect them. Throughout the Great Work he aspired to high professional standards. He had a fine library and a magisterial set of reference books, which he consulted continually. He could sniff out dubious facts like a bloodhound. He believed that nothing need remain obscure for long. In search of unknown documents, he sent his research team to the very ends of the archival earth. His own detailed knowledge was formidable. Above all, he had enormous enthusiasm for recent British history. He demanded at all times to be fed with new material. I once sent him what I knew to be a fine diamond from New York, a complete set of the letters which his father had written to the American politician Bourke Cockran at the turn of the century, and awaited with some complacency his warm approval. To my chagrin I received a telegram which, while starting 'COCKRAN STUFF EXCELLENT', continued imperatively: 'PLEASE GET MORE'. He was quite right; no research ever really comes to an end.

Randolph's telephonic exhortations were often equally maddening. He could be rude, raucous and relentless, both in person and at a distance. The later after midnight, the more impossible his demands seemed to become. The mispronunciation of a single word could lead to fury. No researcher ever found safety in absence: his buzzer reached every corner of the house, except, by a merciful oversight, the Strong Room, where the documents were kept. His telegrams could reach Limbo and penetrate Hell itself. 'PLEASE RING SOONEST. RANDOLPH': these four words were always on the wires. Letters of complaint, written in the most fear-inducing tones, could be followed by even more violent letters announcing that one was sacked. When angry, Randolph could not be soothed. Explanations were twigs cast into an inferno. At his most violent, he was intolerable. But these moments quickly passed; and in the morning all was forgiven.

Although Randolph often appeared to be malicious, he was, I believe, totally without malice. Indeed his magnanimity was on a lordly scale. Often a hard taskmaster, he was always a generous one. The memory of his encouragement and kindness far outbalances the recollection of those horrific moments when storm clouds more fierce than any in nature would burst open. Once, when I evinced a liking for the Boss, his friend Michael Foot said sympathetically: 'Then you belong to the most exclusive club in London—the friends of Randolph Churchill.'

The Lion in Autumn

by

Franklin R. Gannon

(Franklin Gannon, an American, was a postgraduate student at Jesus College, Oxford, when he first started working for Randolph Churchill. After two years at Nuffield College, Oxford, he taught for a year at the London School of Economics before returning to the U.S.A. in 1969; author of The British Press and Germany, 1936–1939)*

I first went up to Stour on a dim November Friday in 1965 to be looked over as a new research assistant. There were other people to luncheon that day, and after introductions all round, and the soon-to-be-familiar injunction to take a drink, I was ignored until just before it was time to leave for the train back to London. Then we were alone with only the firelight to hold back the dull November at the windows, and he spoke quietly and intensely—and as if there were more than three minutes to spare for the train—about his determination to make his Life of his father a monument which would last definitively fifty years and be spoken of ever after as a model of its kind. Would I like to be a part of that Great Work? Would I begin immediately? I said that I certainly would, but that I must leave immediately now or miss the train. He picked up the phone and buzzed Miss Twigg. 'Have them hold the train for Frank, will you please?' he asked casually. I began work the following week, and never looked back.

It was all pretty overwhelming for a young American abroad for the first time. I was fascinated by the endless stories, reminiscences, and anecdotes about 'my Pa'. In the early evenings, as we would sit reading from the galleys or chapters in progress of the Great Work, he would punctuate the reading with remarks, epithets, jokes, and expressive grunts, just as if he were hearing it for the first time, and just as if it were a report of contemporary events. 'Just wait and see what my Pa says about that!' 'Not bad for a young man, what!' 'That's it! That's the stuff! Ho!'

He would move only to use the telephone or to cross the room to make himself a drink. It was not his habit to read anything, but to have everything read to him. He said that hearing words gave him a better sense of their weight and value. The surprising thing was that this method really worked. He would spot a dropped preposition or mis-read phrase from something that had been read to him several hours or even days earlier.

His concentration was visible, almost caricaturish. As he sat in the large green chair, listening intently, staring ahead or into the fire, the ever-present cigarette in his hand and the glass on the table beside him, his shoulders would hunch and his brow furrow. Suddenly he would pick up the phone and call someone about some seemingly unrelated matter. His involvement with the subject and material was so deep that it was impossible to divine the contemporary connexions or associations which some incident or phrase from the past would stir up. The call completed, he would begin to dictate the Great Work in an easy and measured flow.

I had to apply for a work permit, and Randolph had to write to the Home Office explaining why he had not hired an Englishman. He ended his letter by saying, 'Incidentally, since my father was half American, and was an honorary American citizen, I do not really regard Americans as foreigners.'

He was, of course, first and foremost an Englishman, and many times weekend visitors would take me aside and say that they hoped I didn't mind his going on about the faults of 'those United States'. Although he considered America rough and uncultured, he appreciated, as had his father, that the fierce equality and essential democracy which America represents in history is a notable and noble thing. He could not tolerate pretension or fools, and the outspoken strain in the American character which tells such people where to get off was very naturally appealing to him. Like most Englishmen of his class and interests, he loved to mimic an American accent, and like most of them, he did it very badly (on the other hand, his Beaverbrook imitation was almost perfect).

He was in love with the Kennedys, and perhaps the only thing he bitterly held against America was the murder of J.F.K. He could never speak of him without tears. It is probably just as well that Randolph himself was almost past understanding when it was whispered to him that Robert Kennedy had been shot down in Los Angeles. They died not many hours apart.

Any time the then Secretary of Defense was mentioned, Randolph would give a loud rendition of *Macnamara's Band*. Once he began a song, nothing, especially the melody, stood in his way, and nothing could stop him from completing it, his hand beating loud but erratic time on the nearest chair or table. He gave one such memorable rendition of *Lloyd George Knew My Father* to some confused and amused Kennedys while he sat nor'-easter-covered and spray-drenched on the after deck of the *Honey Fitz* off Hyannis. Next to actually being selected to write his father's Life, I think that Randolph's proudest moment was when Senator Robert Kennedy asked him to inscribe one hundred copies of the first volume of the biography of his father as Christmas gifts for the Senator's special friends.

His devotion to Mrs Jacqueline Kennedy was romantic in the chivalrous sense of the word. He was her champion, against the vulgar intrusion of the popular Press, and against the indiscretions of the author of *The Death of a President*. He saw Mrs Kennedy whenever he came to America, and when we were working in the Swiss Valais for a month in 1965, it was like a knightly quest when he chartered a helicopter to take him thirty-five minutes over the Alps to luncheon with her at Gstaad.

Randolph's sense of humour was a very American one. He would enjoy the most sophisticated joke, but just as frequently he would repeat the apocryphal *Variety* headline about the mad rapist who fled 'Nut Screws and Bolts'. He liked the new wave of stand-up comics like Mort Sahl and Shelly Berman, and Bob Newhart's Eisenhower-welcoming-Khrushchev routine was his favourite.

He was a great fan of Tom Lehrer's, and playing at least one side of the latest Lehrer record became part of the nightly after-dinner ritual, along with the ten o'clock news, and the reading aloud, usually from the 'Courtship and Marriage' chapter of Volume Two (with the charming letters between his father and mother) or the section on the 'Naming of the Battleships' (with the King's Secretary's classic line: 'Monosyllables are as a rule a mistake when applied to Battleships . . .'). Lehrer's offhand phrase 'or one of that crowd' (as in 'Mozart or one of that crowd') became a standard part of Randolph's speech, like his unvarying reference to the Luce magazines as '*Time, Life,* and Misfortune'.

One Saturday David Frost brought Tom Lehrer to luncheon. Preparations for a Royal visit could hardly have been more elaborate. A piano was hired and a special menu devised. The meal centred on a *pâté de foie en croûte,* and an hourly kneading schedule was arranged for the dough. Everyone was called upon, and after eighteen hours of virtually continuous kneading, the crust was a deserved triumph.

He derived a mock-blasphemous enjoyment from the fact that I, as a Roman Catholic, could be amused by Lehrer's song *The Vatican Rag,* and wherever we might go where there was a piano, he would insist that I perform it:

> You can do the steps you want if
> You have cleared them with the Pontiff.
> Everybody say his own *Kyrie eleison*
> Doin' the Vatican Rag.

He was also given to readings aloud from Gibbon of the sins of the anti-Pope John XXIII ('the most scandalous charges were suppressed; the vicar of Christ was only accused of piracy, murder, rape, sodomy, and incest . . .') whenever the subject of the Roman Church arose. He said he believed that nothing, except perhaps a boundless void, existed after life, but that he would be willing to entertain direct Divine revelation to the contrary. He claimed to be appalled with the 'bloody-minded God' of the Old Testament, but what religion did appeal to him was mainly of the blood and thunder sort. At his memorial service at St Margaret's, Westminster, which I suspect Randolph himself would have found a great bore, his friends had suggested Ephesians 6 : 10–12 for the lesson:

> Finally my brethren, be strong in the Lord, and in the power of his might.
> Put on the whole armour of God, that you may be able to stand against the wiles of the devil.
> For we wrestle not against flesh and blood, but against principalities, against powers, against the rulers of darkness of this world, against spiritual wickedness in high places.

But the more refined susceptibilities of the Rector of St Margaret's, Westminster intervened and Harold Macmillan read the lesson: Ecclesiastes 3: 1–8, 15, which produced a more touching service, but one which I daresay Randolph would have stormed out of midway:

To everything there is a season and a time to every purpose under heaven. . .

Stour was his home, and as long as he had the newspapers, the telephone, and a steady stream of visitors, he was quite right in saying that he would be a fool ever to leave it. It is a beautiful house, painted a pale pink, set in acres of grounds and gardens. From the broad terrace, a croquet lawn descends to a tennis lawn, and then fields stretch down to the River Stour. Just across, the square tower of Dedham Church stands up above the treetops. Although in the last years he rarely even went out to it, he loved the garden and was very proud of it. He gave Garden Openings for charity which he organized and oversaw as if they were major military operations. The house was in an uproar for days before. The year before he died, when he had to go to the South of France and miss one of the openings, we were all assigned our posts before he left, and he required that we keep hourly records of the attendance and the weather, and he rang just after the closing to get the blow-by-blow account of the afternoon.

Although he was master of his house, in some few important areas the staff had imposed their will on him. Such an area was that of puddings, and perhaps my most significant, certainly my most enduring, contribution to the life at Stour was the restoration of the pudding to its proper place. Randolph had a great sweet tooth, but I was the first ally he found in the battle of sweet against savoury.

When I first arrived at Stour, I duly ate the bit of toast and cheese or egg and anchovy savoury which was served up after dinner instead of a pudding. Then one night we had ice-cream, and I mentioned that this was more to my taste and liking. Randolph, on the spot, put me in charge of devising a pudding menu for the week. The pudding had staged a come-back. Ice-cream was his favourite dessert, but since he required that it be freshly made in the kitchen, we did not have it too often. Usually it would be a soufflé, pastry, or sometimes his other great favourite, Boodles'

Orange Fool. In the summer, we had unlimited fresh strawberries, raspberries, and peaches from the kitchen garden. After I stopped working for him, whenever I would go up to Stour for a weekend, a special pudding would be laid on in my honour, and he took great delight in my reaction to it.

The last entry on his calendar just days before he died noted an impending visit with my mother and sister, for luncheon; it read 'Frank and two Gannons. Have a good pudding.'

Books were even more important than puddings to the life of Stour. They spilled over from the library into the sitting-room, and, finally, when he acquired the books from his father's library at Chartwell, he had shelves built all around. He had a special bookplate saying 'This book is from my father's library' designed to go along with his own which pictured the dogs sitting at the terrace door looking out over the Vale of Dedham.

He had several complete sets of his father's works, including the rare *Mr. Broderick's Army*, and the pamphlet *For Free Trade*. He had a lively interest in the collectors' value of his father's books and paintings and occasionally he would put a set of books on the market to test the price. This would involve elaborate communication links and secret procedures which would even have made John le Carré gasp. It was great fun, especially for Randolph.

He was proud of his specially bound set of inscribed first editions of his friend Evelyn Waugh. He often told the story of Waugh's speech proposing him for White's Club, when he had used three arguments in Randolph's favour: that he was a member of a distinguished and notable family, that he was an outstanding journalist and political observer, and thirdly that he would not avail himself of the facilities of the club very often.

Everything, however, revolved around only one book: the Great Work. He was determined that his Life of his father would be so complete and so magisterial that it would stand unassailable for at least half a century; after that, the passage of time would allow retrospective reappraisals, but even these would be beholden to the Great Work. He really could not believe that anyone working on the Great Work could have a life independent of it. When I finally had to return to Oxford to work full-time on my thesis, he wrote to me, 'I am indeed grieved that your stern masters require you to leave me. But I look forward to your return in the long vac.'

In these last years, his health was particularly susceptible to the state of the Great Work. When I first went to Stour, he was involved with the final preparations of Volume One. He insisted, as had his father, that galley proofs be prepared in specially bound volumes. Dozens of people were called upon to read them and submit comments. Then the bundles of page proofs began to arrive, and there were endless readings aloud of each chapter. The discovery of some hitherto overlooked typographical error or mis-spelling was saluted for the major accomplishment it was.

Then suddenly the last page proofs had been sent back, and it was all over but the waiting. The waiting was the worst part. He tried to occupy himself with the beginnings of Volume Two, but the tension was too great. He began to sleep later into the afternoon, and to be more irritable. He would constantly shift the conversation back to what he was thinking about all the time: how would it be received; who would they get to review it in the *Sunday Times*, in the *T.L.S.* . . . Would the countless people to whom he had been rude, whom he had cut, who had mocked his life as frivolous and flamboyant, who had objected that so great a work should have been entrusted to a competent professional historian—would these people now write their reviews of Randolph S. Churchill instead of the book he had laboured five years, laboured in fact all of his life, to produce?

Randolph's impact on a young and impressionable American was tremendous. He was in many ways a fantastic character like Auntie Mame, right down to the insistence upon immediately look-ing up every uncertain word in the *Oxford English Dictionary*. And he was certainly a subscriber to her belief that 'Life is a banquet and most poor sons of bitches are starving to death'. But he had lived his own life not wisely but too well, and he was now paying the accumulated wages of his sins.

A few days after I began working for him, we put in our first all-nighter. To this day I don't know whether it was a standardized test administered to every Young Gentleman. We talked for hours, and then he began to read. He read Belloc's 'In Praise of Wine'; then selections from John Betjeman (his favourite was 'The Arrest of Oscar Wilde'); then several of his father's speeches from *Step by Step*. Then, for some reason, he picked the *Rubaiyat* from the shelf. I had never heard all the poems read aloud, and by the time he reached the end, after many hours of reading, he was whispering hoarsely, breathlessly.:

> And when Thyself with shining Foot shall pass
> Among the Guests Star-scatter'd on the Grass,
> And in Thy joyous Errand reach the Spot
> Where I made one—turn down an empty Glass!

He closed the book and then rose, stirring up the dogs with the usual, 'Come on, doggies, out you go for a minute. Annie! Boycott!', and went about getting ready for his customary sleep till noon. When I went up to my room, the dawn mist was already rising over the Vale of Dedham. The chill autumn air had made the covers very cold, but I scarcely noticed. I was still transfixed by his extraordinary reading of those extraordinary poems. We were much closer after that night. We were friends then, and when he died less than three years later, I lost a friend.

I last left him as I first saw him: sitting in the great green chair by the fireplace. But everything was different. November had turned to May, and for all the springtime pressing over the terrace, the room was dark and foreboding, His last words, as we rushed for the train, were the usual ones: 'Do keep in touch, Frank. Don't be such a stranger.' I do keep in touch; so frequently a bit of reading or a phrase of conversation will bring him back to mind. And whenever I work or write, I do turn down an empty glass for Randolph. I remember him, and I miss him.

Could You Come Please ...

by

Barbara Twigg

(Private secretary to Randolph Churchill)

This phrase was to become the *cri de cœur*: it was to dominate five years of my life. So much so, that nearly two years later I still have to restrain myself from picking up a ringing telephone, wherever it may be—in someone else's office, private house or even a shop—and from making calls regardless of the hour of day or night. Buzzers still haunt me and at the sound of one my mind is automatically galvanized into action thinking of what excuse I can make this time for not being there at the first buzz.

On 16 March 1963 I was on my way to East Bergholt thinking of the cutting in my bag which said 'Mr Randolph Churchill requires an extra resident secretary at his home in the country: excellent shorthand and typing essential . . .'. I became increasingly nervous at the thought of the word 'excellent' but managed to pass my interview with the shorthand notebook I had been given in readiness for a test still firmly in my handbag. And so the accuracy and speed of my shorthand were never tested.

And so it was that I became Randolph's secretary in May 1963 and remained with him until his death in June 1968. His pursuit of the apposite phrase, the stinging comment or the unusual word made his dictation exceedingly slow and I eventually evolved an abbreviated form of longhand which only I could understand. But Randolph, with supreme confidence in the people he chose, later suggested that I enter the Secretary of Britain contest. I appreciated the compliment but declined the invitation, feeling that although he claimed to know the judges it was best to leave well alone when one would obviously be outclassed, or more likely not in a class at all.

Communications played a large part in Randolph's life. He was fascinated by anything that gave him a sense of increased efficiency, no matter in which department of his household. He had two telephone lines (being at one time the largest private subscriber in the country) with nine extensions, one of which boasted forty feet of cable and enabled him to telephone from his armchair on the terrace in the summer.

These gadgets were imported (often at vast expense) to assist in the fast production of the work in hand, and because of this he was intolerant of any misuse of them or early misunderstandings of the intricacies they might present to their operators. The telex was the greatest example of this. Installed to further communications with Winston in Israel at the time of writing their joint production *The Six-Day War*, it was a baffling machine even to the initiated. The post office's official instructor was firmly told when he came to install it: 'Do not come to my house and tell my secretary how to use a typewriter: she already types at 150 w.p.m.' And as pound notes were burnt in seconds on the telex (which incidentally is very different from a typewriter, having only three rows of keys instead of four) it much reduced the early profits on the book! One evening not long after it had been installed Randolph was sitting on the terrace: I was in my office. The buzzer went and I heard the familiar call 'Could you come please.' I went and without batting an eyelid he dictated the following letter: 'Now that you have become a qualified Telex Operator I would like you to take £1 a week extra.' I typed the letter and laid it on his desk: it was signed and my new salary took effect.

The call could come at any time. I lived in a cottage a mile away from Stour, the house that Randolph bought in 1954 and which was built on the site of the birthplace of John Constable. Oblivious of time, Randolph would think nothing of ringing in the early hours of the morning, and I remember many such calls. 'Could you come please? Where did you put my article for the *Evening Standard*?' 'Could you come please, and see why the radiator in the drawing-room is cold?' 'Could you come please and make some soup and sandwiches for so-and-so who has just arrived?' 'Could you come please and take such-and-such an article to the station: it must be on the editor's desk by 9 a.m.?' And so it went on. . . . Randolph preferred to sit up until dawn and then to sleep until lunch-time: he read the newspapers in the afternoon and liked to work far into the night.

Despite it all, I developed a warm affection for this immensely complex man and little realized how much I should miss him. He was not a man who won the hearts of casual acquaintances—nor indeed did he try to—but to those who gave him their affection and above all to those who worked for him and showed him their loyalty he was the truest and most genuine of friends. His generosity, his humility (though few would believe this) and his ability to bear no malice stand out in my mind. He was demanding of one's time— never believing one had any other life to lead—but he took the precaution of making one learn at the earliest opportunity, and never allowing it to be recited with any faint heart, the following verse:

> The heights by great men reached and kept
> Were not attained by sudden flight
> But they while their companions slept
> Were toiling upwards through the night.

'Box On'

by
Michael Wolff

(One of R.S.C.'s 'Young Gentlemen', he directed the research on the first two volumes of the biography of Sir Winston Churchill)

Once a week, every week for seven years, I make the journey down to Stour. Every week the welcome is the same.

'Ho!'

The black pugs, startled from their 6 p.m. slumbers in front of the smoking log fire, yap around my ankles. 'Boycott! Annie!' Randolph commands. 'Come on, now! Good dogs: don't be silly! Annie! Boycott!' And by now he has hauled himself to his feet from the depth of his green armchair, partly in an unnecessary attempt to pacify the pugs, partly out of an instinctive courtesy to his newly-arrived guest.

'Take a drink, dear.' All friends are 'dear', irrespective of age or sex. 'Have you brought a paper?' He means an evening paper; or, to be more precise, he means the last available edition of the *Evening Standard*. He is incredulous if the occasional visitor confesses that no paper has been brought. 'Left it on the train! Dear, I do wish you'd remember. Never come down without a paper. We country bumpkins depend on it to know what's going on.'

(In the old days we also used to have to bring something from Gow's, the fishmonger near Liverpool Street. A lobster, a dressed crab perhaps—at worst a pound or so of cod's roe. But that was before the itinerant fishmonger came once a week from Lowestoft.)

Randolph again settles down in the big armchair by the fire. 'What news from the great wen?' If there were another 'Young Gentleman' with him, he has been sent out by now, so that the new arrival can impart his information in strictest confidence. Randolph is one of the best-informed men in the country—probably because everybody racks their brains simply to provide him with a tit-bit of new news. But before you have got very far, the telephone rings, and we're off on a new tack. Presently you are given leave to withdraw. 'I expect you'd like to go upstairs to see what's waiting for you.'

'Upstairs' is the Book Office—Arabella's old nursery converted into three separate rooms which serve as research room, office and typists' pool. There, in one of the filing trays allocated to each researcher, is material he asked the secretaries to type or photocopy the previous week. Here, too, are the proofs that have arrived in the last few days, letters that require an answer, and any bits of information or intelligence that belong to your period which may have been picked up by one of the other researchers. On the whole, Randolph lets the secretaries get on with their work without interfering between them and the Young Gentlemen. But Miss Harryman, the archivist, will tell you that quite early in the morning the day you are due to come down he will demand to see what has been done.

It isn't long before the buzzer goes. 'Will you come down and bring anything you've found.' This is the time—one hour before dinner and the hour or two after—when Randolph likes to see the fruits of research. Or rather, he likes to hear it, for he rarely reads an original manuscript or even a typescript copy. He likes 'reading aloud', and though he himself can read a familiar poem or prose passage most eloquently, he prefers the Young Gentlemen to do the reading. Any dinner guest who happens to be around provides a natural captive audience. If the material to be read is designated by Randolph as 'lovely grub' every other researcher in the house is summoned. 'Lovely grub' is original, hitherto unpublished material from either the Chartwell Papers in the strong room or from other archives in London, or from a university library, or from some old lord's muniment room.

It is often 'lovely grub'; and on great occasions the reading takes place from the Disraeli Desk in the window of the library. The Disraeli Desk is a handsome early-Victorian stand-up affair, believed to have belonged to and been used by the great Dizzy himself. It was presented to Sir Winston during the war. By day Randolph uses it occasionally to read a document or sign a letter—or simply to lean over it and gaze at the view of the Stour Valley across the garden. But it is for reading aloud that the desk really comes into its own.

An hour before dinner, perhaps two hours, even longer, afterwards. But it should not be imagined that the reading continues uninterrupted. Even assuming that the dogs settle down right away, there is no guarantee that they will not set up the most fearful barking and yapping every time someone gets up to fetch a drink or shifts in the armchair and pushes off one of the dogs lying on his lap. Nor naturally is the reading without continuous interruption from the telephone. Even when there is no national or international crisis, no election and no war, that telephone rings. But it doesn't ring half as much with outside calls as Randolph uses it to make calls himself. Six calls an hour, an average of five minutes a call—that's half an hour of reading aloud gone.

Nor should it be imagined that the remaining half-hour is uninterrupted. The essence, indeed the charm and the educational value, of reading aloud is contained in the continuous flow of commentary from Randolph that enhances and embellishes it. A name in a manuscript triggers off a fusillade of reminiscence and anecdote, some of it perhaps scarcely germane to the document concerned, yet generally fascinating and nearly always illuminating. Nor is it only anecdotes that these letters spark off. 'Lady Hester—now was she the sister or the mother of the Duchess? Look it up, dear, will you?' And off you go, or someone else, or even the reader himself, to look it up in Burke's or Debrett's or the *Complete Peerage*. Nor will it do just to look it up and find out whether she was the sister or the mother. If it's the *Complete Peerage*, nothing less will suffice than to read out the whole of the relevant biography, where the Duchess and the Duke were buried, how much money he left, and how many acres comprised the estate in 1883. As for the footnotes—once you get involved in them it can be goodbye to the reading for half an hour.

Sometimes it is a phrase that sets off the 'search for truth'. 'I remember my father saying the same thing when he was asked by Max why. . . . He got it from Macaulay.' And Randolph himself gets up to pick out, unerringly, the right volume from the shelves. He fumbles for his glasses, puts them on, adjusts the Angle-poise lamp and within a minute he finds the right place. And then the

'reading aloud' is interrupted for a few minutes by Randolph himself reading aloud—his voice a little hoarse, but full of expression
and sometimes, at a much-loved passage, with emotion. Tears come
easily to his eyes, though he wipes them away as quickly with a
'Warrah! Warrah!'

Words, too, are a frequent source of interruption. He has a
remarkable vocabulary, and he is anxious that his friends and
colleagues should acquire one too. The slightest word that is unusual sends someone scurrying off to the *Oxford English Dictionary*—the big fourteen-volume set—and another reading within the
reading is set in train. Derivation—definition—first recorded use—
all are declaimed and savoured. Not that we confine our activities
to the word under consideration. Any other word on the same page
that happens to catch the eye is brought forward for inspection.
Thus have we chawbacons many a time fossicked over the entries
in the *O.E.D.*

And when the anecdote is at an end, the *Peerage* combed, the
quotation tracked down, the curious word nailed—then Randolph
sits back, takes a sip at his drink and calls out to the reader 'Box on'.
It's a funny, prep-school expression; boys in the ring, in a clinch, a
knockdown or a stumble, the master in charge calls out 'break' or
'stop'; then—'box on'. It is the motto of Stour.

The reading aloud finishes around 11.30 p.m. or midnight. Those
who are not house guests are punctiliously escorted to their cars,
those who wish to retire may do so—all except the Young Gentleman on duty. On the first night of your weekly stay, it is certainly
you, on the second and third probably.

Now the real work begins. Out come the draft text, the current
chapter, the background material to go with it, the files and the
photostats, the relevant books 'flagged' in the right place, the
Annual Register, and, of course, the chronology. The chronology is
something we started right at the beginning—looseleaf, Winston's
life on the right-hand page, general events on the left-hand side,
references to page numbers or files in the archives in square
brackets to each entry. If the chronology is all right, there is no
difficulty in feeding the facts to Randolph. If it isn't there is delay
and exasperation. It isn't always all right. I don't think it ever was.
But Randolph laments: 'I don't know why you haven't kept it up
properly, dear.'

But we make progress. 'The story so far . . . Winston writes to Asquith . . . Asquith replies . . . But that is only a day before Lloyd George said in the House of Commons . . . The historians seem to differ at this point. Taylor says . . . but Jenkins says . . .' Randolph listens, thinks, walks around the room, sits down again, broods, dictates. ' "When Churchill found that" . . . take in that first letter . . . no, why just an extract, let's have it all . . . "Asquith replied to this in magisterial fashion." Colon quote. Take in Asquith's letter . . . Why not all of it? . . . Yes, all right, just an extract . . . Now I want to compose a paragraph about Lloyd George.' Pause for rendering of *Lloyd George Knew My Father*. (If it was about the Prince of Wales, as it was frequently in Volume One, pause for rendering of *God Bless the Prince of Wales*.) Walk out on terrace for some night air: dogs rush out; refuse to come back; scratch at door as soon as Randolph is settled. He gets up to let them in (hardly ever asks you to do it for him), settles down again. 'Now where were we? Ah yes! Box on!'

He dictates slowly—no need for shorthand, though some of the purple passages come with a bit of a rush and it is a good thing to have a few hieroglyphics up your sleeve. Two or three hours of this is as much as you can take. About 2 a.m. you make a move to go to bed. 'You're not tired, dear, are you? Well, let's just finish this bit.' Another half-hour, perhaps an hour. Then you're practically dropping, and your writing gets more and more illegible as you take down Randolph's dictation. You finally insist on going. 'Take a drink. No? All right then—lie down a short while before breakfast. Good night. Thank you very much.' Randolph always says thank you at the end of the day, or when you're leaving at the end of your visit.

He stays on, reading. He usually has two books running at the same time: one on a current topic, usually politics or political biography; the other a new work dealing with the period or with a personality associated with his own great work. He reads carefully, almost minutely, making marginal notes with a pencil and cross-referencing the page numbers on the fly-leaf. Sometimes he will sit reading for two hours, even three. If you're sleeping at the back of the house you may hear him call in the dogs after he has let them out just before going upstairs to bed. You glance at your watch. Five o'clock.

The outside secretaries arrive at 9 a.m. so there is no point in wasting their time. If you haven't done it before going to bed you get up early enough in the morning to make sure that they can type out the previous night's work, insertions and all, first thing in the morning. And while they go ahead with that you start preparing for the coming evening's work, or look for some good grub, or simply get bogged down in the administration answering tom-fool letters. The early-morning hours are valuable, for at 11.30 Randolph buzzes. 'Good morning, would you come down a minute?'

'Down' is his bedroom. But in fact he has been awake an hour or two, reading the papers, making telephone calls, breakfasting. 'What are you up to this morning?' he asks straight away. 'Have you found anything?' He tosses over the morning mail. 'What do you think of this? What shall we do about that? That's a rum one!' The day's plans are run over—who's coming to lunch, what new instructions should be given. The morning news is discussed—the result of the morning phone calls analysed. 'I'll be down in half an hour. I hope we'll have something ready.'

By noon the previous night's work is typed, corrected and collated. Fourteen hundred words. Pretty good—but par for the course, that's all. Downstairs again, Randolph has it read over to him. He makes corrections, he fights some of the same arguments he had been over only ten hours before, but in the end this draft is accepted and passed by him—destined for repolishing four or five months later.

After luncheon—never lunch—there may be a further reading if there is a visitor who is interested. (The evening readings are for all guests whether they are interested or not.) Otherwise, after a walk around the garden, back to the book in hand, or to hear (privately) some 'lovely grub' until 6 p.m. when, for an hour, Randolph is given a foretaste of the evening's work ahead.

The routine rarely varies. (Though when there are trips abroad, or wars to be fought, everything is brought to a standstill.) Weekday or Sunday—there is virtually no difference. For the three-days-a-week Young Gentleman there are the frustrations, but there are also the rewards. Time is short, and we want to get on. Randolph, pressing the buzzer assiduously, is the worst interrupter. But then, he interrupts himself too until he remembers the task in hand. 'Box on,' he says to himself.

'Must you go? There's plenty of time before the train leaves.' Actually, there are exactly nine minutes, but he knows it should not take more than eight to get there. When there are only seven and a half left, he says anxiously, almost reproachfully: 'Well, I really think you ought to get going if you're to catch the train.'

He gets up; the dogs spring up with him, yapping around my ankles. Ceremoniously he escorts me to the front door. He has remembered my wife and caused a splendid bunch of flowers to be picked from the garden. 'My love to Rosemary. . . . Thank you. . . . Keep in touch. . . . Hurry back.'

The car drives off. The dogs run after it. 'Boycott! Annie! Come on, now! Good dogs: don't be silly! Annie! Boycott!'

Friends

Hugh Trevor-Roper
Xenia Field
Sir Isaiah Berlin
Arthur Schlesinger, Jr
Jacqueline Onassis
Aristotle Onassis
The Rt. Hon. Harold Macmillan
Lady Diana Cooper

Randolph Churchill

by

Hugh Trevor-Roper

(British historian and writer: Regius Professor of History at Oxford; author of The Last Days of Hitler, Historical Essays, *and many other works)*

The late Bernard Berenson used to divide humanity, for some purposes, into two classes: the life-enhancing and the life-diminishing. It is a categorization which I have found very convenient—indeed, for social purposes, academic appointments, etc., absolutely fundamental. Randolph Churchill was one of the most life-enhancing of all my friends. Perhaps some people found him at times *too* life-enhancing; but I am not at the moment concerned with those other people: I am concerned only with our direct relations.

How often the telephone would ring—even that neuter instrument would seem, in retrospect, more positive, more imperative when it was to be the channel for his voice. 'Mr Randolph Churchill', the discreet feminine voice would begin—one of the *équipe* at Stour —but would scarcely finish the syllables before being overtaken by the more commanding tones of the Master. One expected a command. Even invitations were commands. So, of course, were self-invitations.

For instance, there was that invitation to a televised weekend at his house. He had commanded the B.B.C. to be present to record our conversation. Would we attend? There would be an elegant, sophisticated party. It was time that the lower classes realized, through the medium of the goggle-box, how their betters lived, how cultivated, sparkling and wide-ranging was their conversation over the candle-lit decanters. . .

We duly arrived at Colchester station. A young man—another of the *équipe*—had been despatched to meet us. He could not drive the car, but of course his protestations had not been heeded: theirs not to reason why. At the village of East Bergholt all was confusion. B.B.C. vans besieged the house, cables entwined the banisters, an army of technicians, as required by union rules, got in one another's way. The guests gathered for their instructions: the ladies were told to 'look decorative and keep their traps shut': only masculine conversation would be worth recording. Then there was a brief general rehearsal, and we relaxed for a night and a day to ease ourselves into the appropriate conversational stride.

I am afraid that that elegant evening, which cost the B.B.C. an astronomical sum to record, was never transmitted to the culture-hungry lower classes. It was not that the conversation was lacking. We all talked brilliantly, even some of the ladies who, while waiting to be joined after dinner, were skilfully misled into believing that they were actually being recorded and almost burst themselves to exhibit their culture. Indeed, even when masculine conversation was in full swing my wife, who was obeying her orders to be decoratively silent, received a sharp kick from Randolph, followed by the command 'look more animated!' But in the end, as sometimes happened even in that highly-organized household, a technical hitch ruined all. In his desire to keep up the level and pace of conversation, Randolph had assumed the posture of an orchestral conductor, and had placed himself more strategically for that purpose than conveniently for the camera. Those who saw the programme privately exhibited in Broadcasting House reported that human voices could indeed be heard, but on the screen only Randolph's bottom could be seen, as he stood, leaning forward, to encourage and regulate the conversation.

Randolph was a great believer in civilized after-dinner conversation, even when the lower classes were not looking, and he was not to be denied this pleasure by any alternative arrangement. There was once an unfortunate episode when he was so denied. I record it—much softened—as he described it to me afterwards. He was coming to Oxford to bring his son Winston back to college, and they had arranged to spend the night with their cousin, the Duke of Marlborough, at Blenheim Palace. At first all had gone well. They had changed, they had come down to dinner. But what was Randolph's dismay when he saw, confronting them at table, a television-screen. Such a thing had never been endured at Stour, and it was not to be endured at Blenheim. Randolph rebuked his ducal cousin, pungently I have no doubt, for this plebeian welcome: a gentleman, he said, expected something different, especially on a rare visit from a distance. The dialogue, as afterwards reported by Randolph, was in the high style, for the duke is not noted for returning soft answers, or the other cheek; but as I have it by hearsay only, I shall (though with difficulty) resist the temptation to recapitulate it. Suffice it that Randolph, unwilling to compromise on so important an issue, was turned out of doors—'We shall be very pleased to see *Winston* again' were the last words he was conscious of hearing from his host—and soon afterwards two insulted figures appeared at our house in Oxford, seeking hospitality for the night. I was very sorry that we happened to be away from home when they arrived. The narrative of their sufferings was vivid enough afterwards. At the time, it would, I am sure, have been even more memorable.

As this story shows, Randolph did not always (or should I say 'ever'?) accommodate himself to his company. He was a law to himself; and whereas his close friends would allow him to be as outrageous as he liked (for he was a good friend, a foul-weather friend, and to such everything is forgiven), there were hazards in introducing him to strangers. I well remember one evening when he telephoned to propose himself after dinner. It happened that we had a dinner party that night, and I was not certain how Randolph would fit in with some of our guests, whom I hardly knew myself. However, a chance remark saved all. 'Surely,' Randolph said to me, in response to some observation, 'surely that showed supine in-attention on your part?' 'You are quoting Gibbon,' said Sir Ronald Syme, the Camden Professor of Ancient History, who happened to be of the company; and he completed the quotation: 'but how shall we excuse the supine inattention of the pagan philosophers. . . ?' Randolph, like his father, was a great admirer of Gibbon. I think that I know my Gibbon too. So does the Camden Professor. So from that point we were off. Quotation followed quotation, each more outrageous than the last. I am not sure that the clergyman present altogether approved of the passage about 'the virgins of the warm climate of Africa, disdaining an ignominious flight . . .'. But there was safety in numbers.

Randolph had a real taste for and command of the English language. Like his father, he learned from good masters, and he was a stickler for right usage, but he wielded it with power, flexibility and a full-blooded buoyancy of spirit, so that his correct diction never seemed laboured or pedantic. When he took trouble, he was a first-class political journalist. This was partly because—again like his father—he enjoyed 'the great game of politics', seeing the comedy as well as the seriousness of it and rising, irrepressible and only superficially bruised, after every fall. I think that this is what made him so sympathetic to Harold Macmillan, who also enjoyed that great game, and so unsympathetic to Lord Avon, who did not.

When I think of Randolph, I always feel a rush of pleasure to the memory or the heart, or wherever the seat of pleasure is. This, indeed, is what is meant by life-enhancing. Every man who adds to the life of others must sometimes give out more than he can generate and feel the void of that evacuation; but if Randolph was ever depressed, I never saw him in that state. Even when I visited him in hospital, after a serious lung operation, I was surprised to find him in the highest of spirits, wreathed in tobacco-smoke, dispensing champagne, and ready for some new adventure. But my most vivid memories of him are at Stour, the charming house which he organized, under the trade name of Country Bumpkins Ltd, as a *scriptorium* or writer's factory. And I think particularly of the remarkable household which he had organized there: what I have called the *équipe*.

I can only describe the *équipe* from outside, as I observed it: its inner organization and functions were always a mystery to me. Basically, it seemed to me, Randolph organized his life by drawing on a small but specialized pool of labour and exploiting it on his own terms. He discovered a series of young men who were prepared to accept a kind of employment more familiar in an Oriental court than in our modern society. These young men no doubt had some fixed duties of a literary or scholarly kind. They also enjoyed the social opportunities of Randolph's house. They met the great and fed, at times, on caviare and champagne. At the end of their service, they were planted out in the City or elsewhere. But meanwhile they paid a price. No union protected them from the caprices of their employer. They were half-courtiers, half-slaves. They might be sent, at any hour, on any errand. They might be made to read to their master, to climb a tree, or dance a gopak. Occasionally I was reminded of the 'young Levite' described by Macaulay, the chaplain maintained by the Tory squire of the seventeenth century, who, besides his professional duties, and his functions as the most patient of butts and listeners, would 'save the expense of a gardener or of a groom'. 'Sometimes the reverend man nailed up the apricots, and sometimes he curried the coach-horses. He cast up the farrier's bill. He walked ten miles with a message or a parcel.' Etc., etc. Randolph's young men needed, above all, a sense of humour. Fortunately those whom I knew always had one. No doubt it was written into the contract.

The other aspect of Stour that lives in my memory is the garden. In his last years Randolph became an expert and enthusiastic gardener. His garden had a beautiful position, looking over the valley of the Stour—Constable's country—and he set out to exploit its possibilities with great imagination. I shall never forget our last visit to him there. It was May. Great clusters of wistaria hung over the trellised walk; the *Clematis montana* had been carried up to the treetops and was in flower; the woodland garden was crowded with peonies. Randolph had grandiose plans of future development and he expounded them, as always, with *brio*. But I must confess that it was on that occasion that I first listened to him with a sense of melancholy. When a man thinks of planting trees, says Dr Johnson, it is a sign that he is growing old; and Randolph, on that occasion, looked old: he had suddenly aged. And yet his great task, the Life of his father, towards which the whole *équipe* was groaning and travailing, was still to come. Would he ever complete that vast undertaking? I asked myself. Walking in that delightful garden, with its prospect of the river and the gentle Suffolk hills, I recalled the sensations of Randolph's (and my own) favourite author, in his garden overlooking the Alps and the Lake of Geneva, that 'two causes, the abbreviation of time and the failure of hope, will always tinge with a browner shade the evening of life'.

Gardening with Randolph

by
Xenia Field

(British journalist: Garden Editor of the Daily Mirror; *an early crusader
for prison reform)*

His hands were small and strong, but somehow they were shy
and almost afraid of the touch of the soil.

He was pushing fifty when he made his first planting. I brought
him a box of pink button-daisies from Colchester and gave him the
know-how for planting them. He rushed off into the garden with a
trowel and tremendous enthusiasm to put them in, and hovered
round the plants with a watering-can in hand throughout the weekend. It was a great misfortune that not a pink daisy survived.

From this day onwards Randolph determined that he was not
cut out for a labouring gardener and regarded his function as that
of a constitutional monarch as defined by Bagehot: 'to be consulted,
encouraged and to warn'.

Stour was a skilfully designed garden on the Suffolk–Essex
border with particularly fine limes, cedars and oaks that framed an
authentic Constable view of Dedham Vale and church tower.

The house stood on the crest of a hill and the lawn sloped down
towards the Stour valley and river, that appeared every now and
then in the changing light.

The garden work he really enjoyed was watering, with hose and
as many modern gadgets as available and if possible with a listener
with a political bias to help him sort out his ideas for his weekly
article for the *News of the World*. Water flowed freely day and night
during deluge or drought; whatever the cost or shortage the self-
styled 'watering boy' kept at it.

The garden was suffering certain neglect when R.S.C. took over
in 1954. There were armies of weeds and no flowers, but the neglect

if anything showed off the beauty of the view for there were no distracting et ceteras.

There then followed a further year during which the garden was still uncared for, Randolph being completely absorbed by the possession of the first home of his own. Bright décor, pictures and furnishings and in particular apricot flock wallpaper in his sitting-room delighted him. Meanwhile, the lawn fast became a hayfield and nettles, thistles and docks sprang up everywhere. The garden deteriorated to jungle land.

It was not until his wife June left him, his irritated newspaper editors upbraided him, and his money became insufficient to meet his generous spending that he turned to gardening, perhaps as an escape. It was a welcome outlet during a troubled period.

Two (or was it three?) head gardeners came and went but neither they nor Randolph could make head or tail of one another and there were scenes, tantrums and rages, about what should or should not be done. Finally after a volcanic upheaval he appointed himself his own head gardener.

This arrangement proved fairly peaceful but the weeds remained in command, there were few flowers and no vegetables. However, the lawn that was first priority was to some extent recovered, but not without sweat and tears. Through Randolph's over-enthusiasm the turf was treated to an overdose of fertilizer that burnt and blackened the grass.

I received a series of telegrams on the subject. 'Lawn ruined. Grass funeral black, my summer wrecked: Come as soon as possible.'

When I arrived at Stour Randolph insisted on my getting in touch with Fison's to ask them to come and see 'the devastation'. A representative from the firm duly arrived on Sunday morning and there was an immediate rumpus on the lawn.

Randolph was in his pyjamas, which kept on tumbling down in the funny unaccountable way that his trousers often did. Nothing could persuade him that the lawn was not ruined. He let loose a torrent of oaths, threats and his special swear words, all the while shaving with an electric gadget he had recently been given while in America. Servants and secretaries popped their heads out of the windows to watch, and the four or five black pugs looked up and pricked their ears. It was just one of those upsets that happened from time to time, loud and disrupting and holding up everything while they lasted. Upsets that friends understood and accepted but that quite naturally shook a visitor. By luncheon the rumpus was forgotten by everybody but the Fison representative, and the lawn returned to a satisfactory green after a noisy thunderstorm a few days later.

In 1958, infuriated by the fast-increasing plantains on the lawns, Randolph organized a 'plantain sweepstake', certainly the first of its kind. The winner would be the child who could pull from the Churchillian lawns the plantain with the longest root. The prize was £5 and there were to be four consolation prizes.

Printed posters advertised that 'Operation Plantain', an open competition, had as its object the eradication of weeds from the Stour lawns for all time. Its instigator hoped that the scheme might well spread throughout the country.

Ice-cream was served to the workers while Randolph harangued them as to the knack of the job: 'to pull, to twist and then to ease up gently'. His daughter Arabella and I were among the judges who measured the plantains and Nancy, Viscountess Astor, presented the prizes.

The prize of £5 for the longest plantain pulled by a child between the ages of eight and sixteen went to the gardener's son, who staunchly refused to tell Lady Astor what he was going to do with the money. 'I am not interested in gardening at all,' he said bravely, 'I want to be a vet.' Among grown-ups who had a try at pulling was a Kensington visitor who won a consolation prize for a fourteen and a half inch root.

In spite of unusual onslaughts on the weeds disorder triumphed, and Randolph ceaselessly wandering around his garden became disconsolate. Nature was getting the better of him. It was about this time that his neighbour Colonel Corke, late Indian Army (retired), offered to take over.

It was a crazy and unsuitable plan unlikely to succeed, but it came off. The dear patient colonel slogged with the minimum of equipment and inferior assistant labour to bring chaos under control.

And because Randolph knew that the new 'head' would give notice if tried too far he bit his lip and behaved himself even when itching to let fly. 'I'll go in and write my art-i-cle,' he'd bravely smile, adding under his breath: 'The Colonel's bitching up that border.'

Randolph's forced self-control and Mike's Army discipline and training enabled the relationship to last two years. It finished in friendship when Mike and his wife decided to build a house in a different part of the country.

An excellent head gardener, Mark, was engaged to take over, and the garden at long last found itself in capable professional hands.

Randolph now concentrated on training a canopy of wistaria, honeysuckle, roses and clematis over a colonnade on the terrace, much used for eating out. He was the arbitrator whose job it was to see there was fair play between the fragile clematis and the rampant honeysuckle. He had a bias for the climbing Ena Harkness, and I remember getting a telegram 'Come, Ena in explosion'.

He supervised the work of clearing a path through the wood round the wild garden and back through a planting of nuts where cowslips had been introduced into the meadow grass. The cowslips were, as they so often are, unwilling to naturalize at short notice and Randolph soon lost patience with the 'obstinating buggers'.

The path around the wood and wild garden was cleared when he was fit and well but he explained that it was to be finally widened to take an invalid chair when he reached old age. He also made plans for a waterfall to rush by the banks where he had planted his much-loved specie roses—when finances allowed. But when money became available it was passed at lightning pace to other more urgent ploys.

Among other innovations were a lime avenue—unsuitably sited beneath immense and veteran limes that overshadowed the newly planted tunnel—and plantings of peonies and 300 dwarf alpine evergreen azaleas from the Rothschild nursery which led a thirsty existence on a desert-dry shady bank in the wood. Randolph, impervious to argument, was determined that these plants enjoyed the heavy shade. They might well have died altogether had not a gale blown down a number of the biggest trees, thinning out overhanging branches.

For some time Randolph had had a fancy for a herbaceous border and he finally ordered one *en bloc* of some two hundred plants, at the cost of some eighty pounds. It was a dull border lacking character, *sans* taste, *sans* colour, *sans* everything. But to Randolph who seldom discriminated between plant and plant, it was a herbaceous border and filled the bill. He had done it his way, ordering it off his own bat and that was important to him.

On the terrace immediately below the balustrade and against the house there were masses of tulips in the spring. He got to like the lily tulips and 'China Pink' went well with the Suffolk pink of the house.

Wallflowers and forget-me-nots were followed by dahlias, a rich medley, planted without design. He preferred it that way and with no eye for colour was inclined to belong to the school of thought that believes that flowers do not clash. If two dahlias flowered happily together cheek by cheek it was by chance.

Now to the most exciting adventure that Randolph made in his garden, the blue polyanthus river that travelled through the woodland.

Half an ounce of blue polyanthus seed, at £15 an ounce, was ordered from Suttons of Reading. It was sown and pricked out by Mrs Corke, Mike's wife, the seedlings planted out in the autumn of 1960. In 1961 the river was in full flood and gorgeous, the yearling plants being in their prime. It was an enchanting display with a touch of Churchillian genius, the inspiration of a literary man rather than a gardener.

In the autumn of the following year the plants were divided and the river extended both north-east and south. But as primula fans well know, divided plants have not the vigour of the yearlings, and there was a deterioration in both size and colour of bloom. Now Randolph, wishing to reinforce success, had the unfortunate idea that a fringe of yellow polyanthus would suggest a river edge of foam.

But the picture he had in his mind failed to reproduce itself in the woodland and the creams and yellows were a sad disaster, spoiling the original effect.

It is hoped that the blue river will never cease to flow at Stour and that it will remain the mark of Randolph Spencer Churchill, together with the yellow aconites that he loved and dubbed the 'golden herald of the snowdrop'.

Randolph got little enjoyment out of other people's gardens and found enchantment only in his own.

To the last days he would look out of his window to the Constable view, Dedham church tower and valley and ask his friends, 'Aren't I lucky to have this garden? How can people live in London? Will the white wistaria flower this year? I've given it lots and lots of splendid grub. It should be grateful. Look, watch the river now in the changing light.'

Randolph

by

Isaiah Berlin

(British historian and writer: Fellow of All Souls; President of Wolfson College, Oxford; Chichele Professor of Social and Political Theory 1957–67; author of Karl Marx, The Age of Enlightenment, Two Concepts of Liberty, *and other works)*

Randolph, if not altogether house-trained, seemed to me altogether free from fear, almost too fearless, if it is possible to be so, both morally and physically. He was liable to suit the action to the word more or less instinctively, which led to consequences which were, at times, counter-productive.

I remember that one afternoon, just before the celebrated Fulton Address delivered by his father in the late spring of 1946, the door of my office in the British Embassy in Washington was flung open, and Randolph appeared, dishevelled, with one of his trousers slightly torn at the knee. He was violently flushed, and was pressing a handkerchief to a bleeding wound just below his left eye. In answer to my inquiry, he said—so far as I now recollect—something like this:

> I went to see a man in the State Department, called, I believe, Braden [Spruille Braden]. He seems to have occupied some kind of post in the Argentine. I believe he was American Ambassador there. I tried to interview him about Latin America. In the course of the interview he made highly offensive remarks about England and her policies. I struck him at once. I always do that to anyone who attacks my country; don't you?

Randolph was not entirely suited to peacetime conditions. But he was rich in military virtues. His views were sometimes those of a very young, ungrown-up undergraduate, but he was brave, simple, uncalculating, truthful, loyal, eccentric, and at times wildly enter-

278

taining. There was something arrested about him; he was given to romantic fantasies both personal and political, and these seemed to me to spring from appalling frustration and misery. His violence and lack of control which sometimes took alarming forms, were at the same time pathetic, disarming and childlike. Sober, and in the company of those with whom he felt secure, he was peaceful and courteous. He drank a good deal, and could then be a terrible bore: yet even then he could inspire affection, and was capable of deep affection himself. There was something at once disturbing and sweet about his expression in repose. His world was as black and white as his father's. He believed in the simple maxim of being amiable to his friends and appallingly rude to his opponents. He was a staunch and loyal friend; his enemies (as opposed to those who merely found his behaviour on occasion offensive or embarrassing or barbarous) were, on the whole, men a good deal inferior to himself.

Randolph Churchill

by
Arthur Schlesinger, Jr

(American historian and writer, winner of two Pulitzer prizes: Albert
Schweitzer Professor of Humanities at the City University of New York;
author of The Age of Jackson, A Thousand Days: John F. Kennedy
in the White House, *three volumes of* The Age of Roosevelt, *and*
other works)

I saw Randolph from time to time through the years. mostly with
two people of whom he was genuinely fond—Kay Halle in Washington and Charles Wintour in London. One has a montage of
memories: Randolph arguing with a cop in Georgetown who had
dared stop a car he was driving rather uncertainly down 29th
Street sometime in the 1950s; Randolph, red-faced and exultant at
the Democratic convention in Los Angeles in 1960, rejoicing over
the nomination of John Kennedy, whom he adored; Randolph
telling with relish of a dinner given by Otto Preminger in Hollywood in which he successfully insulted so many guests that eight
people, he claimed, had left the table; Randolph conducting a marvellous discourse on the Munich period in which he gave the leading characters a series of Joycean names—Chamberpot and
Holyfox and Mountbottom; Randolph drinking beer at Claridge's
while he discussed the way he proposed to organize the writing of
his father's Life.

I found him, nearly always, courteous, entertaining and no more
disagreeable than the occasion demanded. Perhaps because I saw
him so often in the company of people he really liked, I missed
most of the historic rages that appear to have adorned his social
progress. There were, of course, exceptions. In the spring of 1963
he came to Washington to receive on his father's behalf the
Honorary American Citizenship bestowed by President Kennedy
as the result of the long campaign by Kay Halle. The night before
the ceremony, I went over to Kay's to see Randolph. Let me quote
the account in my journal:

I arrived late and found Randolph obviously in a bad temper. After dinner he led me back into the dining-room, shut the door, poured a drink and complained about 'gabby American women'. We stayed there drinking for the next couple of hours, while the party continued in the living-room. Having separated himself from the women, Randolph became exceedingly charming and interesting. He told a great story about his father. During his first lecture tour to the United States, the American Winston Churchill presided over his meeting in Boston. The British Winston said to the American Winston, 'Why don't you run for the Presidency of the United States? Then I will become Prime Minister of England, and we can amaze everybody.' I asked Randolph about his impressions of F.D.R. Randolph praised his domestic policy but felt that his foreign policy during the war had produced great mischief. He had only met him a few times and felt him to be rather a 'feminine' figure with visible prima-donna traits of jealousy. Then he added, 'But his voice—a great voice—instinct with courage. Even more so than my father's.'

This particular evening ended with a quarrel between Randolph and Kay about the circumstances of a luncheon which took place after F.D.R.'s election in 1932. Randolph had invited Kay and Jimmy and Betsy Roosevelt to lunch with his father at Chartwell. Randolph insisted that Joe Kennedy also was there. Kay denied this, trying to remind Randolph of his dislike for Joe Kennedy and saying that he would not possibly have invited him to Chartwell. As for Kay, she recalled Mr Churchill's having drawn an inter-twined dollar and pound sign and giving it to Jimmy to take to his father. Randolph said irritably that, while his father on occasion had drawn such symbols, he had not done so then. They argued back and forth, with Kay signalling covertly to me that Randolph had drunk too much; finally he decided to call Jimmy Roosevelt and settle the matter. Jimmy produced a Solomonesque resolution: Joe Kennedy, he said, had *not* been at the luncheon, and Winston Churchill had *not* given him a drawing to take to his father.*

* Editor's note: As Jimmy had been awakened at 2 a.m. by Randolph's calls, the following day he affirmed the truth of the 'dollar-sterling' happening. See Kay Halle, *Irrepressible Churchill, A Treasury of Winston Churchill's Wit*, New York: World Publishing, 1967.

The next afternoon the ceremony conferring the honorary citizenship on Winston Churchill took place in the Rose Garden at the White House. Randolph, resisting, as he later told me, the temptation to mimic his father, read the letter of acceptance with great dignity. The crucial sentence in his father's letter was a majestic rejection of the view which relegates Britain to a 'tame and minor' position in the world. This was obviously aimed at Dean Acheson for his statement that Britain had lost an empire and had failed to find a new role. Dean was present and, during the reception afterwards, remarked, 'Well, it hasn't taken Winston long to get used to American ways. He was not an American citizen for three minutes before he began attacking an ex-Secretary of State.'

I remember, too, another evening at Kay Halle's with Randolph, Franklin D. Roosevelt, Jr., and Robert Kennedy. Bobby, though much the youngest, somehow dominated the evening with his urgent vitality and teasing wit. One wondered a bit about families. Winston Churchill and Franklin Roosevelt were incontestably greater men than Joseph P. Kennedy. Yet Randolph and Franklin Jr., both men of talent and charm, seemed to have lived lives beneath their promise and capacity; while the sons of Joseph Kennedy, endowed somewhere with a capacity for self-discipline, had risen beyond their father, and no doubt, because of him.

The sadness of Randolph's life was the wrecking of his great gifts and hopes, though the wounds, of course, were largely self-inflicted. The happiness came when his remarkable qualities at last found magnificent fulfilment in the biography of his father. By now this once robust man had grown wan and frail. He looked much older than his years. He confined his drinking to beer. His manner had a surprising gentleness, and his skin was acquiring an illusion of transparency. One felt that he knew he had only a short time to live.

But the volumes he wrote showed no diminution of vigour. They are magnificently done, and his father would certainly have been proud of him. In spite of himself, Randolph left a monument behind.

Randolph

by
Jacqueline Onassis

(Wife of Aristotle Onassis; widow of the late President John F. Kennedy)

Dear Kay:

I can't write what I feel about Randolph.

He was my friend.

You know how Jack and Bobby loved him—but did you know how my son John loved him?

It started when John was 4 or 5 and Randolph came to the Cape. He was fascinating to children—at least to John. He was completely himself—and never changed gears for them.

Randolph had decided to have first editions of all Winston Churchill's books beautifully bound, and was going to give them to Jack's Library. He told me that at the time of Runnymede.

But one day after he had left Hyannis Port he wrote me that he disapproved of giving things to institutions—and he sent them all in a painted tin trunk, to give to John. They are 49 volumes and they are in the bookshelves in the dining-room, beside Jack's Marlborough, which he read when he had scarlet fever as a boy, and the Churchill books he had at Harvard.

At supper the children have invented a guessing game— 'which of Winston Churchill's books are they thinking of?' They used to stump Bobby with it, and be so delighted, as he would always guess the ones we have all read—and they would rattle off, *London to Ladysmith via Pretoria, Painting as a Pastime, Savrola, Liberalism and the Social Problem, Malakand Field Force, The Sinews of Peace*, etc.

John is always taking one out—together they cover about 10 running feet—and asking me what it is about.

It is because he enjoyed Randolph that he cares about the books.

If, when he is older, he finds in them what his father found in them—that would be this strange, touching legacy of Randolph's. Winston Churchill and Randolph outlived Jack—but maybe Randolph will be the one to draw John to the books that shaped John's father.

That sounds too sentimental. Maybe John won't like books at all—but it touched me so when Randolph did that—and I thought you might not know it.

Sometimes you hear people describe him as such a flamboyant character—but all I can ever think of about Randolph is his incredible sweetness.

Love,
Jackie.

I remember Randolph, on a spring day after rain, with the afternoon sun streaming into the Green Room.

We sat around a table—Randolph and young Winston, Sissie and David Harlech, Kay Halle and Jean Campbell, with glasses of warm champagne—and I was so happy for Randolph, I wished that moment to last for ever for him.

It was the day Jack had proclaimed Sir Winston Churchill Honorary Citizen of the United States. There had been the ceremony in the Rose Garden, a reception in the White House. Now Jack had gone back to his office, the last guest had wandered out, and we had gone to sit in the Green Room to unwind together.

Jack had cared about this day so much.

We met in his office. Randolph was ashen, his voice a whisper. Someone said he had been up most of the night. 'All that this ceremony means to the two principals,' I thought, 'is the gift they wish it to be to Randolph's father—and they are both so nervous it will be a disaster.'

The French windows opened and they went outside. Jack spoke first but I couldn't listen—every second was ticking closer to Randolph. Then the presentation.

Randolph stepped forward to respond: 'Mr President.' His voice was strong. He spoke on, with almost the voice of Winston Churchill, but they could imitate Sir Winston, and Randolph's voice was finer.

He sent his words across the afternoon, that most brilliant, loving son. His head was the head of his son beside him—Randolph and Winston—those two names that would for ever succeed each other as long as Churchills had sons. And Randolph speaking for his father. Always for his father.

But that afternoon, the world stopped and looked at Randolph. And many saw what they had missed.

After—in the Green Room—the happy relief—Randolph surrounded, with his loving friends—we so proud of him and for him—he knowing he had failed no one, and had moved so many.

I will for ever remember that as Randolph's day.

Randolph, my Friend

by
Aristotle Onassis

(*Greek shipping magnate and businessman: a close friend of the late Sir Winston Churchill*)

Most sons are born to redeem the evils or the virtues of their fathers.

It is easier to redeem the evils of a father, far more difficult to redeem his virtues.

If this principle is coupled with the fact that Randolph had an excess of the qualities needed to redeem the virtues of his father, we can perhaps think that he was confused in the process of the struggle.

His was such an exuberance of talents. Without exaggeration, I believe that the brilliance, the nobility of feature, the rhetoric, the voice, all such vital generators of public appeal—Randolph had these in excess of his father.

Sometimes I wonder if he was not a victim of his own most rare and valuable human qualities, particularly in the domain of public life.

He was as stubborn as he was loyal, and as loyal as only one as stubborn can be; whether to a cause or to individual friends.

Such qualities, as beautiful as they are, are an anathema to flexibility. For one who aspires to political life, or by inheritance is predestined for it, ignoring or lacking flexibility is like being a pagan, who, refusing to accept the dogma of a creed, is doomed to perish.

Randolph—A Tribute*

by
Harold Macmillan

(Prime Minister and First Lord of the Treasury 1957–63)

The death of Randolph Churchill at a comparatively early age, although not unexpected, has been a sad shock for his many friends, especially perhaps his older friends. For one who knew him from his early youth, it creates a real gap—a sense of deprivation; for at any time of day or night, on any occasion of importance, or at any crisis, for any discussion, grave or gay, in person or by telephone, there was always Randolph.

If you did not choose to telephone to him, he would be sure to ring you up and you always answered; although sometimes you rang off, or thought fit to be cut off.

When I was in active politics I was accustomed to Randolph coming round to obtain or, more often, to impart information. There were occasions when these interventions were not altogether welcome—there were even times when they might lead to subsequent difficulties—but they were always fun. And then he was so disarming. I might be angry about an indiscretion—very angry, but not for very long.

Most of those who have written about him stress the difficulty of his position—as the son of so great a father. They felt that he was overshadowed by the size and quality of Sir Winston's dominating personality.

To use a phrase of his own, he seemed by comparison 'a small sapling living under the shade of a great oak.' In a sense this is true;

* Reprinted from *The Sunday Times* of 9 June 1968.

but if he was dominated, he was never overawed and seldom silenced. One of Sir Winston's favourite admonitions to young ministers in his cabinets was 'fight your own corner.' Randolph fought his, always stoutly if sometimes tediously. But it is equally true that Randolph's deep affection for and devotion to his father gave purpose to his own life.

During the last war, when I saw a good deal of both father and son, it was clear that they enjoyed an almost unique relationship. Sir Winston was never content unless he could arrange for Randolph to come to meet him during his journeys. Sometimes, indeed, he was present at inconvenient and inappropriate occasions, and would not hesitate to give advice to his superior officers in his father's presence.

Some resented this; but I always thought it good fun—and a little irreverence was quite useful from time to time in these exalted gatherings. In these and subsequent years there would be frequent discussions, arguments, and even quarrels between them; and yet each was absolutely devoted to the other.

There will, of course, be some who will only remember the less attractive sides of this strange, romantic, and curiously sensitive man. It is true that he could be intolerant, overbearing, and fatiguing. Being much older, I naturally did not see too much of these aspects of his behaviour. In any case, I prefer to remember him as a man who, once his friendship was given, never went back on it; who had the highest standards of personal loyalty and devotion; who behind all the seeming appearance of arrogance suffered in reality from a certain diffidence which this outward behaviour was used to cloak.

Since from his earliest youth he rallied with ardour to his father's defence, and employed all the pungency of his biting tongue and pen against those with whom Sir Winston was at the moment in conflict, he was, during the long years of his father's political isolation, apt to make as many enemies as converts.

The father was able to survive these events; the son continued to suffer from the antagonisms which his filial loyalty had created. Nor, to be frank, did he take much trouble to soften them. He gloried in controversy—even when the old battles had been fought and won.

Randolph was a first-class journalist. He had a natural power of reporting events and of seizing the main points in any issue. He was also a remarkably good historian. His life of Lord Derby is the best picture of the politics of that period that I have read. The first two volumes of Sir Winston's biography are brilliantly devised, and the theme of the work, 'he shall be his own biographer,' is loyally carried out. But the author's own contributions are of notable value. It is sad indeed that Randolph has not lived to complete the work to which he hoped to devote his remaining years, and for which his life had been a long preparation. Let us hope that enough has been completed under his direction to allow the great story to be unfolded on the scale and with the dignity which he had planned.

Of course it would be foolish to pretend that Randolph did not make many enemies in all walks of life—especially among the powerful and great—for he was by nature a fighter. But many—among whom I am proud to be—will mourn him sincerely, and cherish the memory of a man who always proved as loyal a friend in bad times as in good.

Dear Randolph

by
Lady Diana Cooper

(Daughter of the 8th Duke of Rutland and widow of A. Duff Cooper, 1st Viscount Norwich: took a leading role in Max Reinhardt's play The Miracle; *President of the Order of Charity; author of three volumes of memoirs:* The Rainbow Comes and Goes, The Light of Common Day *and* Trumpets from the Steep)

Our dear Randolph was bound to make enemies because he could not compromise or tell a lie or trim his sails. He told me once that he did not know the feeling of shyness. Shyness is a great protector. For these same reasons he could make ardent friends. I know—I was one of them.

I saw his dawn, beautiful as an Olympic athlete. I watched his satisfaction in the incentive of his great father's biography, to finish which he fought to live. I saw his afterglow, when he was robbed of his vigour, though mellowed and deeply touching. Always there was his adrenalized vitality, his foolhardy courage and dauntless spirit vanquished by greedy death at fifty-seven. He willingly turned his face to the wall and gave up the ghost.

Death can't wrench him from those who had desire and reason to love him. I had great reason, for in my life's most tragic hour, in 1954, it was Randolph who succoured me, guarded me, and showed me how true a heart he had. He had been a devoted friend and supporter of my husband. Both he and his father, Winston, cried when Duff resigned over Munich—salt tears of admiration I need not say.

The wrangles, vituperations, brawls, gaieties and feastings were over and it was Randolph who organized, collected the funds from our friends, and arranged the constitution of the Duff Cooper Literary Memorial prize. He did not consult me or maybe anyone else. He simply designed and ordered it and I was wholeheartedly grateful.

I fear that the dear boy was a bitter disappointment to himself. His confidence and ambitions suffered cruel frustrations. There was everything in his favour except his stars, which he could not defy. Some bastard meteor crossed the fortunate pattern. Hilaire Belloc said of the heroes and villains of his choice, 'He was a good man. He'll find himself in Paradise.' I think that Randolph with his exuberance, violence and blustering love is Heaven bent. Not everyone will mourn him but the few will mourn him very much, and I one of them.

Index

One notable entry not in this Index is Randolph Churchill himself
—because he is the book!—K.H.

Smith, F. E. (see 1st Earl of Birken-
head)
Soames, Rt Hon. Christopher, 152,
153, 186
Socrates, 76
Soustelle, Jacques, 126, 127, 128
Stalin, Joseph, 83, 87, 195, 225
Stancliffe, Michael Staffurth (Rector
of St Margaret's, Westminster), 250
Stewart, Janet Rhinelander, 161
Stirling, (Archibald) David, 88, 89
Sulzberger, Arthur, 241
Sutro, John, 43, 44, 47, 48, 51, 141
Sutro, Leopold, 53
Swift, Jonathan, 161
Swope, Herbert Bayard, 73, 74, 75, 77
Sykes, Christopher, 43, 49
Syme, Sir Ronald, 269

Talbert, Ansel E., 129
Taylor, A. J. P., 240, 261
Tito, Marshal, Josip Broz, 4, 8, 9, 83,
83(*n*), 84, 85, 85(*n*), 86, 87, 88(*n*), 91,
92, 93, 95, 96, 132, 136
Toch, Ernst, 77
Togliatti, Palmyro, 165
Trevor-Roper, Hugh, 239, 267
Trott, Adam von, 49
Truman, President Harry S., 10, 195

Twigg, Barbara, 233, 246, 254
Tynan, Kenneth, 146

Vanderbilt, Mr, 42
Verwoerd, Dr Hendrik, 122, 125
Viertel, Berthold, 77, 78
Viertel, Salka, 77, 78

Walpole, Horace, 187, 199
Warner, Jack, 78, 79
Washington, President George, 10
Waugh, Auberon, 118
Waugh, Evelyn, 4, 9, 10, 12, 40, 46,
47, 49, 60, 91, 95, 118, 155, 251
Weizmann, Dr Chaim, 224
Wilde, Oscar, 252
Williams, Corporal, 99, 104, 105
Wilson, Rt Hon. Harold, 11
Windsor, Duchess of, 106
Windsor, Duke of 34, 35, 57, 106,
107, 108, 111, 244
Wingate, Major-General Orde, 43(*n*)
Wintour, Charles, 280
Wolff, Michael, 238, 257
Wolff, Rosemary, 263
Wolfson, Sir Isaac, 161

Young, Colonel Desmond, 113